Introducing UNIX and Linux

Mike Joy, Stephen Jarvis and Michael Luck

palgrave
macmillan

First published 2002 by
PALGRAVE MACMILLAN
Houndmills, Basingstoke, Hampshire RG21 6XS and
175 Fifth Avenue, New York, N. Y. 10010
Companies and representatives throughout the world

PALGRAVE MACMILLAN is the global academic imprint of the Palgrave Macmillan division of St. Martin's Press, LLC and of Palgrave Macmillan Ltd. Macmillan® is a registered trademark in the United States, United Kingdom and other countries. Palgrave is a registered trademark in the European Union and other countries.

ISBN 0–333–98763–2 paperback

This book is printed on paper suitable for recycling and made from fully managed and sustained forest sources.

A catalogue record for this book is available from the British Library.

10   9   8   7   6   5   4   3   2   1
11   10   09   08   07   06   05   04   03   02

Printed and bound in Great Britain by
Antony Rowe Ltd, Chippenham and Eastbourne

Contents

Preface

UNIX is an operating system which has seen substantial growth in its popularity over the last few years and is used by many universities and colleges, as well as in industry. Linux is a UNIX-like operating system for PCs which is freely available and has become a serious alternative to proprietary systems such as Windows. This book is a *beginner's* guide for students who have to *use* UNIX and/or Linux. No prior knowledge of programming is assumed, nor is any experience of using computers. We do, however, expect our audience to have a serious interest in computing, and a typical reader might be a student in the first year of a degree or HND course.

UNIX is more than just a computer operating system: it is a philosophy of programming. Learning UNIX involves becoming familiar not only with the commands it affords the user, but also with the methodology it employs. It is a very powerful tool in the hands of an experienced practitioner, but it can be daunting for the novice. We introduce enough detail for the reader to be able to utilise the facilities in UNIX, but no more.

In 1993 an International Standard was published, known as 'POSIX.2', which specifies the constructs and commands that a UNIX system should have available to its users. This book follows that standard. However, POSIX is a 'minimal' standard, and most UNIX or Linux systems contain much more. We discuss in this book *all* the basic constructs and commands of UNIX (as defined in POSIX.2), sufficient for the reader to be able to use each of them, together with some of the more common and useful extensions. We do not delve into any in fine detail; part of the UNIX philosophy is that such information is available online. The reader who requires more sophisticated use of UNIX after reading this book will know how and where to find the extra information they need.

To get the most from this book, you should have access to a UNIX computer system or a PC running Linux, as much of the text relies on your being able to try out examples. If you have a PC running Windows, we discuss in Chapter 3 how you can install Linux on your PC.

This book is a new version of *Beginning UNIX*, which is no longer in print. The material covered in chapters 4 to 11 is substantially the same as the corresponding chapters in *Beginning UNIX*, but the remaining chapters are new. We have expanded the coverage to include discussion of Linux and related issues, including installation and maintenance on a PC. A new chapter on Perl has been included. Technical material is now consistent with current Linux distributions in addition to Solaris and other versions of the UNIX operating system.

NOTE

Acknowledgements

Grateful thanks are due to Nathan Griffiths and Steve Matthews for commenting on draft versions of this book. Thanks also to Hugh Glaser for encouragement and feedback, and to students at Warwick and Southampton for valuable input.

NOTE

Trademarks

Adobe, Acrobat and Framemaker are registered trademarks of Adobe Systems Incorporated.

BeOS is a registered trademark of Be, Inc.

Eudora is a registered trademark of the University of Illinois Board of Trustees, licensed to QUALCOMM Inc.

Internet Explorer, Outlook, Windows, Windows 95, Windows NT, Windows 2000 and Windows XP are registered trademarks of Microsoft Corporation.

Java is a trademark of Sun Microsystems, Inc.

KDE, K Desktop Environment and KOffice are trademarks of KDE e.V.

Linux is a registered trademark of Linus Torvalds.

MacOS is a registered trademark of Apple Computer, Inc.

Mandrake and Linux-Mandrake are registered trademarks of MandrakeSoft SA and MandrakeSoft, Inc.

Mozilla is a trademark of the Mozilla Organization.

Netscape Navigator is a registered trademark of Netscape Communications Corporation.

Opera is a trademark of Opera Software AS.

PalmOS is a registered trademark of Palm, Inc.

Pentium is a registered trademark of Intel Corporation.

PostScript is a registered trademark of Adobe Systems, Inc.

Red Hat and RPM are registered trademarks of Red Hat, Inc.

SPARC is a registered trademark of SPARC International, Inc.

StuffIt is a trademark of Aladdin Systems, Inc.

SuSE is a registered trademark of SuSE AG.

TeX is a trademark of the American Mathematical Society (AMS).

UNIX is a registered trademark of The Open Group.

VMS is a registered trademark of COMPAQ Computer Corporation.

VMware is a registered trademark of VMware, Inc.

WordPerfect is a registered trademark of Corel Corporation.

X Windows is a registered trademark of the Massachusetts Institute of Technology.

All other trademarks are the property of their respective owners.

The Computing Environment

CHAPTER OVERVIEW

This chapter

▶ reviews basic notions of computer hardware and software;

▶ outlines the different kinds of software program;

▶ introduces the basic philosophy of UNIX and Linux; and

▶ provides a brief description of the history of UNIX and Linux.

If you pick up any book over ten years old on the subject of computing, you could get quite different ideas of how people use their computers. The basic ways of using computers haven't changed, but modern computing places an unimagined amount of control and power with the individual user. This means that the user now has the ability (and quite often the need) to deal with issues relating to the administration of the computer to get the best out of it. In this book, we'll be explaining just how to understand what this involves, and how to minimise the amount of effort required for effective use of your computer.

We start in this chapter by reviewing some basic concepts of computing in a non-technical way, so that if you really are a beginner, reading through this chapter should bring you up to speed. If you are already familiar with the ideas of hardware and software, input and output, processors, systems software, and applications programs, you may choose instead to move swiftly on to Chapter 2.1, or simply to skim this chapter.

1.1 What is a Computer?

In very basic terms, there are essentially two kinds of "thing" involved in computing. There are things you can kick, actual bits of machinery that you can pick up and take away, including the computer itself, printers, screens and other physical devices (digital cameras, scanners, disk drives, CD drives, etc.), which are collectively and individually known as **hardware** Thus, hardware includes the devices you use to communicate with a computer system (such as the mouse, keyboard), the actual components that make up that system, and any other devices.

Unfortunately, the hardware won't work by itself and needs detailed instructions, or **programs**, to make it do what it should. In addition to the hardware, therefore, it is also necessary to have a set of programs that tell the hardware what to do. These programs, which refer to the actual instructions rather than the medium on which they are stored, are collectively known as **software**. Software is needed for the basic operation of computers (like the software that is the subject of this book, UNIX and Linux) as well as for the more common applications that you may already be familiar with, such as word-processing, spreadsheets, games, MP3 playing, and limitless other possibilities. By themselves, hardware and software are not enough to do the things we want of computers — it is the combination of hardware and software that enables effective use of modern computers.

Below, we describe the different kinds of hardware and software in a little more detail.

1.2 Hardware

1.2.1 Processors

The most important part of the overall system is the **processor** (or **central processing unit**, **CPU**) on which the computer is based, and which does the main work of the system. In recent years, the advance of the PC has been fuelled by progress in such processors, which are becoming ever faster and more powerful. In PCs, these have included the series of Pentium processors developed by Intel, with alternatives from companies like AMD. Other computers have different processors, like Sun's SPARC processor. Whichever processor your machine uses is not important for now — there may be variations in speed and power, as well as in some other more technical differences, but the key point to note is that this is the main component of the machine.

> **ACRONYM**
>
> *AMD = 'Advanced Micro Devices, Inc.'*
> *SPARC = 'Scalable Processor ARChitecture'*

1.2.2 Input Devices

Although the processor is most critical, it is of little use if you can't display the *results* of the computation it performs, or if you can't specify and modify the *kinds* of computation you want it to perform. For this reason, we need **input** and **output** devices — hardware components that allow users to interact with the processor in easy and convenient ways.

In order to instruct a computer to perform a task, we require a way to provide instructions as input. Perhaps the most recognisable input device is the **keyboard** (typically of the 'QWERTY' variety because of the layout of the keys, similar to a typewriter), which nearly all computers use to receive textual and numeric input. The keyboard is the most usual way in which people write programs or enter data on which those programs might operate. However, there are also many other ways to provide input to a computer. For example, many people now have scanners to enable graphical images to be provided as input. Similarly, digital cameras, bar-code readers in shops, and even sound recorders offer different ways of getting data to the processor. In this book, we will focus on the standard keyboard as our main input device, but we also note that the **mouse**, with the purpose of enabling the selection and movement of items displayed on the screen, is a vital part of modern computer systems.

1.2.3 Output Devices

Output devices are also varied, and we will focus primarily on the **screen** or **monitor** (or even **visual display unit** — **VDU** — to use a somewhat out-of-date expression) that typically comes as part of the package with the processor and the keyboard.

In the past, people used so-called **dumb terminals**, which are largely redundant now. A dumb terminal consists of a keyboard and a screen, and can display only the same sort of text and simple characters as a typewriter. On the screen is a **cursor**, which is either a block (a filled rectangle the size of a letter) or an underscore, marking the point on the screen at which typed characters appear, and also where any message the computer writes will begin. The equivalent of a dumb terminal is now more commonly referred to as a **command window** in many systems.

These days, modern computers typically use a screen (to display both the input that is provided through keyboards, for example, and any results of the processing performed), a keyboard and a mouse. The configuration is sometimes referred to as a **graphics terminals**, to distinguish it from a dumb terminal. These are capable of much more sophisticated output. In particular, the screen is a high-resolution display (nearly always colour), allowing complex graphics to be drawn as well as simple characters. Usually, a system is employed by which the screen is divided up into rectangular areas called **windows**, with which to communicate individually. The computer itself may be a PC, as shown in Figure 1.1, a **workstation** or a laptop, but that is not important. We will assume the use of a command window, which applies to all equally. If you are using any of these, you can create such a window, which behaves as if it were itself a dumb terminal, having its own cursor. Typically, there is also a global cursor that moves each time you move the mouse; you can select which window the keyboard will communicate with by moving the global cursor so that it is within the chosen window.

The look and feel of the various kinds of computers can vary enormously, as can the way in which windows on a screen are manipulated. Either a **window manager** or a **desktop manager** can be used to control the windows on a screen, and though the distinction between the two kinds of software is somewhat blurred, a desktop manager typically has more features and capabilities than a window manager. We will go into more details about these later on in Chapter 3.

Figure 1.1 A typical computer, with screen, keyboard and mouse

These basic components of processor, screen and keyboard are the key pieces of the modern computing system, and their combination underlies all of the details that follow in this book.

1.3 Software

1.3.1 Input and Characters

When communicating with UNIX, users send to the system a **stream** of characters. Each time a key on the keyboard is pressed, a character is sent to the machine. Usually, the computer **echoes** the character so that it is displayed on the screen. Similarly, to communicate with the user the system sends a stream of characters to the user's computer, which is able to interpret the particular character coding and display the characters on the screen accordingly.

While interacting with the system, a user types in lines of text from the keyboard, terminating each line by pressing the **Return** (or **Enter**) key. These lines are interpreted as instructions to UNIX, which then responds accordingly, and displays messages on the screen. On a graphics terminal, this dialogue is between the keyboard and a specific window (typically the window over which the cursor has been placed). Manipulation of other devices such as a mouse also results in the transmission of characters to the UNIX machine. However, these are interpreted as relating to the management and display of the windows only.

Commands sent to UNIX are executed by a program called the **shell**. We shall see later that the shell is just one example of a program that can run on a UNIX system, but is special since it is the principal interface between a user and the very heart of the system software, known as the **kernel**.

Most characters that we shall use are the **printing characters**. These, which include letters, digits, punctuation marks and the other symbols marked on the keyboard, are displayed in the obvious way. However, other characters, known as **control characters** (listed in Table 1.1), are sometimes required by a UNIX system. Each is stored as a number using a **character encoding** such as **ASCII**. For instance, the character whose code is 7 and is sometimes referred to as 'bell', if printed on your terminal, normally causes the terminal to make a noise (typically a 'beep').

Each control character has a name, typically an acronym of its description. For character number 7, this is **BEL**, short for 'bell'. Control characters can be typed by pressing a key while holding down the **Ctrl** key. For BEL, this key is G, and for this reason BEL is often written as **ctrl-G** or ^G. Some of the other control characters have anachronistic names that also relate to the functioning of a teletype, but most of them will not concern us here.

Control characters have purposes which, for the most part, are obscure. Many are used by operating systems (not necessarily UNIX) to structure data, and have meanings with historical relevance only. Some of the more useful control characters include the following. The character **TAB** has the effect, when sent to the screen, of moving the cursor to the next tab position (usually columns 8, 16, 24, 32, etc.). The key marked TAB or →, when pressed, transmits a TAB character to the computer. The character **NL** (Newline) causes the cursor to move down to the left-hand side of the next row on the screen. This character is provided as input to the machine whenever the key marked RETURN (or ENTER or ↩) is pressed. The escape character, which would not normally be

Table 1.1   ASCII control characters

Code	ctrl-key	Name	Description
0	^@	NUL	null
1	^A	SOH	start of heading
2	^B	STX	start of text
3	^C	ETX	end of text
4	^D	EOT	end of transmission
5	^E	ENQ	enquiry
6	^F	ACK	acknowledge
7	^G	BEL	bell
8	^H	BS	backspace
9	^I	HT	horizontal tab
10	^J	NL	newline (linefeed)
11	^K	VT	vertical tab
12	^L	NP	new page (formfeed)
13	^M	CR	carriage return
14	^N	SO	shift out
15	^O	SI	shift in
16	^P	DLE	data link escape
17	^Q	DC1	device control 1
18	^R	DC2	device control 2
19	^S	DC3	device control 3
20	^T	DC4	device control 4
21	^U	NAK	negative acknowledgement
22	^V	SYN	synchronous idle
23	^W	ETB	end of transmission block
24	^X	CAN	cancel
25	^Y	EM	end of medium
26	^Z	SUB	substitute
27	^[	ESC	escape
28	^	FS	file separator
29	^]	GS	group separator
30	^^	RS	record separator
31	^_	US	unit separator
127	^?	DEL	delete

displayed on a screen at all, is sometimes required when typing in data. There should be a key on your keyboard marked ESC or ESCAPE.

1.3.2 Application Programs

As mentioned earlier, the hardware alone is not enough. To do anything useful with a computer, you need to run software, or programs, on the hardware. Programs can be used to do pretty much anything you want, but commonly include word-processing, scientific calculations and games, and even support the development of yet more programs. What is important to note here is that for each different application, you need a different **application program** to run on the computer. Thus, if you want to do some word-processing, you'll need to get a word-processing program to execute; word-processing can't be done directly by the computer otherwise.

Programming Languages

The processing units inside a computer understand a language called **machine code**, and all the calculations that a computer performs use this code. Machine code, which is a 'low-level' language, is specific to the particular make and model of computer on which it runs, and is not designed to be read by humans. Any instruction given to a computer must be translated (somehow) to machine code before the computer will understand it. It is unlikely you will ever need to come into direct contact with machine code.

Typically, programs are written in high-level languages that are easily readable by humans, but not by computers. They require **compilers** and **interpreters** to perform a translation into the machine code that computers can understand.

1.3.3 The Operating System

The final piece of the jigsaw of modern computing, to make the hardware and software work together, and to make the different bits of hardware like the screen, keyboard and processor talk to each other, is what is known as the **operating system**, which is **system software** as opposed to application software. The operating system is a complex program (or collection of programs) that controls the internal operation of the computer to ensure that all of the different things that are taking place at the same time are done effectively and sensibly. For example, while the computer accepts input from the keyboard and displays output on the screen, it may also be processing some data and accessing the hard disk, all at the same time.

Just as there can be different processors, different screens and keyboards, and different application programs, so there can be different

operating systems. If you've got this far, then we should be able to
assume that you know that your particular operating system is (or is
likely to become) UNIX or Linux, but you may also be familiar with
Microsoft's **Windows**, with **DOS**, or with some other operating systems
such as **CPM**, **MacOS**, **Multics**, **BeOS**, **PalmOS** or **VMS**.

1.3.4 System Administration

Traditionally, UNIX systems have been multi-user systems with
individuals simply gaining access as users. In these situations, there is
usually someone, somewhere, who is in day-to-day charge of the system,
and known as the **system administrator**. If you are using this kind of
system and have problems that neither you nor your colleagues are able
to resolve, then the system administrator will either be able to help, or at
least point you in the direction of someone who can. You should find out
who your system administrator is, and make sure that you are in
possession of any documents that he or she wishes users of the system to
have.

More recently, however, there has been a move towards the use of
UNIX for individually-run personal computers, especially with the recent
success of Linux. If this is your situation, then it is you who will act as
the system administrator for your machine, and will be responsible for its
maintenance. In particular, if you are using Linux on your own personal
computer, make sure you read the handbook supplied with the operating
system in conjunction with this book. If there are any differences, it will
be an invaluable help.

Finally, there is one user of the system who is called the **super-user**. He
or she has special privileges on the system, and is allowed to perform
certain actions forbidden to ordinary users, such as having the
unrestricted right to change and to delete files on the system. The
super-user may or may not be the same person as the system
administrator.

1.4 History of UNIX and Linux

The first UNIX system was built at **Bell Labs**, the research division of the
US telephone corporation **AT&T**, in 1969. Prior to that date, Bell
(together with **General Electric** and **MIT**) had been engaged in developing
a large-scale operating system, known as 'Multics'. This collaboration
between industry and the academic community had begun in 1964, but
five years later it became clear that the three participants had different
goals for the project. By this time a vast amount of work had gone into
Multics, but more needed to be done for it to fulfil the aspirations of any
of the participants. Accordingly, Bell Labs pulled out of the project.

Faced with not having a state-of-the-art operating system with which to work, a number of researchers at Bell, led by Ken Thompson and Dennis Ritchie, decided to create a new operating system 'from scratch'. Multics had become complex, and it was felt that a much simpler system was needed — the name 'UNIX' arose to emphasise that difference between it and Multics. The experience gained during the development of Multics contributed much to the design of UNIX.

A number of fundamental design decisions that were taken pervade the whole of UNIX. Programs written for UNIX should be simple, and should each do a single task well. This was different from the style adopted in some other operating systems, where large programs would be developed with many different capabilities, and would be commensurately complex. Also, programs should be designed so that they could easily be linked together, the output from one becoming the input to another. Thus it would be possible to build more complex programs by joining simple ones together.

Part of the philosophy underlying the design of UNIX was that the core system software, or kernel, should be as small as possible, and only perform those functions that are absolutely necessary — all other tasks should be the responsibility of the shell. At the same time as UNIX was being written, the language **C** was being designed, and in 1973 a UNIX kernel was written using C. C is a high-level language, and as such is machine-independent, so the new (small) kernel and shell could be transferred to a different machine easily. This was found to work well, and Bell Labs was happy to allow the source code for the kernel to be distributed to universities.

In the next few years, work on UNIX was undertaken principally by Bell Labs and by the University of California at Berkeley. These two organisations, however, developed their own versions of UNIX, known respectively as **System V** and **BSD**. Industrial users tended to use System V, whereas BSD UNIX was common in universities and colleges.

By the late 1980s UNIX had been implemented by many manufacturers, each of whom had developed versions which, although based either on System V or on BSD, had their own features. It became apparent that the popularity of UNIX, coupled with the proliferation of 'dialects', had resulted in a pressing need for a recognised standard for UNIX to be developed. This was taken on board by the **IEEE** under the name **POSIX**. POSIX consists of a number of interrelated standards. Now part of the **PASC** project, there are more than nine proposed POSIX standards, but not all are yet completed. In this book we only deal with POSIX.2, since the other standards are not necessary for understanding the UNIX shell.

In 1991, a computer science student at the University of Helsinki in Finland, Linus Torvalds, decided to create his own version of UNIX, which he named Linux. It was in 1994 that he released version 1.0 of

---

NOTE

The kernel is discussed in Chapter 2.1

ACRONYM

BSD = 'Berkeley System Distribution'

ACRONYM

IEEE = 'Institute of Electrical and Electronics Engineers, Inc.'
PASC = 'Portable Application Standards Committee'

Linux. Very quickly it became clear that Torvalds alone would not be able to develop a complete operating system, so he chose to open up his project to allow others to contribute to its development. On the Internet, Torvalds announced his project and called for volunteers to assist; in doing so, the source code was made freely available.

As a result of this model of allowing developers from around the world to contribute to the development of Linux, a Linux community was born, and has now grown to millions of users, numerous different Linux distributions, and over a hundred developers just for the Linux kernel. It is now an effective and successful operating system that competes on many platforms with commercial offerings. The latest version at the time of writing is version 2.4.

1.5 Conventions

Several different fonts are used in this book. **Bold face** is used when names or concepts are first introduced, and occasionally for emphasis. When dialogue with a machine is displayed, `fixed width font` is used for messages that the UNIX system prints, and **`(bold) keyboard font`** for instructions typed by a user. If a word that would normally appear in such a dialogue appears in the text, `fixed width font` is again used.

For most purposes in the book, the words 'UNIX' and 'Linux' are interchangeable, and unless otherwise stated use of the word 'UNIX' should be understood as meaning 'UNIX or Linux'.

CHAPTER SUMMARY

▶ Modern computer systems are made up of both hardware and software.

▶ Hardware comprises processors, and input and output devices.

▶ Software can be application programs or system software like operating systems.

▶ UNIX and Linux are operating systems with a long academic tradition.

UNIX and Linux Design and Organisation

This chapter

▶ introduces the basic organisation of UNIX and Linux;

▶ describes the key underlying concepts;

▶ outlines the basic technical components necessary to get started; and

▶ gives details of how to get a copy of Linux.

2.1 The Kernel and Shell

In order for a computer to do any useful work, it must also perform 'housekeeping'. It needs to understand that it has various devices such as printers connected to it, and it needs to know when a user wants to run a program. These tasks, are performed by an **operating system**, together with many others that are required for the computer to function effectively, but are not of interest to the user. An operating system is a program, or collection of programs, that runs whenever the computer is switched on. It controls the computer, allows the user to type in instructions to the computer, and performs many other necessary functions. UNIX is an operating system.

A UNIX system can be split into two parts. While the system is operational, a program called the **kernel** is constantly running. This is what forms the core of the operating system and is central to UNIX. In this book, we will not be concerned with how the kernel functions, since it is not information which the user needs to know.

The other part of a UNIX system is a **shell**, which is the interface between a user and the system itself. It allows the user to instruct the machine and to run programs. A shell communicates with the kernel, but keeps the user at arm's length from it, as illustrated in Figure 2.1. In order to use a UNIX system, it is sufficient to understand a shell; the kernel can remain hidden from the user.

Figure 2.1 The UNIX kernel and shell

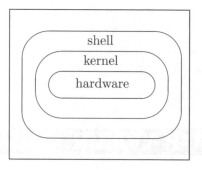

The kernel is always present, but the shell is only active when someone is actually using the UNIX system. Since the shell enables the user to instruct the system to perform tasks, the instructions that can be given to the shell must be easy for a person to understand. Different individuals have had different ideas about exactly how a shell should be designed, and a number of different shells have been devised in the past. They are all similar to each other, but differ in details. The first shell, historically, is the **Bourne shell**, known as **sh** and named after its creator. This shell is still used today, although newer shells with more powerful features have been created which are effectively extensions of the Bourne shell. These include the **Korn shell** (**ksh**), the **Z shell** (**zsh**), and **bash**. A programmer familiar with the Bourne shell should have no trouble using any of these three other shells. Indeed, if such a programmer were not using the extra features provided by these shells, he or she would be unaware that the shell was not the Bourne shell.

ACRONYM

bash = 'Bourne Again SHell'

The **C shell**, known as **csh**, has a syntax that resembles that of the C programming language, and is markedly different from any of the shells based on the Bourne shell. A programmer familiar with the Bourne shell would not be able to use the C shell without learning the differences between it and the Bourne shell. Just as there are shells that are extensions of the Bourne shell, so the C shell itself has been developed into shells with extra facilities. The most common of these is the the **tcsh** (pronounced 'teesh').

POSIX.2 defines the 'standard' shell, and is modelled principally on the Bourne shell. The POSIX.2 shell contains features that have been added to the Bourne shell in the light of experience gained with other shells. Much of what is discussed in this book will thus be true for the Bourne shell. It is likely that as existing shells derived from the Bourne shell, such as ksh and zsh, are developed, each will be amended so that its specification conforms to POSIX.2.

2.2 Files

On any machine there will be a large amount of information (or data) that must be stored, including programs, text, and the UNIX operating system itself. Each unit of data — which may be small (for instance, a few words of text) or large (like parts of the UNIX operating system itself) — is stored in a file. Files are simply sequences of bytes, stored somewhere on the system, perhaps on magnetic disks, CD-ROMs, or other storage devices. We are not interested in exactly where the file is stored, merely in its contents.

Each file has a name, which should consist of any letter, digit, or the characters . (period), - (minus sign), or _ (underscore). Other characters are also acceptable in a filename, but are discouraged in order to promote clarity. When we use files, we will normally refer to them by name. Some examples are:

```
test    11a    My_File    prog.c    p-1
```

2.2.1 Networks

ACRONYM

CPU = 'Central Processing Unit'

Computer systems contain at least one computer. However, it is becoming increasingly difficult to define what is meant by 'a computer' — until a few years ago, a computer would have had a single CPU, which would perform all the computational tasks.

Nowadays, a computer may contain several processing units around which the workload will be distributed. In addition, several computers may be connected together in a **network** where each constituent computer can communicate with others in the network.

In some cases, the computers in a network are very intimately connected, and the network appears to a user as a single but very large computer. We use the word **system** to mean either a single computer or a network of computers that appear to the user as a single entity. A campus-wide UNIX network would be an example of such a system; a more loosely-connected network such as the Internet would not be. When using a terminal on a network, users are still communicating with a specific machine. Each window allows a dialogue with a single UNIX machine, and it is that target UNIX machine with which we shall be concerned in this book.

2.3 Technical Basics

2.3.1 Bits, Bytes, Words and Characters

Data inside a computer is stored as a sequence of binary digits. Each such digit is called a **bit**. Exactly how bits are stored does not concern us here, but several different methods can be used depending where on the computer system the data is required. Bits are grouped together in groups of (usually) 8 to form a **byte**. Bytes are then grouped in 2s, 4s or 8s to form **words**, the number of bytes in a word depending on the machine being used.

Figure 2.2   A 4-byte word

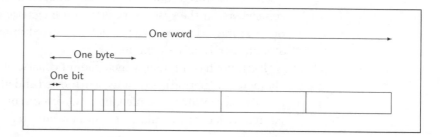

It is rarely necessary to enquire what individual bits are stored on a computer. Normally, the byte is regarded as the most basic unit of storage on a machine. Since a byte contains 256 permutations of eight binary digits, a byte can represent any number between 0 and 255 inclusive (or between −128 and +127, or other such ranges).

Just as with a typewriter, communication with UNIX is character-by-character. Unless you are dealing *bit-by-bit* with the data stored in the system's memory, it is helpful to think of each byte representing a character, such as the letter 'A' or the symbol '@', since there is a correspondence between characters and the numeric codes (between 0 and 255) that can be stored in a byte. The most common coding scheme used is called **ASCII**, in which codes for the upper-case letters 'A' to 'Z' are 65 to 90, for lower-case letters 'a' to 'z' they are 97 to 122, and for the digits '0' to '9' they are 48 to 57. Other codes are used for other symbols. The codes are summarised in Table 2.1.

In the earlier days of computing, the electronic components were often unreliable, and the final bit in a byte was used as a **check digit** whose value is determined by a simple calculation from the other seven bits. If one of the other seven bits is changed, the value of the eighth, which is referred to as a **parity bit**, is also changed. This parity check can then be used to identify bytes whose contents have been accidentally altered.

ACRONYM

ASCII = 'American Standard Code for Information Interchange'

Table 2.1   ASCII characters

Code		Description
0-31		control characters (see Table 1.1)
32		space
33	!	exclamation mark
34	"	double quote
35	#	hash
36	$	dollar
37	%	percent
38	&	ampersand
39	'	single quote
40	(	left parenthesis
41	)	right parenthesis
42	*	asterisk
43	+	plus
44	,	comma
45	-	minus
46	.	dot
47	/	slash
48-57	0-9	digits
58	:	colon
59	;	semicolon
60	<	less than
61	=	equals
62	>	greater than
63	?	question mark
64	@	at
65-90	A-Z	capital letters
91	[	left bracket
92	\	backslash
93	]	right bracket
94	^	caret
95	_	underscore
96	`	backquote
97-122	a-z	lower case letters
123	{	left brace
124	|	bar
125	}	right brace
126	~	tilde
127	DEL	delete (control character)

Parity checking is an unsophisticated form of error detection, and modern equipment seldom uses it, thus allowing 256 character codes to be stored in a single 8-bit byte, rather than just 128. Usually the first 128 match the ASCII character set, and the remaining characters are used for extra symbols, such as currency symbols and accented letters from languages other than English. One such code is known as **LATIN-1**. For the symbols used in this book these two codings are identical. Other codings do exist, however, perhaps the best known being **EBCDIC** and the 16-bit **Unicode**, but for the purposes of this book, we shall assume that ASCII is being used.

Note that if you total the number of letters, digits, punctuation marks and other graphics symbols, there are nowhere near 256 of them — some codes relate to *non-printing* characters. These are characters which, rather than representing a symbol that can be printed on a computer screen, denote other actions that the computer display can perform.

> **ACRONYM**
>
> *EBCDIC = 'Extended Binary Coded Decimal Interchange Code'*

2.4 How to get Linux

For many years there has been a tradition in universities of freedom of information, and results of academic research are typically easily accessible. Furthermore, software created during that research is often made available free of charge, either as public domain (where copyright no longer applies) or as shareware (where, although copyright still applies, the copyright owner permits copying). The source code for that software may also be available, and much software is now **open source**, where the source code is distributed and the user licence prohibits sale of the software without the source code. Linux is open source.

You may have access to a UNIX system via your university or college. If you don't, or you would like to use UNIX on your PC at home, Chapter 3 tells you how to get and install your own copy of Linux.

CHAPTER SUMMARY

▶ The kernel is the core of the UNIX operating system.

▶ The shell is the interface between the kernel and the user.

▶ Data inside a computer is organised in bits, bytes, words, characters and files.

▶ There are several different shells and character codings.

Installing Linux

This chapter

▶ shows you how to collect system information about your computer;

▶ introduces you to the different options for setting up Linux;

▶ provides guidelines on how to install Linux; and

▶ highlights some of the everyday features which Linux will provide.

The purpose of this chapter is to arm you with the necessary information to install your own version of Linux. There are a number of Linux configurations you might consider and the choice you make will be influenced by the capabilities of your computer. This chapter is designed to help you recognise these choices and their limitations.

3.1 Starting out

If you want to download a freely distributed version of Linux, you can do no better than starting your venture at `www.linux.org`. As well as documenting general Linux information, details of the various Linux applications and on-line Linux tutorials, this official web site also plays host to the distribution of the numerous Linux packages.

The distribution of Linux is now extremely well supported and you will find that there are references to English and non-English language versions. There are also links to mirror sites where you can download Linux free of charge; there are details of Linux vendors and on-line reviews of some of the free Linux distributions.

At the last count there were at least 40 versions of Linux which could be downloaded from this site. This chapter does not deal with the specifics involved in downloading any one of these distributions, but you will find that the on-line documentation provided with each package is quite adequate. However, there are a number of fundamental choices of which you should be aware when installing Linux; it is to these that we turn our attention in this chapter.

3.2 Preliminaries

Before you begin with the installation of Linux it is important that you establish a match between the requirements of your chosen Linux download and the capabilities of your computer system.

Linux turns out to be extremely versatile and it is therefore likely that your computer will be able to run Linux in one form or another. The 'build' you choose may, however, depend on the amount of processor power you have available, the amount of **RAM** and the amount of hard disk space you are able to commit to Linux.

ACRONYM

RAM = 'Random Access Memory'

3.2.1 Collecting information about your system

If your computer is already running a version of the Microsoft Windows operating system, then you can find information about your system by clicking on the 'Start' button and selecting 'Settings' and the 'Control Panel'. From here you should click on the 'System' icon; this will bring up a window entitled 'System Properties'.

The easiest way to capture the information that the 'System Properties' windows provide is to print a System Resource Report. You can do this by selecting the system properties 'Device Manager' window and then clicking 'Print'. At the print menu you should select the 'All devices and system summary' option and then press 'OK'.

If your computer is still using one of the older versions of Windows (3.1, 3.2, etc.) then you can gather and print the same system information by running the MSD.EXE utility from a DOS command prompt.

Among the information provided with each of the Linux distributions will be listed the minimum system requirements. Before you decide on which version of Linux to install, it is worth making sure that your System Resource Report meets these requirements.

3.2.2 Installation options

A second issue likely to affect the type of Linux distribution you choose is the way in which you intend to use Linux on a day-to-day basis. You might want to install the Linux operating system as the sole operating system on your computer. If this is the case then you should probably install Linux as a 'single boot'. This means that when you turn your computer on it only recognises the one operating system.

If, however, you want to retain the use of your existing operating system, for example, you would like to be able to run Linux *or* Windows, then you should choose a **'dual boot'** option. This means that the computer is aware of two different operating systems when it is turned on. It is also possible to run one operating system inside another with the aid of an **emulator**.

The next sections provide some of the detail which you will need to be able to choose between installation options. Note the pros (+) and cons (-) of each method; you should also be aware that the installations have very different hardware requirements and that your choice may to some extent be determined by the capabilities of your computer.

3.3 Single boot

If you are installing Linux on an old computer (without a CD drive, with 32 Mb of memory or less, or with a 75 MHz processor or thereabouts) then you will find that the way in which you install Linux is already limited. In this case you must install Linux as a 'single boot' system. This means that you must essentially forfeit your previous operating system for your new version of Linux. While this is not always what people want (as you may still want to use Windows from time to time), this is the simplest way to install Linux on your machine.

You need to partition your hard disk before Linux can be installed. It is therefore worth checking whether the version of Linux you have chosen has its own partitioning software as part of the software bundle. If not, you will have to use the DOS/Windows **FDISK** program.

The single boot option does have a number of benefits. For example, it provides a fast, reliable and easy to use system.

3.4 Dual boot

If you possess a more up-to-date computer, or you are keen not to lose the use of your previous operating system, then you should install Linux as a 'dual boot' system. This has the overwhelming advantage of allowing you to switch between operating systems (Windows and Linux for example) and being able to use the applications provided by each. There are a number of possible dual-boot set-up configurations, which we consider next.

3.4.1 Booting from CD/floppy

Many of the Linux packages come with a boot floppy disk. If you download Linux free of charge then you can create your own boot floppy from the download; you can also order these disks online or purchase a package with a free distribution copy inside.

NOTE

(+) reliable install
(+) less disk and processor
(−) can only run one OS

ACRONYM

FDISK = 'Fixed disk utility'

NOTE

(+) minimal install
(−) not as fast as a hard disk boot

The advantage of this approach is that you only need to do a minimal installation (of approximately 150 MB) for your system to be Linux usable. The disadvantage is that you need to keep your boot disk handy and may require your CD or floppy for other purposes.

3.4.2   Booting from your hard disk

Dual booting Linux from the hard disk is a popular option. It allows you to select which of your two (or more) operating systems you wish to use when you boot-up your computer and it will leave any CD or disk drives free for other use. Although this mode of working does not allow you to run both operating systems simultaneously (see the Section 3.5 on emulators if this is your requirement) it allows you to maximise the speed at which both operating systems are able to co-exist and run independently on your computer.

3.4.3   A partitionless install

It is possible to provide a dual boot system without any repartitioning of your hard disk. However, repartitioning is a way of keeping the file systems and operating components of your two operating systems completely separate, see below. As a result you may find that you achieve a more reliable build if a dedicated Linux partition is provided.

If you are aiming to set up a dual-boot Linux on a non-partitioned disk — an option which is often offered with many of the Linux distributions — then you should search for a distribution of Linux that uses **UMSDOS**. This allows Linux and DOS to coexist in the same partition and uses the Linux loader **loadlin** to boot between each.

While this might seem like a good solution, it should be noted that a partitionless dual-boot installation may have serious implications for your existing operating system. Rather than take this risk, and to be completely sure that you achieve a clean installation, it is better to opt for a dedicated Linux partition.

3.4.4   A dedicated Linux partition

If you have enough disk capacity, then you can allocate a complete partition (or indeed disk) to Linux. If you are serious about running a safe, clean and reliable Linux alongside an operating system such as Windows, then this is a good option. Recognising this fact, many of the Linux installers provide a GUI-based partitioning package that is fairly simple to use. Partitioning is discussed in more detail in Section 3.6.2 below.

3.5 Emulators

Operating system emulation allows you to run multiple operating systems concurrently without having to reboot. At best it allows you to run a full version of Windows inside Linux through the creation of something called a **virtual computer** — see subsection 3.5.1 below on VMware.

Alternative solutions include those systems that allow Windows applications to run under Linux without modification. Although this is not regarded as true emulation, it does provide a considerable level of Linux and Windows compatibility — see subsection 3.5.2 below on WINE.

NOTE

(+) runs Windows and Linux simultaneously
(+) unrivalled capabilities
(−) speed hit on guest OS
(−) costs around $300 at the time of writing
(−) "commercial software"

3.5.1 VMware

VMware is a commercial software package that allows you to run more than one operating system simultaneously. This is done by setting up a *host* operating system and one (or more) *guest* operating systems, each of which runs in an unmodified state.

Each guest operating system runs in a secure virtual machine; the beauty of VMware is that when using these virtual machines it is as easy to swap between operating systems as it is to swap between windows. In fact, if you run the virtual machine window in full screen mode, it is as if the guest operating system (OS) is the only OS on your machine.

Such sophistication must come at a price. Firstly, you will need a machine with a bare minimum of 256 MB of RAM and a 400 MHz processor. You will also need at least 500 MB of disk for the guest OS and the associated applications. Secondly, there will be a speed reduction when using the guest OS. This can be as much as 50%, which may be a problem if your machine is at the bottom end of the hardware requirements.

VMware is very well supported and you can configure your system so that the host operating system is chosen from any of Windows XP, 2000 and NT, Red Hat Linux, SuSE Linux and Mandrake Linux; the guest operating systems include all of the above and also the Windows 3.x/9x series.

You can find out more about VMware at `www.vmware.com`.

3.5.2 WINE

ACRONYM

WINE = 'Wine Is Not an Emulator'

WINE allows most Windows applications to be run natively under Intel versions of UNIX. WINE does this by providing low-level compatibility for Windows programs running under Linux. As a result, the applications run faster than they will under an emulator.

One of the main reasons for choosing WINE over an emulator is that it does not require extensive hardware resources. If you have a processor sufficiently powerful to run Linux then you will be able to run both

NOTE

(+) WINE is free
(+) applications run fast
(−) some applications
don't work

WINE and Microsoft Windows applications under it. As far as disk space is concerned, you only need approximately 250 MB of free disk to be able to store and compile the source code plus an additional 18 MB of /tmp space (see below) and 50 MB of disk in order to do the install. Another advantage of WINE is that it is free.

Corel has been using WINE to port its WordPerfect Suite to Linux, so there are some well-documented success stories. However, there are difficulties with some of the Windows applications, so it is worth looking at the Application Database on the WINE web page before deciding whether this is going to be appropriate for your needs.

Once you have set up WINE on your computer, you can install Microsoft applications by invoking a terminal window and typing `wine` followed by the name of the set-up program. A similar procedure is used to run the application once it has been installed.

More details on WINE can be found at `www.winehq.com`.

3.6 Installing Linux

Once you are satisfied that you have chosen an appropriate version of Linux that matches the capability of your computer and also meets your own needs, you are ready to begin the installation process.

3.6.1 Installer software

ACRONYM

`YaST` = *'Yet another Setup Tool'*

Most of the Linux distributions, including SuSE and Red Hat, have very good installer software. The SuSE distribution includes the text-mode YaST installer which is designed to make the process of installation as painless as possible. You may also find references to the GUI-based YaST2, which, despite being more memory intensive, is easier to use. Each version of Linux has its own tool similar to YaST.

The installer software will probably provide you with a number of installation modes such as **recommended**, **customized** and **expert**. If this is your first Linux installation then you should choose a *recommended* installation. This will automatically install the core components and yet provide you with enough options to maintain control over the amount of memory needed for the installation.

Many of the installation questions are straightforward. The choice is less clear, however, when you are asked whether you are installing as a **workstation**, as a **server (installation)** or for **development**. Again, if this is your first installation and you are planning on using your computer as a stand-alone machine, then you should opt for the 'workstation' mode. You should also select a security setting if prompted to do so; something around 'medium risk' should be adequate if you are planning on connecting your computer to the Internet.

3.6.2 Linux partitioning

Disk partitions allow the hard drive on your computer to be sectioned into a number of different areas. This is useful as it allows programs to be stored separately from data and it allows multiple operating systems to be resident on the same disk.

If you are used to a Windows system then you will be familiar with the alphabetic labelling of your disk drives. The labels A: and B: are reserved for floppy disk drives. If you have two hard disks, which is true of many computers these days, then you will find that C: and D: are normally used as labels for the first primary partitions of each of these drives. If your two hard drives are sub-partitioned then these would follow the lettering E: for the second partition on the first drive and F: for the second partition on the second drive. When accessing files under Windows you specify the drive, directory and filename.

Linux uses a style of disk partitioning that differs from the Windows equivalent. The names given to Linux partitions are derived from the type of the drive, the drive letter and the partition number. This leads to some slightly obscure names such as hda1, for example. However, the equivalent of typing 'dir C:\' in DOS is to type 'ls /' in Linux. The relationship between the directory name (e.g. /) and the partition which forms the associated storage area (e.g. hda1) is set up through the **mounting** process.

When selecting a Linux distribution you should choose a version of Linux that provides nondestructive disk partitioning during installation, otherwise you will have to use the destructive application called **FDISK**.

If you do go for this latter option, then before installing Linux you should back up your hard disk, as you will not be able to recover your files after it has been run. Once you have backed up your hard disk, it is worth running scandisk to correct any disk errors that might be present. It also makes sense to run the Windows defrag program, which tidies up the data stored on your disk, if you want to create a separate partition for your Linux installation.

If you opt for a Linux distribution that provides disk partitioning — and this should be your preferred option — then you will be taken step-by-step through the automated process of disk partitions and mounting. Your resulting Linux partitions should look something like those illustrated in Table 3.1.

Table 3.1   Linux partitions

/	root partition, stores Linux installation and program files
/boot	stores Linux kernel (might be found under root partition)
/home	used to store your personal files
/usr	used to store your program files
/tmp	used to store temporary files
/var	used for variable size data including unprocessed email etc.
/swap	used as extra memory by working files and applications

The sizes you choose to set for each of these partitions depends on your needs. One option is to allocate 10% for the / (root) and /var partitions, 30% for the /home partition and 50% for the /usr partition. The size of your /swap partition will vary, but a good rule-of-thumb is for the size of swap partition to be double the size of your RAM. The installer software will create, format and mount these partitions and then begin the installation proper.

The installer will allow you some control over the software that you decide to install. In the first instance, it is sensible to install all of the packages that are recommended. You will be able later to uninstall some of the packages if you later find that they are of no use to you.

User accounts

When you are using Linux you will be logged on as an account holder. Therefore, when Linux is being set up, you will need to add some account names and passwords. You will be asked to set up one of these accounts, called **root**, by default. The root account is the Linux **administrator account** and with this you will be able to change the system configuration, install new system software and create new accounts. For your normal day-to-day working you should use an account other than **root**. This will ensure that you do not inadvertently change your system set-up.

3.6.3 LILO

ACRONYM

LILO = 'LInux LOader'

The information stored on each disk begins with the partition delimiters — where the disk partitions start and stop — and also the location of the **boot loaders**, which start loading the operating system when your computer is turned on. The Windows boot loader is called **IO.SYS** or **DOS.SYS**; the Linux boot loader is called **LILO**. Running LILO causes the kernel of the Linux operating system to be activated and the operating system to be loaded.

During the installation you will be required to supply information about the other operating systems that you are running on your computer. Once you have done this the Linux loader will be configured so that you can move between operating systems. You might also be asked to create a custom boot disk, which you should store safely in case anything goes wrong with your computer. If you are installing a dual boot system, and the other operating system is a Windows NT/2000/XP system, then the configuration is more complex, and you should consult your documentation (or a site such as www.linux.com).

ACRONYM

KDE = 'K Desktop Environment'

The installer should then set up the X server configuration (see below). **X windows** provides the basic component of the Linux desktop, but your installer may also provide one of the new desktop environments such as KDE or GNOME (see below). It is possible to start up Linux in text mode (which requires you to type startx after you have logged in) or alternatively you can specify that X windows is run automatically on startup.

At the end of the installation process you will need to re-boot your computer, after which you will have a computer that boots up in Linux and which offers you Windows as a secondary option. If you choose Linux, you will be required to enter your name and password, and then you can use the system.

3.7 Using Linux

3.7.1 The window manager

One of the main benefits of Linux is the ability to select and configure your desktop environment so that it suits your working needs. This has been made possible through the development of a component-based windowing system.

At the core of the Linux desktop is the X windows system, a portable, network-transparent graphical user interface whose design since the mid-1980s has been geared towards its use with the UNIX operating system.

The design of X windows is different from that of Microsoft Windows in that it separates the 'what to do' part of a graphical application from the 'how to do it'. This means that the part that interfaces with your computer hardware is not mixed up with the application itself. The Linux world has made good use of this and, as a result, has developed the 'what to do' application-side in the form of a number of so called **window managers**. The window managers look different and provide a range of different behaviours. Better still, each is highly customisable and so can be tailored to suit your needs. One of the best known UNIX window managers is the **Tab Window Manager** (**TWM**) and its virtual-desktop counterpart **VTWM** (see `www.visi.com/~hawkeyd/vtwm.html`). Though dated, this still provides a good GUI interface to Linux for little hardware overhead. Another of the older and more stable window managers is **FVWM** (`www.fvwm.org`) which, through its development, has acquired lots of customisable elements known as **themes**.

A new breed of Linux desktop environment has been developed in response to the growth in the number of custom environments and the increased impact of Microsoft Windows. These desktop environments, like Windows, are now highly developed and provide a range of integrated applications to the user as well as a more comprehensive interface to Linux.

The window manager and/or desktop environment that is provided with your Linux download will vary. Three of the more popular options include **KDE** (`www.kde.org`), **CDE** (`www.opengroup.org/desktop/`) and **GNOME** (`www.gnome.org`)

NOTE

Sometimes called Tom's Window Manager, after its principal author Tom LaStrange

ACRONYM

FVWM= 'F Virtual Window Manager'
CDE = 'Common Desktop Environment'
GNOME = 'GNU Network Object Model Environment'

KDE (K Desktop Environment) is the default interface for many of the Linux downloads. It provides an excellent graphical front end to UNIX as well as a window manager, a help system and a number of developed utilities. We will consider KDE in more detail below.

GNOME is also cutting-edge, though currently less stable than KDE. GNOME not only provides a desktop environment, but also a development platform — providing tools, libraries, and components with which to develop UNIX applications — and GNOME Office, a set of office applications.

3.8 KDE

The K Desktop Environment (KDE) is an easy-to-use contemporary desktop environment for the UNIX operating system. The major advantage of KDE over something like Microsoft Windows is that it is completely free. KDE is also open source; this means that the development of the desktop has not been restricted to one individual or one company. The result is well supported and professional and benefits from a wide range of applications, upgrades of which can be downloaded directly from the Internet.

When you run KDE on your computer you are presented with a default desktop configuration that contains the following:

▶ A **panel** at the bottom of the screen that is used to start applications and switch between desktops. This default panel is customisable.

▶ The **taskbar** at the bottom of the screen that is used to manage currently running applications.

▶ The **desktop** of files and folders. This desktop represents only a quarter of the total desktop work area. You can move between the desktop areas by selecting the numbered buttons found in the KDE panel.

3.8.1 Desktop help

You should familiarise yourself with the on-line KDE Help browser. This can be run by clicking on the KDE Help icon in the KDE panel, or alternatively by clicking on the K icon and selecting KDE Help from the selection menu (see Figure 3.1). It is possible to navigate your way around the help system via a set of links and by using the options in the 'Goto' menu and the tool bar.

KDE Help is a valuable source of information. Here you can find all the necessary details about the KDE system, including a short history of KDE should you be interested, and documentation on all the KDE applications, details of which are regularly updated on the complete on-line KDE Help web pages.

In KDE Help there is also a reference to a short tutorial to the K Desktop Environment. It is well worth spending some time working through this tutorial, as it is not overly detailed, yet covers most of the important features you will need.

Finally, KDE help is connected to the underlying UNIX help system. You can find out more information about any UNIX commands by selecting 'search' from the KDE file menu.

Figure 3.1   The KDE desktop displaying KDE Help

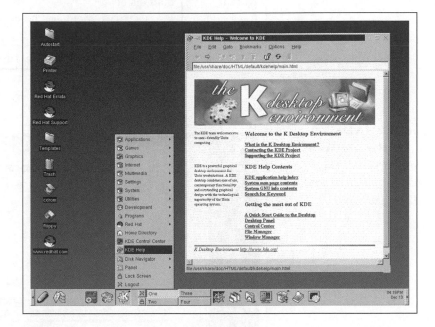

3.8.2 Applications

The KDE applications available to you do not have the same full-blown features of some of the more familiar Microsoft Windows applications. However, it is worth noting that they are all free and that upgrades can simply be downloaded from the Internet.

There are a number of applications available with the default KDE desktop. To start an application simply click on the K button on the KDE panel. Table 3.2 lists some default applications, and Figure 3.2 shows a typical screen shot.

Table 3.2   KDE
applications

KEdit	a simple text editor
KOrganizer	a calendar, 'to do' list, appointment organiser, etc.
Games	ranging from poker to mahjongg
KFax	a fax viewer
KGhostview	a postscript viewer
KPaint	a bitmap paint program
KMail	mail client
Kscd	a fast CDDB enabled CD player for the UNIX platform
KFM	a file manager and fully featured web browser

Figure 3.2   KDE
running the AbiWord
word processor, the
KDE file manager and
a CD player

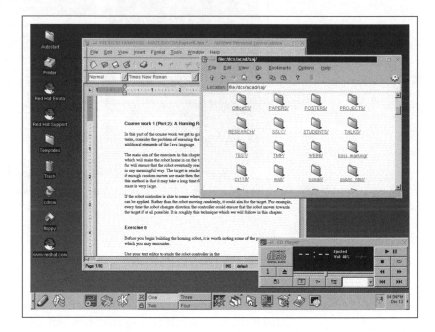

There are many more default applications than this and if you are looking for something that is more Microsoft Office-like in nature, KDE does have an office suite called KOffice (which can be downloaded from `www.koffice.org`), containing applications listed in Table 3.3.

Table 3.3 KOffice applications

KWord	a frame-based professional standard word processor
KSpread	a spreadsheet application
KPresenter	a fully-featured presentation program
Kivio	a flowchart application program
Kontour	a vector drawing application
Krayon	an image manipulation program
Kugar	for generating business quality reports
Kchart	a graph and chart drawing tool

All the components of KOffice are compatible and you can therefore embed one KOffice component in another. For more information consult the web site.

There are many more non-KDE applications which you might like to explore; two applications of note are StarOffice, a popular Linux alternative to Microsoft Office, and Gimp, an image manipulation tool similar to Adobe Photoshop.

3.8.3 The KDE Control Center

The default KDE desktop can be customised using the KDE Control Center so that it suits your own working style. The Control Center allows you to modify your desktop including the background, the colours and the style of windows etc. It is also possible to make modifications to the behaviour of the windows environment and to the configuration of input devices and sound, etc.

3.8.4 File access and the command prompt

You can access the files in your home directory by clicking on 'K', followed by 'Home Directory'. The file manager is very similar to that of Microsoft Windows, so it is possible to drag and drop files from one place in your file system to another; creating, deleting and moving files is also easily done through the file manager system.

If you wish to gain access to your files (and your computer) through the UNIX command prompt, click on the 'K' button in the KDE panel, then select 'utilities' and then 'terminal'; alternatively click on the shell button in the KDE panel.

CHAPTER SUMMARY

When installing Linux you should:

▶ Collect information about your computer using the 'System Properties' screen in Windows.

▶ Match your system capabilities to an appropriate installation. You will need to choose between a single or dual boot, and a partitioned or partitionless installation. VMware and WINE provide alternative options.

▶ Installing Linux is best done using the YaST set-up tool (or similar).

Once you have Linux installed the KDE desktop environment provides an easy to use contemporary desktop environment for your new UNIX operating system.

Getting started

CHAPTER OVERVIEW

This chapter discusses

▶ conducting a simple dialogue with a UNIX machine;

▶ simple use of the text editor Vi;

▶ getting help via the command man;

▶ using email with UNIX

▶ input and output streams; and

▶ input and output redirection and pipes.

This chapter describes how you start (and finish) a session on a UNIX computer, together with some of the basic commands which you can use. We assume that you are now using a UNIX or Linux system which has a system administrator. If you are using a stand-alone Linux system, then *you* are the system administrator. From now on, any reference to UNIX should be interpreted as 'UNIX or Linux', since the two operating systems appear virtually identical to the user.

4.1 Using UNIX

4.1.1 Usernames

In order to use your UNIX system you will need a **username** and a **password**. The username is a code which will allow you to access the system, and to distinguish you from any other users. For the rest of this book, we shall assume you have been given the username chris. The password verifies that you are in fact the person allowed to use that username, and is similar to the PIN (4-digit code) of an ATM (cash machine), but longer and more secure. You should already have been told what arrangements have been made for allocating you a username. If not, you must ask your system administrator.

ACRONYM

PIN = 'Personal Identification Number'
ATM = 'Automated Teller Machine'

31

You will either be asked to choose a password, or you will initially be allocated one, in which case you will have the opportunity to change your password at a later time. When choosing a password, which can normally be up to eight characters long, bear in mind that you don't want anyone else to guess what it is. Some simple rules will help you. *Always* use a mixture of upper-case and lower-case letters, together with digits or other symbols. *Always* choose passwords which are eight characters long. *Never* choose as password a word that occurs in a dictionary, or which is the name of a person. If you ever think that someone has discovered your password, *change it immediately and tell your system administrator.* It is also good practice to get into the habit of changing your password every few weeks as a matter of routine.

4.1.2 Logging in

Once you have found a terminal, or you have set up your own Linux machine, you are in a position to use the system. Sit down *and make yourself comfortable.* Make sure you can see the screen clearly and that you can reach the keyboard easily. Not only can an awkward body posture be uncomfortable, it can be dangerous, contributing to **RSI**, if held for more than short periods of time.

ACRONYM

RSI = 'Repetitive Strain Injury'

Check that your computer is turned on — you may need to press the *Return* key since some computers darken their screens, or run a screensaver, after a period of inactivity. Adjust the screen's brightness so that it is at a comfortable level. Somewhere on the screen you will see the line

```
login:
```

If your computer has a graphics terminal with windows, use the mouse to ensure that the cursor is within the window containing the `login:` message. Now type in your username followed by *Return.* The computer will then print on the screen the message

```
Password:
```

and you should then type in your password. *What you type in as the password will not appear on the screen,* for obvious security reasons. If there are other people in the same room as you, be discrete when typing in the password, and make sure no-one is standing looking over your shoulder. If you make a mistake typing in your username or password, don't worry — you'll be given another chance. If you forget your password, your system administrator can allocate you a new one.

Be careful when you type that you distinguish between upper-case and lower-case letters — UNIX treats them as different. If your username is `chris`, and you enter **Chris** at the `login:` prompt, the system will not allow you to log in.

Most UNIX systems appear different to their users in many superficial ways. For instance, types of computer display will vary. The messages displayed on the screen when you log in to the system can be changed. If you are using a UNIX system at a University or College, it is likely that a document is produced by your institution to explain how to use the UNIX machines, and *you should consult that document*. It will clarify the differences (if any) between your UNIX system and the standard version described here.

4.2 Logging out

NOTE

Sometimes the system will be set up so that ctrl-D fails to work, in which case you should type exit *instead*

When you wish to finish using UNIX — known as **logging out** — there are two things you need to do. Firstly, in each command window you should type **ctrl-D** on a line by itself. Secondly, you must close down the window manager by following the menu choices to Logout. The machine will respond by giving you a prompt so that the next user can log in.

4.3 Commands

4.3.1 Typing in commands

After you have logged in, and a command window is available, the system will **prompt** you to type in a command.

The prompt is usually **$** (**dollar**), though many systems are able to change this, and you yourself are able to alter it.

NOTE

Linux distributions always have a POSIX shell set up as the default

Beware, however, if you get a prompt that terminates in **%** (percent) — this is usually an indication that the shell you will talk to is either the C shell or a derivative of it, and not a POSIX shell. Although most of the next couple of chapters will still be valid for such a shell, there are significant incompatibilities, and much of Chapters 7–9 will not be correct. In such a circumstance, it may be possible for your login shell to be changed to a POSIX shell (such as `bash`). Again, consult your system administrator. Try now typing **date** (remembering to press the *Return* key at the end). You should see on the screen something like

```
$ date
Tue May 14 20:10:39 GMT 2002
$
```

By typing **date** you have instructed the machine to obey the command called `date`; it has executed the command and has printed on your screen a message (as instructed by the command `date`). When that command completes, you are then given another prompt. Try now typing nonsense

33

— you should get something like

```
$ qwerty
qwerty: command not found
$
```

telling you that it doesn't understand what you've typed in.

The command `date` is the name of a program — it's written in machine code, and you don't need to know the details of *how* it works, just *what* it does. To describe a program such as `date` being obeyed, we use the words **running** or **executing**.

You will have been notified of the command you must type for changing your password; this is usually `passwd`, although some system administrators prefer to install their own command. On some systems `passwd` can work very slowly, and your new password may not take effect until a few minutes after you have entered it, especially if your UNIX system is a network of machines rather than a single computer.

4.3.2 Commands and options

UNIX commands take the form of a name (such as `date`), possibly followed by **options**, and other **arguments** as required. An option is denoted by a hyphen (-) followed by a single character (itself possibly followed by arguments). For example, the command `date` can take only one possible option, namely `-u`. Without this option, the date and time are printed for the local timezone; with option `-u` the time is converted to **UTC** thus

```
$ date -u
Tue May 14 20:10:39 UTC 2002
```

Information about exactly what machine and operating system version are being used can be found by typing `uname` (UNIX name). This command will either give a brief (one word) description (typically the name of the operating system), or more detailed information. `uname` allows several options, including `-a` (all) to display all information about the system. For instance,

```
$ uname
Linux
$ uname -a
Linux box 2.4.10-4GB #1 Fri Sep 28 17:19:49 GMT 2001 i686
unknown
```

The output from `uname` indicates that the operating system is Linux, its (kernel) **release** is `2.4.10`, **version** `#1 Fri Sep 28 17:19:49 GMT 2001`,

NOTE

`passwd` *is not a standard POSIX command, since the shell does not specify* how *to authenticate users*

ACRONYM

UTC = 'Universal Coordinated Time', which is GMT

NOTE

A company which writes a UNIX operating system will have its own name for it, and will update it periodically; major updates are called releases, *minor updates are versions* and the name of the machine you are using is box. The hardware being used (i.e. the type of physical machine, as opposed to the operating system, which is software), is an i686.

Options -m (machine), -n (nodename), -r (release), -s (system name) or -v (version) can be used to print out *part* of the information that -a (all) supplies. With no argument, -s is assumed by default. You can combine options, for instance to print out the release *and* version of your system, and can do so in one of four ways:

```
$ uname -r -v
2.4.10-4GB #1 Fri Sep 28 17:19:49 GMT 2001
$ uname -v -r
2.4.10-4GB #1 Fri Sep 28 17:19:49 GMT 2001
$ uname -rv
2.4.10-4GB #1 Fri Sep 28 17:19:49 GMT 2001
$ uname -vr
2.4.10-4GB #1 Fri Sep 28 17:19:49 GMT 2001
```

Try entering uname with the various options.

You will be communicating with the machine from a **terminal**. The command tty displays the name of the terminal you are currently using. If you are using a windowed display, UNIX treats each **window** as a separate terminal with its own name.

ACRONYM

tty = 'teletype'

Worked example 4.1

What is the name of the terminal or window you are using?
Solution: Use **tty**:

```
$ tty
pts/1
```

and the name is pts/1 (or whatever is printed on the screen by tty). Note that some systems, including Sun's *Solaris*, have more complex names, such as /dev/pts/1

Another command you can try now is who:

```
$ who
chris     pts/1    Dec 3 14:23 (console)
sam       ttyp2    Dec 3 08:38 (console)
jo        pts/4    Dec 3 13:58 (console)
```

NOTE

On some systems who will also display extra information

This command lists those people currently logged in to the system by **username**, together with the terminals they are using and the dates and times they last logged in. In the above example chris logged in at 2.23

pm on Dec 3 to a terminal known as `pts/1`. This command allows several options, including `-u` (unused); try typing the command `who -u`. The output you will get is similar to that for `who` on its own, except that an extra column of information is given, perhaps:

```
$ who -u
chris     pts/1    Dec 3 14:23   .   (console)
sam       ttyp2    Dec 3 08:38 01:03 (console)
jo        pts/4    Dec 3 13:58 00:02 (console)
```

The extra column indicates **idle time** — the amount of time since a user has touched the keyboard. So, `chris` is active at the present moment (a dot is used in place of a time if the user has actually used the system in the previous few seconds). However, `sam` has been idle for 1 hour and 3 minutes (perhaps `sam` has forgotten to logout?), and `jo` has been idle for only two minutes (perhaps thinking about what to do next).

4.4 Communication with other users

A big advantage of modern computer networks is that messages may be sent between users of machines on such a network, or people on the same machine, and email has become ubiquitous. It is also possible to send messages to other users, either on the same machine, or elsewhere on a network, in 'real-time'.

4.4.1 Email

Although most people are familiar with email, through sophisticated mail software such as Microsoft's Outlook or Eudora, it is instructive to look at the basic facility available under UNIX. This does still have uses, for example if you require a shell program to send email without intervention from the user.

The standard utility for sending email is **Mailx**. To make use of this, you need to know the username of the person you wish to send a message to. Type `mailx` followed by the username, and then type in the message terminated by *ctrl-D* on a line of its own. If option `-s` is given to `mailx`, the string following `-s` will be used to denote the *subject* of the message to the recipient. For example,

```
$ mailx -s "Programming Assignment" sam
Hello Sam.
Have you finished the assignment yet?
```
ctrl-D

will send a message to user `sam`. If you have a tilde (the symbol ˜) as the

NOTE

It is always good practice to give an email message a subject

NOTE

If the subject string contains spaces, then it must be enclosed in quotes

first character on any line you type in, this will be interpreted by `mailx` as a management instruction. For instance, if you wish to edit a message half-way through typing it in, type ~v and you will then be editing it using a standard text editor (usually Vi).

If you have a friend who is currently logged in, mail him or her a short message and ask them to mail you one. If not, mail one to yourself. In either case, the mail arrives almost instantaneously.

In order to read mail that has been sent to you, just type `mailx` on its own. If you have mail that you have not read, `mailx` will display a brief list of messages awaiting you, with the date they were received, the name of the sender, and the subject (if specified by the sender). For instance,

```
$ mailx
>N  1 sam Wed Jul 27 15:28  16/465    Programming Assignment
 N  2 jo  Thu Jul 28 19:33  77/1220
```

In this example, you have two messages (each message is given a number), the first from user `sam`, the second from user `jo`. The mail from `sam` has subject `Programming Assignment`, is 16 lines long and contains 465 characters; that from `jo` was sent without a subject specified, is 77 lines long, and contains 1220 characters. While you are reading your mail, at any particular moment one message is **current**, and may be read, deleted, saved in a file, or edited. The > symbol indicates that message number 1 is the current message. The command p (print) will then display the current message on the screen. If you type ? a screenful of *help* messages will be displayed indicating the other commands you can give to Mailx.

Note that this mail is simple text, and does not contain attachments or HTML enhancements, which are now commonplace.

Most UNIX systems are equipped with a collection of other (not POSIX) programs for electronic mail: **Elm**, **Mail**, **Mush**, **Pine**, and **Xmail** coming to mind. These utilities are similar to Mailx, but the sophistication and facilities vary. Check with your system administrator for the preferred mail programs on your system, and if they differ from Mailx for simple use.

NOTE

Most Web browsers include commands to let you send mail

4.4.2 Other communication facilities

Electronic mail is useful for sending messages, but not for holding a 'conversation', nor for sending urgent messages (since not all users will read mail very frequently). Two utilities are provided in UNIX to enable 'real-time' communication between logged in users. The first is `write`: suppose user `sam` is logged on, and you wish to send Sam a (short) message; use `write sam` followed by the lines of the message then *ctrl-D*.

```
$ write sam
```

```
Hi Sam.
It's coffee time
```

The message will be sent across line-by-line. Your message will appear on Sam's screen, preceded by a line telling `sam` who's sending the message:

```
Message from chris@box on ttyp9 at 14:42 ...
Hi Sam.
It's coffee time
```

If `sam` was logged on at several terminals at once (which is possible if Sam has multiple windows on a graphics display), you could specify the terminal the message should appear on, so:

$ write sam ttyp7

Sam can reply to you with the command `write chris`. Whatever `sam` is doing, the lines you type will appear on Sam's screen.

It could be that the recipient of your message does not want this to happen (perhaps he or she is doing a complicated operation and doesn't wish to be disturbed). They can prevent messages being displayed by means of `mesg`. To deny other users permission to write messages to your screen, type `mesg n`. To reinstate permission, `mesg y` will reverse the effect of `mesg n`. If you try to `write` to a user who has denied you permission, you will simply get an error message.

The second communications mechanism is `talk`. Rather than sending lines of messages, `talk` is the nearest you will come to actually talking to another user. It sends messages character-by-character as you type them in, and will work over networks. To run `talk`, the syntax is just as for `write`. After you have typed `talk sam`, a message will appear on Sam's terminal:

```
Message from chris@box
talk: connection requested by chris@box
talk: respond with: talk chris@box
```

When `sam` types `talk chris@box` (or whatever address `talk` specifies) both your screen and Sam's will be cleared and divided into separate regions, one for each of you. When you press a key, it will appear in 'your' part of the screen; when Sam presses a key the corresponding character will appear in 'Sam's' part. You can use the *DELETE* key if you press a key by mistake. Your conversation will be terminated when either of you presses *ctrl-C*. Standard input and standard output are not the mechanisms employed by `talk`. Find a friend who is also logged in and experiment with `write` and `talk`.

ACRONYM

n = 'no', y = 'yes'

4.5 Files

In UNIX, you are able to create, delete and edit files, but before
attempting to perform such operations on your files, you may need to
check which files you have at the moment. The command to do this is `ls`
(list).

If you have only just started to use the UNIX system, you should not
have created any files. If you type `ls` on its own, this should be confirmed
when nothing is printed in response, so:

NOTE

*There may also be
'hidden' files, which we
will discuss later*

```
$ ls
$
```

You will need to create and update files containing text (for example,
programs written in Java, Pascal or C, or word-processed reports). There
are many simple to use **editors** available, and Windows users will
probably be familiar with Microsoft Word and with Notepad. These are
fine for modifying small amounts of text, but are cumbersome if large files
are involved, or if repeated changes have to be made. We look in this
section at editors which are available under UNIX, and which are suitable
for heavy use. In particular, we introduce the standard UNIX editor Vi,
which may at first sight seem relatively tricky to use. Fear not! The skills
you will gain in later chapters will feed back into use of Vi, and allow you
to make complex changes to a file quickly and easily. We also discuss the
other options available to you if you prefer at this stage to use an editor
which is more straightforward for simpler use.

4.5.1 The editor Vi

NOTE

*Vi is pronounced
'vee-eye', and stands for
'VIsual display editor'*

Vi is the 'standard' screen editor on UNIX. Whilst being the editor of
choice for many systems programmers, it has a reputation, arguably
undeserved, for being difficult to use. There is a tradeoff here — if you
use a simple, graphical editor, then you will be able to create files quickly,
and easily make *simple* changes to them. However, complex editing cannot
often be done quickly with simple editors. There is a learning curve for
using Vi, but once mastered the benefits later on are substantial.
Furthermore, the skills needed to use Vi overlap substantially with those
needed for UNIX shell programming, and include topics covered later on
in this book, such as Regular Expressions and the stream editor Sed.

NOTE

*If you have already
created a file called
`myfile` then choose a
filename you do not yet
have*

The command `vi` invokes the Vi screen editor, which has facilities to
enter text into a file and to change text already there. In this subsection
we discuss only a small proportion of Vi's facilities, enough to allow you
to create and edit files for the rest of this book. To edit the file `myfile`
(say), type `vi` followed by the name of the file:

```
$ vi myfile
```

39

Your screen (or window) will be cleared, and the cursor will appear in the top-left corner of the screen. Along the left-hand side of the screen will be a column of ˜, indicating that those lines on the screen are not (yet) being used by Vi. Additionally, a message may appear on the bottom line of the screen.

Now, type the letter **a** (append text) and type in several lines of text — the *Return* key will terminate each line — followed by *ESC*. Then press **h**, **j**, **k**, **l**, and see the cursor moving around the screen one square at a time, as pictured in Figure 4.1.

Figure 4.1 Cursor movement in vi

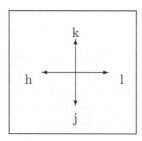

You won't be allowed to move the cursor to any location that does not contain text. Position the cursor near the centre of your text and press **a** again. Type in more text — it will appear after the cursor position. As before, *ESC* will terminate the input. If you're not sure whether or not you have typed *ESC*, then type it again — if you type too many, the extra ones will be ignored and will do no harm. Move the cursor to the centre again, type **i** (insert text), and repeat what you did for **a** — you will see that text is inserted, but this time *before* the cursor position.

To delete text, you can remove one character at a time by placing the cursor on it and typing **x**. To remove a whole line, place the cursor on the line and type **dd**. To remove part of the line from the cursor to the end of the line, type **D**. Try these commands now.

When you have finished making all the changes you desire, type **ZZ** and the contents of the file will be stored on disk and you will be returned to the shell.

There are three *modes* that Vi may be in. There is **command mode**, during which you can move the cursor around the screen, and generally move from one part of the file to another, deleting and altering text at the point of your cursor. When you enter Vi, you always start in command-mode. Secondly, there is **colon-mode**. This is necessary when you wish to perform more complicated operations on your file that cannot (easily) be done with simple keystrokes. Third, there is **input mode** during which you can enter text.

To enter colon-mode, you must be in command-mode, so make sure you are not entering text (type *ESC* if necessary). Then type a colon (:) (not followed by *Return*). The cursor will immediately move to the bottom line of your screen and will be preceded by a colon. At this stage, there are a few colon-mode commands that you must know. If you make a mistake while typing, then the command u (undo), either in colon-mode or in command-mode, will correct it. If you accidentally type a colon, you can return to command-mode by just pressing *Return*. In the following discussion we assume that you are in command-mode unless otherwise stated.

Try using Vi to create in file myfile just two lines:

```
hello
there
```

After you have done this, and left Vi by typing ZZ, use the command ls to check which files you now have. You should find:

```
$ ls
myfile
```

Now edit the file myfile again and remove the two lines by typing dd twice to delete each one in turn. Choose another document, such as a book or a newspaper, and copy a couple of paragraphs into the file. Make sure that you enter them correctly, using the Vi commands we have just discussed to make any corrections. If the file fills more than one screen you can 'scroll' backwards and forwards through the file by typing **ctrl-U** and **ctrl-D** respectively.

Some other cursor-moving commands are useful:

▶ ^ moves the cursor to the start of the current line,

▶ $ moves the cursor to the end of the current line.

The file will contain words, which just as in English are sequences of letters and/or digits:

▶ w moves forward through the file to the *start* of the next word,

▶ e moves forward through the file to the next *end* of a word,

▶ b moves *backwards* to the *start* of a word.

If you know that there is a word, or sequence of characters, in the file that you wish to find, then Vi will search for that string:

▶ typing / followed by the string you are looking for, followed by *Return*, will look *forwards* in the file for the string, and

▶ typing ?, rather than /, searches for a *previous* occurrence of a string.

So, in order to search for the next occurrence of hello, you should type

```
/hello
```

followed by *Return*. If a line is too long, you can split it into two by positioning the cursor where you wish it to be split, and using i or a to insert a *Newline* character. If you have two lines you wish to join to a single one, place the cursor on the first one and type J (join). There are also colon-mode commands for moving about the file. For each colon-mode command you must press *Return* at the end of the command:

▶ :0 moves the cursor to the start of the file,

▶ :$ moves the cursor to the beginning of the last line of the file,

▶ :*n* moves the cursor to the beginning of line *n*.

Practice the other commands listed above and those in Tables 4.1 and 4.2, and get used to them. You will have to create many files, and it is worthwhile getting used to the editor at this stage. Some sites will support a command called `vilearn`, which is a user-friendly program that teaches you how to use Vi, and if it is available you may find it very helpful.

Table 4.1
Command-mode
commands in Vi

a	enter insert mode after cursor position
b	moves the cursor back to the previous start of a word
cw	change the word the cursor is on by deleting it and entering insert mode
D	delete rest of line after cursor position
dd	delete the line the cursor is on
dw	delete the word the cursor is on
e	moves the cursor to the next end of a word
i	enter insert mode before cursor position
J	join the line the cursor is on and the following line together
o	open a new line, position the cursor at the start of it and enter insert mode
w	moves the cursor to the start of the next word
x	delete the character at the cursor
ZZ	write all changes to the file, and quit Vi
^	moves the cursor to the beginning of the current line
C	moves the cursor to the end of the current line
/*word*	search forward for the string *word*
?*word*	search backwards for the string *word*
ctrl-D	move down the file half a screen
ctrl-U	move back up the file half a screen

Table 4.2
Colon-mode
commands in Vi

q	quit Vi, provided you have not changed your file at all since you last saved it (if you have altered the file, Vi will warn you and will not terminate)
q!	quit Vi, and any changes you have made to the file will be discarded and the file left in its original state
w	writes all the changes to the file, but remain in Vi
wq	equivalent to performing command w followed by command q; same as command-mode ZZ
0	moves the cursor to the beginning of the file
$	moves the cursor to the end of the file
number	moves the cursor to the start of line *number*

At this point, mention must be made of an editor called ex. Strictly speaking, ex and Vi are the same animal — think of Vi *permanently in colon-mode* so that after each colon-mode command the cursor is prompted on the bottom line by a colon, and you have ex. The command visual to ex will turn it into Vi. If you are in Vi and in command-mode the command Q (quit) will put you permanently in colon-mode, namely in ex.

4.5.2 Other editors

NOTE

Emacs is not POSIX

Another text editor that is in common use is **Emacs**, and is invoked with the command emacs. The Emacs and Vi editors differ greatly in style, and being competent in using one will not necessarily help you when you use the other. If your system administrator recommends another editor in place of Vi you may wish to use that editor instead, and you should refer to the relevant system documentation. The principal advantage of Vi is that, being a 'standard' editor, you can rely on it being available on all UNIX systems. In common with many UNIX utilities, Vi is somewhat terse, and some people simply don't like it. Advantages of Emacs are that you can 'customise' its commands, and that it includes many powerful facilities not available in Vi. However, these benefits are offset by the complexity of Emacs for the novice user.

Several other editors should be mentioned. The 'simplest' editor is ed (edit), which looks to the user similar to ex in colon-mode. It is used where full-screen editing may be problematic, for instance if you are accessing the UNIX system via a slow communications link such as a telephone line with a 56k modem. If you can use ex, then learning ed should present no major problems. Like ex, ed is a standard editor that you can expect to find on all UNIX systems. The commands available to ed are similar (though not all are identical) to those used by ex, but ed cannot be used as a full-screen editor. The machine can also edit files as

NOTE

*Neither command is
defined in POSIX*

well as the user; this can be done using Sed, which we discuss in
Chapter 10.

Simple text editing can be done with graphical editors, such as **NEdit**
or **KEdit**. These are *point and click* applications, which allow you for
instance to *cut and paste*. They are fine, but complex editing may require
many mouse movements. Also, unlike the Microsoft Windows
environment, there is no standard graphical editor, but they are simple to
use and require no instruction here. There is also an open-source version
of Vi called **Vim**, which supports a graphical interface.

4.6 Input and output

We now leave discussion of editors and return to consideration of the shell.

When you type in text at the terminal, the input is **buffered**; the
characters you type in are not immediately transmitted to the shell. They
are initially stored in a temporary area of the computer's memory called a
buffer; the contents of the buffer are usually transmitted to the shell at
the end of each line, when you press *Return*. A consequence of buffering is
that if you make an error when typing in data on your terminal, you can
correct it. Systems vary in the amount of 'line-editing' they allow, but
you can expect at least the following:

DEL   deletes the most recent character typed in
ctrl-U deletes the whole of the line currently being typed

Once you have typed in a command, and the command begins to be
executed, you may be requested to type in data as **input** to the command,
which will, in response, send messages as **output**. Output consists of the
stream of characters usually sent to the screen. The commands we have
looked at already — `ls`, `date` and `who` — give output but require no
input. Some commands — such as `vi` — will 'interact' with you, and need
you to type in data while they are running. For simple commands that
require input, the input is formed by the characters you type in at the
keyboard. More complex commands (`vi` is in this category) may also have
other input and output, but this description of how a command
communicates with the system will serve us for the present.

Each command has associated with it three input and output **streams**,
as shown in Figure 4.2. They are called **standard input**, **standard output**
and **standard error** (often abbreviated to **stdin**, **stdout** and **stderr**
respectively). Normally, standard input will be taken from the keyboard,
and standard output and standard error will both be sent to the terminal
screen. A command may, in addition, have other input and/or output
streams. Each input/output stream is also given a number: 0 for standard
input, 1 for standard output and 2 for standard error.

Figure 4.2   Input to and output from a command

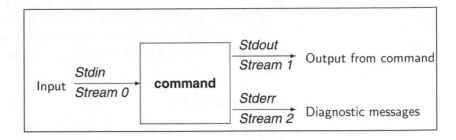

Commands that require input will usually take it from standard input, and the normal output of a command will go to standard output. Standard error is used for other messages, typically warning messages if the command could not be executed as intended (for instance, if you try to print a file that does not exist). Thus, the output from a command and its diagnostics can be separated, as we shall discuss later. The messages sent to standard error are not always error messages, and will include general information of use to you that is not part of the usual output of a command — it's called 'standard error' simply because the majority of messages sent to it tend to be error messages.

To terminate input to a command, type *ctrl-D* on a line by itself. When you log in, each command you type represents a new line of input to your login shell. A shell is simply a program that takes commands as its input. Terminating input to your login shell by typing *ctrl-D* causes the shell program to finish; that's all that logging out really is.

A useful command is `cat` (catenate), which takes the names of zero or more files as arguments and copies them, in order, to standard output. We can use `cat` to display files we have created. If `cat` has no arguments, standard input is copied directly to standard output. For instance, to display the file `myfile` which was created earlier using Vi:

```
$ cat myfile
hello
there
```

NOTE

cat echoes each line as soon as it has been typed in since input is buffered

With no arguments, `cat` will take its input from the standard input:

```
$ cat
abc          ← standard input
abc          ← standard output
def          ← standard input
def          ← standard output
ctrl-D
```

It is possible, indeed common, to **redirect** input and/or output. Instead of input coming from the keyboard, it can be the contents of a file or the output of another command. Similarly, output from a command can be sent to a file or used as input to another command.

The symbol < indicates that standard input should come from a file, and the following will produce the same output as `cat myfile` (Figure 4.3):

```
$ cat <myfile
hello
there
```

So, having created file `myfile`, you can display its contents on the screen in two ways. In the first case, `cat` is given one argument, the filename `myfile`, the contents of which are copied to standard output; in the second, `cat` is given zero arguments and thus the standard input, which has been redirected from `myfile`, is sent to standard output.

Figure 4.3
`cat <myfile`

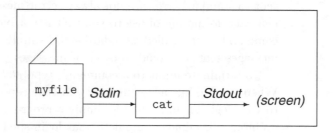

The standard output can be directed to a file. The output from `date`, for example, can be sent to file `xyz` (Figure 4.4):

```
$ date >xyz
```

Figure 4.4
`date >xyz`

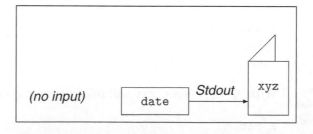

Now, type `cat xyz` to examine the contents of file `xyz`. The symbol > indicates that the standard output from `date` is to be sent to a file whose name immediately follows. In the case of `cat`, we can do the same, but remember that `cat` also requires input from the standard input stream (Figure 4.5). The following replaces the contents of `xyz`:

```
$ cat >xyz
```

have a nice ← *standard input*
day ← *standard input*
ctrl-D

You can copy several files to standard output:

```
$ cat myfile xyz
hello
there
have a nice
day
```

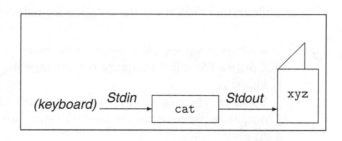

A command can redirect both its input and its output; the following will
create a copy of file `myfile` called `def` (Figure 4.6):

```
$ cat <myfile >def
```

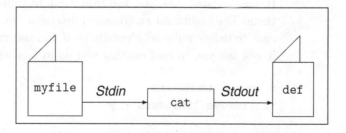

The *effect* of this is the same as if you had *not* redirected standard input
and had given `cat` a single argument `myfile`:

```
$ cat myfile >def
```

Beware that you cannot take input from and send output to the *same* file
— it won't work. The file you try to take the input from will be destroyed
in preparation for receiving the output *before* anything is read from it.
A command that requires a filename as an argument can use the
symbol – (hyphen) to denote standard input. The following dialogue

illustrates this:

```
$ cat myfile -
hello          ← file myfile
there          ← file myfile
Mike           ← standard input
Mike           ← standard output
ctrl-D
```

Thus we can refer to the standard input in situations where simple redirection using < would be inappropriate. The hyphen can be used wherever the name of a file is used, so you can refer to standard input as a file (rather than using the notation for redirection).

Worked example 4.2

Create a file called `theusers` containing a list of those users currently logged in.
Solution: The command `who` will send a list of users to standard output, so we need only redirect the standard output of `who` to the file:

```
$ who >theusers
```

If you now type `cat theusers` a list of users who were logged on will be displayed on the screen.

Having created files, you will from time to time wish to remove some of them. The command `rm` (remove) deletes a file. Take care, as it is very easy to delete a file accidentally — if you use `rm` with option `-i` (inquire) it will ask you to confirm that you do in fact wish to delete the file:

```
$ rm -i theusers
rm: remove 'theusers'? y
```

We can separate standard output and standard error. To illustrate this we set up `cat` so that it produces good output and an error message by asking it to copy two files, one of which (say `myfile`) exists, and the other (`qwerty`, for instance) does not. We send the standard output to file `output` and the standard error to file `error`:

```
$ cat myfile qwerty
hello
there
cat: qwerty: No such file or directory
$ cat myfile qwerty 2>error 1>output
$ cat output
```

```
hello
there
$ cat error
cat: qwerty: No such file or directory
```

NOTE

*This notation will not
work for the C shell and
its derivatives*

By **prepending** the symbol > with the number of the output stream, that
stream is redirected to the named file. When > is used alone, it is
equivalent to 1>, so that the diagnostic messages are still sent to your
terminal unless you explicitly request otherwise.

Although in normal use UNIX commands have only one input stream,
it is possible to write programs that have more than one such stream. In
this case the same syntax applies as for output, namely that 0< denotes
taking input stream number 0 from a file, and 0< is synonymous with <.

If a command redirects output, from whatever stream, to a file using >,
then if that file does not exist it will be created. If the file does exist, then
it will be overwritten and its previous contents will be lost. If you wish to
append data to the end of a file, then replace > by >>. Consider the
following dialogue:

NOTE

*Appending data to a file
means adding it on at
the end without affecting
the data already stored
in it*

```
$ date >outfile
$ date >>outfile
$ cat outfile
Tue Dec 4 20:10:39 GMT 2001
Tue Dec 4 20:10:47 GMT 2001
```

The first time `date` is called, the standard output is sent to file `outfile`;
the second time, the output has been added to the end of the same file.

4.6.1 Scripts

A method of performing several commands, one after the other, is to
create a file containing those commands, one per line, and then 'execute'
that file. As an example, create a file using Vi, called (say) `whenandwho`,
and containing two lines:

```
date
who
```

Now, type `sh whenandwho` and the commands `date` and `who` mentioned in
the file `whenandwho` will be executed, and you will get

```
$ sh whenandwho
Tue Dec 4 20:10:39 GMT 2001
chris    pts/1   Dec 3 07:21 (console)
sam      pts/3   Dec 3 08:38 (console)
jo       pts/4   Dec 3 14:58 (console)
```

NOTE

'Script' for short

A file such as `whenandwho`, which contains commands, is called a **shell script**.

At this stage it is important to understand how UNIX executes commands in a script. When you are logged into your system, you will be communicating with it via a program called a shell. The shell that is run from the moment you log in to the end of your session is your **login shell**. It is possible to run further copies of the shell by typing the command `sh`. In order to execute a shell script, the program `sh` is run, but instead of taking standard input from your terminal, the input comes from the file. Thus while the script is executing there are two copies of `sh` running. The login shell runs one command, namely `sh`, and this shell executes the commands in the file.

When writing scripts, the command `echo` is very useful. This command takes arguments and simply copies them to the standard output, thus:

```
$ echo Hello there
Hello there
```

Worked example 4.3

Write a script called `niceday` to display today's time and date together with a user-friendly message, thus:

```
$ sh niceday
The time and date are now:
Tue Dec 4 20:10:39 GMT 2001
Have a nice day!
```

Solution: We can use `date` to output the date and time, and `echo` to output the messages on lines 1 and 3. To create the file `niceday`, use either Vi or, if your typing is good, simply `cat`:

```
$ cat >niceday
echo The time and date are now:
date
echo Have a nice day!
ctrl-D
```

4.6.2 Here-documents

You will sometimes wish to give input to a command, where that input consists of a small number of lines — for example, if you want to create a script which, after it executes its commands, mails `sam` a message that is more than a single line.

One possibility would be to create a file for the message (`mymessage`, say), redirect the input for `mailx` to come from that file, and include the line

```
mailx sam <mymessage
```

as the last line of the script. This would work, but would involve creating two files (one for your script, and one for the message) rather than just one. In large scripts it might become confusing if too many files have to be created. Note that this would not be a problem if `mailx` was not in a script, as you could take the input to `mailx` from your terminal — but since the input to a script may be redirected from elsewhere this is not always possible.

A solution is known as a **here-document**. Following the symbol `<<` comes a word, and all subsequent lines of standard input are treated as the standard input for the command, up to (but not including) that word. For instance,

```
mailx sam <<END
```
line 1 of message
...
last line of message
```
END
```

The line that terminates the input need not be `END` — any word will do. Try mailing yourself a message using a here-document. Although here-documents work perfectly well interactively, their principal use is in scripts.

4.6.3 Pipes

An extension of redirecting input and output to and from files is to redirect to and from other commands. The syntax for **pipes** is similar to that for file redirection, except that the symbol `|` is used instead of `<` and `>`. If we have a command `X` whose standard output is to be used as the standard input to a command `Y`, we could have

> **NOTE**
>
> | *is a vertical bar*

```
$ X > tempfile
$ Y < tempfile
```

storing the output of `X` in a temporary file `tempfile`. However, this is not elegant, and in some situations impossible (if you require `Y` to process the output of `X` as soon as it is produced). By means of a pipe, we can join the two streams together, as follows (Figure 4.7):

```
$ X | Y
```

Figure 4.7   X | Y

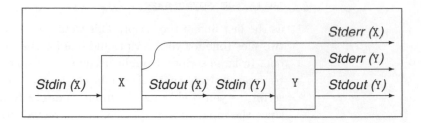

Worked example 4.4

Send an email message to user `sam` to inform `sam` of the current time and date.
Solution: The command `date` sends to its standard output the time and date, and `mailx` sends an email message from the standard input stream. Therefore we can pipe the output of `date` to the input of `mailx`:

```
$ date | mailx -s "Today's time and date" sam
```

Using > or <, different input or output streams can be specified, but pipes only connect standard output to standard input, and cannot be used with the standard error stream.

You can use `write` in a script, and since the input is standard input this can be redirected or piped just as with any other UNIX command. However, you cannot use `talk` in a pipe since it does not use the standard input and output mechanisms.

A script may contain input and output redirection, and pipes.

Worked example 4.5

In a script, mail `sam` a message that says `Running my script now`.
Solution: Using Vi, create a file containing:

```
echo Running my script now | mailx -s "What I'm doing"
sam
```

4.6.4 Making copies of input and output

Suppose you have a command that displays something on your screen, and you wish to save it in a file. So far, we have discussed only how that output can be redirected to a file, so that in order to see it on the screen *and* save it in a file there are two possibilities. Firstly, you could run the command twice (the first time with no redirection, and then directed to a file). Secondly you initially run the command with output sent to a file and then view the file using a pager. Both methods involve duplicating the output to the command, firstly by producing it twice, and secondly by storing it and then viewing the stored output.

The first method is no use if the command you run is *interactive*, conducting a dialogue with you while it is running. If you ran the command twice you might give it different input each time, so the two outputs would probably differ. If your command was time-sensitive, such as `date`, the second method would simply give you the wrong answer when you tried to view the output.

If you wish to make a copy in a file of the input to a command, there would also be a problem. If the command is interactive, so that we cannot store the input in an intermediate file, we have not yet met any mechanism at all which will perform this task.

NOTE

Tee = ⊤

The solution is to use the command `tee`. which duplicates the standard input so:

```
$ tee copy_of_input | command_name
```

This has the same effect as the command *command_name* on its own, except that a copy of all the standard input to the command is sent to *copy_of_input* (which will be overwritten if it already exists).

Worked example 4.6

> Send user `jo` a message and keep a copy of the message in file `jo_message`.
> **Solution**: `mailx` will read standard input as the message; use `tee` to copy it:
>
> ```
> $ tee jo_message | mailx jo
> ```

To use `tee` to copy standard output, pipe the output of a command through `tee`.

Worked example 4.7

> Run the command `who`, but store a copy of the output in file `who_out`.
> **Solution**:
>
> ```
> $ who | tee who_out
> ```

4.6.5 Pagers

A **pager** is a program that will allow you to browse through a file 'one page at a time', moving backwards and forwards through the file with the minimum of keystrokes. The standard pager is `more`, although others may be available on your machine (two other commonly encountered pagers are `pg` (page) and `less`). To invoke `more`, type `more` followed by the name

of the file you wish to examine. For example, to view the file called
`/usr/dict/words`:

$ **more /usr/dict/words**

The following keystrokes will be useful:

Space	view next page
b	view previous page
Return	scroll forward one line
?	display a page of help on your terminal
q	quit

The commands that `more` understands are similar to Vi, and you can, for
instance, type `/hello` to move to an instance of the string `hello` in the
file. The command `cat`, which was discussed earlier, is fine for viewing
small files, but should not be used as a substitute for a good pager for
general viewing of text files.

4.7 Emergencies

What happens if you type in a command you realise you shouldn't have?
It may be that UNIX will provide you with an error message indicating
this; if, however, your command was a valid UNIX command that simply
does something that is not what you intended, then the situation becomes
more complex.

The worst-case scenario arises if your command runs and causes
damage, such as deleting a file you did not wish to delete. In this case,
you probably cannot recover from the error, and you quickly learn to be
more careful in future! Fortunately, such mistakes are infrequent, as there
are few commands that will destroy data. More common is the following:
you write a program, try to run it, and find that either it **hangs** (it sits
there apparently doing nothing) or begins to generate incorrect results.
You know something has gone wrong. The remedy is to **interrupt** the
command, which can be done by typing **ctrl-C**, and will cause the
command to terminate immediately. This is not the same as *ctrl-D*, which
simply indicates to the system that the standard input stream has been
closed. Try this out — there should be a file called `/usr/dict/words` on
your machine; try to display it on your screen using `cat`. It's a very big
file, and will take perhaps a minute to fully appear, so you will have
ample time to press *ctrl-C*.

The file `/usr/dict/words` simply contains a list of English words and
abbreviations, one on each line. If your system does not have such a file,
create a similar file yourself using Vi, since `/usr/dict/words` is used for
several examples later on. If you name this new file `mydictionary`, then
you should substitute `mydictionary` whenever `/usr/dict/words` is

NOTE

*Neither ctrl-C nor ctrl-D
will get you out of Vi*

NOTE

*The meaning of '/' is
discussed in Chapter 5*

mentioned in subsequent chapters. To indicate the words that might
occur in the file, the following is a typical section of `/usr/dict/words`:

```
O'Donnell
odorous
O'Dwyer
Odysseus
Odyssey
o'er
oersted
of
off
offal
```

4.8 Getting help

There is an on-line help facility available on UNIX systems. It goes under
the name of **manual pages**, and the command to get help is `man` (followed
by the topic you require assistance with). The manual pages give very
detailed information about UNIX commands, and may appear
intimidating at first — the manual 'page' for the C compiler `cc` often runs
to 20 or more screens of text. As an example, if we require more
information on the command `who`, we might get:

```
$ man who

WHO(1)                                                    WHO(1)


NAME
      who - show who is logged on


SYNOPSIS
      who [-mTu]


DESCRIPTION
      If given no arguments, who prints the following
      information for each user currently logged on:


          login name      terminal line        login time


OPTIONS
      ...
```

Do not panic! Although the format looks a bit strange, each manual
page is structured in the same way. First of all, on the top line is the
name of the command followed in parentheses by a number — the manual
pages are divided into **volumes**, usually numbered 1 to 8 inclusive. We are

concerned principally with commands in volume 1, which are commands you can type in to the shell. Other volumes give information on other UNIX utilities, such as libraries available to language compilers. The top line may also tell you who wrote the utility, and when it was last updated.

There then follows a sequence of headers (such as NAME) and information under those headings:

NAME	The name of the command, and a short description
SYNOPSIS	The arguments (if any) it expects
DESCRIPTION	A *detailed* description of the command
OPTIONS	A list of the possible options, and what they do
FILES	The files used by the command
SEE ALSO	Related topics or commands with manual pages
DIAGNOSTICS	What to do if the command fails
NOTES	Miscellaneous other useful information

Remember that UNIX commands are usually (though not always) lower-case, and that if you type them upper-case by mistake, the machine will not understand you. In the example of who above, under the heading SYNOPSIS, we have:

```
who [ -mTu ]
```

The square brackets indicate that options -m, -T and -u are *optional* and can be typed in any order and combination. For the meanings of the options and arguments, look further down the manual page.

Worked example 4.8

Find out how to display the current hardware type on which your system is running by using uname.
Solution: By typing **man uname** we get:

```
UNAME(1)                                                UNAME(1)


NAME
      uname - print system information

SYNOPSIS
      uname [-amnrsv]

DESCRIPTION
                          ...

OPTIONS
      -m          Print the name of the hardware type
                  on which the system is running.
```

> ...
>
> and thus the command you require is `uname -m` (machine).

If you are unsure which (if any) command you can use to perform a particular task, type `man -k` followed by a keyword related to that task. You will be given a brief (one-line) description of all commands indexed by that keyword, and can then select which command you would like detailed information on. You can only give `man` one keyword at a time, so if the first keyword you try doesn't indicate a suitable command, try a couple of others.

Worked example 4.9

> You wish to find who else is logged in; which command can you use?
> **Solution**: Use `man -k`; choose a single keyword relevant to the topic, say `logged`:
>
> ```
> $ man -k logged
> who (1)          - show who is logged on
> ```
>
> So you should use command `who`.

CHAPTER SUMMARY

Table 4.3   Commands introduced in this chapter

`cat`	concatenate and print files to standard output
`date`	display current time and date
`echo`	write arguments to standard output
`ed`	basic text editor
`ex`	text editor (see Vi)
`logname`	display your login user name
`ls`	list files (directory contents)
`mailx`	process electronic mail messages
`man`	display manual pages
`mesg`	allow or deny messages on your terminal
`more`	'pager'
`rm`	remove a file
`sh`	the shell
`talk`	talk to another user
`tee`	duplicate standard input
`tty`	display the terminal name
`uname`	display the system name

Table 4.3   (cont.)

vi	full-screen text editor
who	list who is using the system
write	write a message on another user's terminal

EXERCISES

1 Which command will print out just your login name? *Hint*: try
   keywords for man.

2 Using Vi, create a file called Parone, which contains the first
   paragraph of Chapter 1. Make sure you correct any typing mistakes
   you make.

3 What argument would you give to date so that it would give today's
   date and time in the format:
   11:22:35 PM on Tuesday 4 December 2001

4 Suppose you have a file called important; using a *single-line*
   command, make two copies, one in file backup1 and the other in file
   backup2. *Hint*: this can be done in several ways.

5 Write a script that will list the users currently logged in to the
   system preceded with a one-line message:
   The following are logged in:

6 You are editing a file using Vi. You realise that you have misspelled
   the word *vision* as *cision*. What keystrokes could you use to correct
   the mistake?

Files

CHAPTER OVERVIEW

This chapter introduces

▶ the UNIX file structure;

▶ common commands which deal with files; and

▶ the UNIX file access and security mechanisms.

This chapter concentrates on the basic information you need to know about UNIX files and the utilities that relate to them.

5.1 The UNIX directory hierarchy

A typical UNIX system has many users and usernames. The machine stores large numbers of programs and datasets that are either 'system' files (required for the running of UNIX) or files for the benefit of the system's users (such as the UNIX commands we discuss in this book). In addition, each user has their own collection of files. On a large UNIX system it would not be unreasonable to expect to find millions of files occupying thousands of **gigabytes** of space.

> **NOTE**
>
> *A gigabyte is a unit of storage equal to 1024 megabytes*

If I choose to create a file called `myfile` (say), it is unlikely that I will be the only user on the machine to have chosen that particular name for a file. It would be unreasonable to expect me to choose a filename instead of `myfile` that was different from all the files created by all the other users. Therefore, UNIX must impose a structure on the filespace that will make it easy to manage a large number of files. The solution adopted is simple yet very powerful.

We can think of the available file storage for our machine as partitioned into separate **directories**. At any given time you can access files in one particular directory, which we can think of as the **current** directory. You can also 'move' between different directories and so change which is *current*. A directory need not be a contiguous section of disk, and might be fragmented. That is, the various files contained within this storage area that we call a directory may in fact be physically located on different parts of a disk, or even on completely different disks or storage devices. This does not matter to the user — the logical structure of the machine's memory is important, not how it is physically implemented. In order for the machine to know how to find the data in these directories, each has a file, called **dot** and referred to by the 'dot' symbol (.) that stores information about that directory (such as which files are stored within it, how big they are, and precisely where on disk they are stored). The word *directory* is also used to describe a file such as *dot*, which contains the vital statistics for a directory storage area. Since the physical layout of a directory is not important to us, this dual meaning for the word presents us with no ambiguity.

Within a directory are files, some of which may themselves be directories. Directories are organised in a **tree**-like structure. At the base of the tree is a directory whose UNIX name is '/' ('root'). So, we might have the situation in Figure 5.1

> **NOTE**
>
> . = 'period'

> **NOTE**
>
> *Trees grow downwards ...*

Figure 5.1   A typical UNIX directory hierarchy

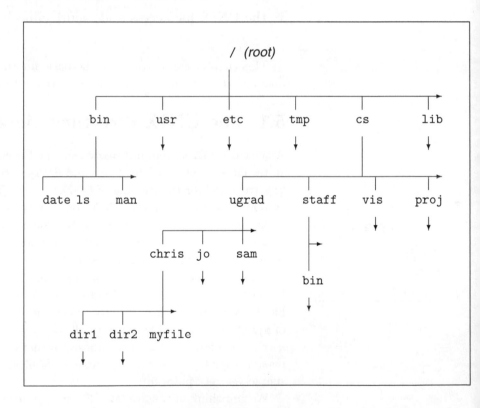

In each directory, in addition to the file *dot*, is a file called **dotdot**, referred to by the symbol '..', which is a synonym for the **parent** of that directory in the tree. Since a file *dot* and a file *dotdot* exist in each and every directory, we do not usually mention them when describing a UNIX directory hierarchy.

There are two means by which we may refer to the name of a file. Either we can name it **relative to** our current directory, in which case we need only use its simple name, such as `myfile`, or we can use its **absolute** filename *relative to the root*. In this latter case, its name commences with a `/`, followed by the intervening directories between the root and the file separated by `/`s, and finally with the filename. Thus in the above tree, file `myfile` has absolute name `/cs/ugrad/chris/myfile`. If a filename commences with the character `/` then it is an *absolute* name, otherwise it is *relative*. Each file thus has a *unique* absolute filename. Moreover, since these filenames can be as long as required and the *depth* of the tree can be as great as needed, we can cope with a UNIX system containing as many files as desired. Since the current directory has several names, there will be several names for an individual file; if the current directory is `/cs/ugrad/chris` then the following names all refer to the same file:

```
/cs/ugrad/chris/myfile
myfile
./myfile
../chris/myfile
././././././myfile
../../../cs/ugrad/./chris/myfile
```

When logged in to the machine, you are always in a current directory somewhere. When you initially log in, you start in your **home directory** in which you can create your own files. This directory has a synonym, `~`, which you can use whenever you need to refer to your home directory. To find your current location within the file system use the command `pwd` ('print working directory'). For example,

```
$ pwd
/cs/ugrad/chris
$
```

It is not always convenient to have your home directory as the current directory, since this might involve much typing of absolute filenames if you wish to access a file elsewhere. By means of the command `cd` ('change directory') you can move around the filesystem. By typing `cd` followed by the name of a directory, you can make the directory become the current directory (if it exists — if not, an error message will be output and your current directory will not change). For instance, to move to user `sam`'s home directory, and then to a non-existent directory called `/squiggle`:

```
$ cd /cs/ugrad/sam
$ cd /squiggle
/squiggle: No such file or directory
```

You may also want to know what files exist on the machine. The command `ls` ('list') which we have already met will accomplish this. By default, `ls` lists the files in the current directory; if, however, you give `ls` one argument that is the name of a directory (either relative or absolute) the files *in that directory* will be listed. For instance:

```
$ ls /
bin etc tmp usr lib cs
$ cd /bin
$ pwd
/bin
$ ls
date ls man
$
```

Try this on your own machine. The output will not look exactly the same, and there will be many more files that are listed. If you give `ls` an argument that is an ordinary file, not a directory, just that filename will be displayed. Do not be afraid of 'getting lost' by changing to different directories — you can always return to your home directory by typing `cd` with no arguments (alternatively `cd ~`). Since ~ always refers to your home directory, you can always refer to files relative to that directory, so if ~ is `/cs/ugrad/chris`, then `/cs/ugrad/chris/myfile` could equally well be referred to as `~/myfile`

If you follow ~ by the name of the user, it refers to that user's home directory — so if you are `chris` then ~ is equivalent to `~chris`, and `sam` has home directory `~sam`.

Worked example 5.1

> What files does `sam` have in `sam`'s home directory?
> **Solution**: Use `ls` followed by the name of `sam`'s home directory:
>
> ```
> $ ls ~sam
> ```

NOTE

Pronounced 'eye-node'

When a file is created, space to store it is found on the machine. That space is given a unique number, called an **inode**, which remains with that file until it is eventually deleted. At creation, the file is also given a **name**. The file is created in a directory, and at creation the directory is updated so that it contains the name of the file and the inode where that file is stored.

5.2 Filesystems

UNIX does not have the notion of 'a disk' that the programmer is allowed to work with. Not only is this concept somewhat vague, but developments in hardware and in storage devices may well mean that thinking in terms of disks might be inappropriate in the future. Instead, it uses the concept of a **filesystem**, within which inodes are unique, and which is named and known by the machine, and associated with a specific directory in the file hierarchy. Each filesystem is set up with an allocated amount of storage space which the user cannot change.

When manipulating files, you will occasionally get error messages telling you that a filesystem is 'full'. In order to discover the amount of free disk space we can use the command df ('disk free'), which will also give information on which filesystems are set up for the system:

```
$ df
Filesystem    1024-blocks    Used Available Capacity Mounted on
/dev/id000a         10637   10103      -529     106%  /
/dev/id001b        186723  155666     12385      93%  /usr
/dev/id000f         93033   42924     40806      51%  /export
/dev/id000d         46508   15384     26474      37%  /var
/dev/id001a        373463  266931     69186      79%  /usr
/dev/id001h        124263   93306     18531      83%  /usr/local
/dev/id001e         57802   39182     12840      75%  /var/tmp
/dev/id000g        747582  600260     72564      89%  /cs/staff
/dev/id001f         61803   50714      4909      91%  /cs/ugrad
/dev/sd8e          863422  700676     76404      90%  /cs/seng
/dev/id002h        560203  456846     47337      91%  /cs/res
/dev/sd8d          878162  562567    227779      71%  /cs/acad
/dev/id001d        186723  184473      2250      99%  /ex/swap2
/dev/id002f        524542  393609    130933      75%  /ex/swap
/dev/id000e         93033   80079      3651      96%  /ex/root
```

We see the storage for the machine divided into the filesystems, and their sizes are listed together with how much of each is in use, and where within the directory hierarchy it is placed. Notice that, in this example, /dev/id000a is more than 100% full — this is not a printer's error! For each filesystem, normally only 90% of the physical space on that device is available. This gives UNIX leeway to warn a user if they attempt to use more of a filesystem than actually exists. Without this extra space, the kernel might find itself without enough workspace to continue, and the system might crash. However, the super-user is allowed to use the final 10% of a filesystem, and the capacity is measured relative to the normally allowed 90% of the filesystem. Although most UNIX systems are set up in this way, the 90% is not cast in stone, and the super-user may change it as local circumstances dictate.

5.3 Manipulating files

There are lots of things you can do with a file. You can create, destroy, rename and copy it, and you can protect it so that only certain users have access to its contents. These simple actions have corresponding UNIX commands, which are generally simple. **Directories** contain information about files other than themselves, unlike ordinary files, and operations on them are in consequence more complex. We shall start by looking at directories.

5.3.1 Creating directories

To create a new directory, the command `mkdir` ('make directory'), followed by the name you wish it to have, will make a new directory with that name. For instance, we can create a file called `dir1` in the current directory:

```
$ mkdir dir1
```

Conversely, to destroy a directory, use `rmdir` ('remove directory'). Note that `rmdir` will only work if the directory you are trying to remove contains no user files. You should get used to structuring your home directory so that it contains structured subdirectories. If you do not, and you have more than a very small number of files, then you are likely to find difficulty keeping track of which data you have stored where. A common way of organising your filespace is to use the same conventions that are used on the system files. This involves creating directories with 'standard' names, such as shown in Table 5.1, for instance.

Table 5.1   Standard directories

`bin`	commands you have written
`src`	source code for the commands you have written
`doc`	documentation
`tmp`	temporary files

Worked example 5.2

Create a directory called `tmp` in your home directory.
Solution: Firstly, change your current directory to your home directory by typing `cd`; check that no file called `tmp` already exists by using `ls`; and then type `mkdir tmp`.

Figure 5.2   A typical user's directory hierarchy

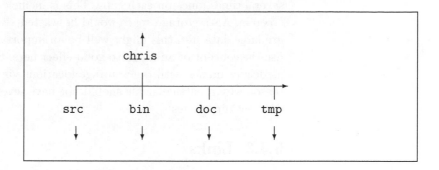

5.3.2 Creating files

The first thing that must happen to a file before anything else is that it must come into existence. This may happen by design of another command (when you create it with an editor, for instance) or as a side-effect. You will frequently find that the current directory contains files you don't remember anything about! When the data held in a file is no longer required, you may wish to delete the file. Just as for file creation, this may be explicit or implicit (some automatically created files may disappear spontaneously).

Suppose you have created a file called `myfile`. You can create another file with a copy of the contents of `myfile` using the command `cp` ('copy'). If you decide that the name of a file needs to be changed, the command `mv` ('move') will do exactly that. For instance:

```
$ ls
myfile
$ cp myfile foo
$ ls
foo myfile
$ mv myfile bar
$ ls
bar foo
```

When the command `cp` is called, a completely new file is created, *with a new inode*. The directory in which the new file is to be located is amended with the information about the new filename and the new inode. The data in the file being copied is not changed at all.

Sometimes it is useful to give a file several different names. This can often happen if you have data that needs to be accessed in several different directories, and any changes to it need to be made consistently. If you created several copies of the file, you would have to perform updates several times, once on each copy. This is inefficient, and errors might creep in. Also, storage space would be wasted — and if the files concerned are large data files this might well be an important consideration. We can use the concept of an inode to good effect here. Since a directory associates names with their storage locations via inodes, there is no reason why a particular file should not have several names, perhaps in different directories.

5.3.3 Links

To create a second name for a file that already exists, we can create a **link** — sometimes called a **hard link** — to it using the command `ln` ('link'). With two arguments, which must be filenames, provided the first file does exist and the second does not, we can create a link from the first to the second. For instance, if user `sam` whose home directory is `/cs/ugrad/sam` has a file `datafile` that I wish to have in my own home directory under the name `samsdata`, then the command `ln` can be used to create a link between the two:

```
$ ln /cs/ugrad/sam/datafile samsdata
```

We say that `samsdata` has *two links*, and it has two names, one `samsdata`, the other `/cs/ugrad/sam/datafile`. The file has a single inode, however. When `samsdata` is amended, the contents of `/cs/ugrad/sam/datafile` are changed at exactly the same time (and vice versa). If we delete `/cs/ugrad/sam/datafile`, we actually delete that file*name*, and the file continues to exist, but with only one name (`samsdata`) and one link. The kernel will keep track of how many names (links) an inode has, and when this drops to zero the filespace allocated to that inode is released for use elsewhere. There is one important point to note here — inodes are unique only within a single filesystem, and therefore you can only link a file to another file within the same filesystem. We can check precisely which inodes are allocated to which files by using option `-i` ('inode') to `ls`:

```
$ ls -i
total 561
241563 myfile     43532 dir1     86475 dir2
567721 prog.c    563341 foo     563341 bar
```

In this example, files `foo` and `bar` have the same inode, namely `563341`, and have therefore been linked. Note that two linked files do not necessarily have to be in the same directory.

At this point, it is worth discussing briefly what a directory actually is. If you type `ls` while in a particular directory, any directories contained within it (referred to as **subdirectories**) will appear as if they were files. In a sense, this is correct — every directory can be considered as a file, each with its own inode. This 'file' contains — in a form that need not concern us — information as to where the files in that subdirectory are stored. By typing cd followed by the name of a directory, the file representing that directory is examined, and the data in the file that indicates where it is stored is retrieved and used to work out where the new current directory is stored.

Worked example 5.3

> What is the inode of your home directory?
> **Solution**: First of all, type cd to change to your home directory. If you then type ls -i the inodes of the files contained in that directory will be given; the manual page for ls indicates that option -d ('directory') will list directories like other files, rather than listing their contents. So you require
>
> ```
> $ ls -id
> ```

5.3.4 'Dot' files

Change to your home directory, and type ls -a ('all') and you will see displayed the names of the files in that directory including some other names that ls on its own does not produce. These 'hidden' files all have names beginning with a dot (.). You will recognise the name of the current directory *dot* and the parent directory *dotdot*, but some others will also be there. Typically you may expect .profile, .mailrc and .xinitrc; these files are all used by a UNIX utility to enable you to customise that utility, and many of them end in rc ('run commands'). When a utility requires such a file, the manual page explains what data it should contain. *Never* delete or edit a dot file unless you know what it should contain, even if it's empty — that's why ls does not normally list them, to prevent you accidentally changing them.

If you wish to access a dot file, the procedure is exactly the same as for any other file — it's just ls that hides them.

5.4 Protecting files

Some data you store on the machine should not be readable by other users. If you are doing a programming assignment for your course, for example, other students should not read it. If your institution has purchased software which has conditions attached to its use (as is often the case nowadays) it may be necessary to restrict its use to a specific group of users.

You may also wish to prevent yourself accidentally overwriting a file and destroying important data.

In this section we look at a basic mechanism for enabling file protection. First, however, we must explore UNIX's formal notion of a *group of users*, which is important for understanding how to protect files.

5.4.1 Groups

The system administrator manages a database of **groups**. Each group is a list of users and is given a name (such as `ugrads`, `general` or `proj`). The reason for having groups is that when access to software or data needs to be restricted, a group can be used to specify this. Each user is a member of one or more groups, and each file is allocated to exactly one group. At any particular time, for each user there is a group that is the default group for new files they create.

Each group has a unique name and also a unique number (its **group-id** or **GID**). The command `id` ('identifier') is used to interrogate the database, and on its own displays the user's name together with the groups they are a member of, both names and numbers, and the user's user-id and current group-id. If you give `id` an argument that is another user's username, then the information for that user will be displayed instead. For example,

```
$ id chris
uid=145(chris) gid=12(ugrads) groups=12(ugrads),417(proj)
```

shows that user `chris` is a member of groups `ugrads` and `proj`, with GID numbers 12 and 417 respectively. Currently `chris` is allocated to group `ugrads`. Notice also that `id` has displayed a number for `chris`, namely 145 — each user is also allocated a unique number, their **user-id** or **UID**. In order to change your current group-id, command `newgrp` ('new group') should be invoked. Followed by the *name* of a group *of which you must be a member* this will perform the required change. With no argument, it will return you to your default group-id as defined in the password file. For example, if you are user `chris`, and wish to change your allocated group to `proj`, so that you can control access to users in group `proj` when you create new files:

```
$ newgrp proj
$ id
uid=145(chris) gid=417(proj) groups=12(ugrads),417(proj)
```

5.4.2 File access control

UNIX has a flexible method of protecting files to deal with the situations we described earlier. First of all, each file on the machine divides the users of the machine into three categories:

▶ the file's **owner** (normally the user who created the file)

▶ a **group** of users

▶ **other** users.

For each of these categories of user, that user may be either given or denied the following **access privileges**:

▶ **read**

▶ **write**

▶ **execute**.

If a file has *read* permission, it can be examined at a terminal, printed (if it is a text file), viewed by an editor, and so on. If it has *write* permission, the contents of the file can be changed (for example, by an editor), and the file can be overwritten or deleted. If it has *execute* permission, and is a binary program or a shell script, that program can be run (but copied only if it also has *read* permission). An example is given later on.

Access control is determined as follows. The system first of all checks to see whether the user is the *owner* of a file, and if so the *owner* permissions are used. Otherwise, it checks to see if the user is a member of the group allocated to that file, and if so checks *group* file permissions. If the user is neither the file owner nor in the file's group, they come under the heading of *other* users. The group to which a file has been allocated must be a valid group the that system administrator has already set up, as discussed above. The owner of a file can change the group to which the file has been allocated.

Access privileges for directories have a different meaning than for ordinary files. If a directory has *write* permission, files in that directory may be created or deleted. If it has *read* permission, it is possible to see the files that are contained in that directory (using ls, say); if it has *execute* permission it is possible to cd to it. A directory with *execute* but not *read* permission is useful if you wish to allow someone else to run one of your commands located in that directory, but do not wish them to see what other files you have.

To find out the access privileges for a file, use ls. As an example, consider user **chris**, who has six files in the home directory (including two subdirectories). By typing ls -l ('long') the following output might be seen:

NOTE

On BSD systems you need ls -lg

```
total 561
-rw-r--r--   1   chris   ugrads    122 Dec 21 18:40 myfile
drwxr-xr-x   2   chris   general   512 Dec 22 14:55 dir1
drwx------   2   chris   general   512 Dec 22 14:55 dir2
-rw-r-----   1   chris   proj     9912 Nov 22 17:55 prog.c
-r-x------   2   chris   general   147 Dec 22 17:56 foo
-r-x------   2   chris   general   147 Dec 22 17:56 bar
```

In fact, `ls -l` will display most information you are likely to need about files for routine work. The general format for the output is:

```
-rw-r--r--   1   chris   ugrads     122 Dec 21 18:40 myfile
```

access   links owner   group   size last change name

The access privileges are presented as a string of 10 characters. The first character is usually either a `d` or a `-`, indicating that the file is a directory or an ordinary file respectively. There are other possible values, which we discuss later. Characters 2–4, 5–7 and 8–10 describe the access privileges for the owner, the group and for others respectively. Each of these 3-character substrings denotes whether read, write and execute privileges have been allowed or denied.

For *read* privilege, the first character will be `r`, otherwise `-`; for *write* privilege the second will be `w`, otherwise `-`. Lastly, for *execute* privilege, the third will be `x`, otherwise `-`.

For example, file `myfile` above can be read by anybody, but only Chris can write to it (that is, change the contents of the file in any way). File `prog.c` can only be written to by Chris, but users who are members of the group `proj` can also read it. File `foo` can be read by Chris, and also executed, but no-one else can access it at all. Nor can Chris write to it — this is not necessarily a mistake, it is often useful to deny yourself write access to a file to prevent yourself accidentally deleting the file if it contains important data.

If a directory does not have write permission, then files in that directory cannot be deleted, nor can new ones be created. However, files within that directory that *do* have write permission can have their contents changed.

The other information that `ls -l` provides is as follows. The number of **links** to a file is printed, followed by the owner of the file and the group the file is currently assigned to. Then comes the size of the file in bytes and the date and time the file last had any of its contents changed. At the end of the line comes the name of the file.

5.4.3 Changing privileges

A file has precisely one group associated with it; this can be changed to another group by `chgrp` ('change group'). For instance, suppose our directory has the same contents as before, and recall that we have linked `foo` and `bar`, we might have the following dialogue:

```
$ ls -l
total 561
-rw-r--r--    1    chris   ugrads       122 Dec 21 18:40 myfile
drwxr-xr-x    2    chris   general      512 Dec 22 14:55 dir1
drwx------    2    chris   general      512 Dec 22 14:55 dir2
-rw-r-----    1    chris   proj        9912 Nov 22 17:55 prog.c
-r-x------    2    chris   general      147 Dec 22 17:56 foo
-r-x------    2    chris   general      147 Dec 22 17:56 bar
$ chgrp proj foo
$ ls -l
total 561
-rw-r--r--    1    chris   ugrads       122 Dec 21 18:40 myfile
drwxr-xr-x    2    chris   general      512 Dec 22 14:55 dir1
drwx------    2    chris   general      512 Dec 22 14:55 dir2
-rw-r-----    1    chris   proj        9912 Nov 22 17:55 prog.c
-r-x------    2    chris   proj         147 Dec 22 17:56 foo
-r-x------    2    chris   proj         147 Dec 22 17:56 bar
```

Note that the other file linked to foo has also had its group changed, and that the access privileges for the file are not changed. chgrp allows one option, -R ('recursive') — with this option, if its file argument is a directory, all files and subdirectories will also have their groups changed.

The above information does not tell us that foo and bar are linked — it merely states that each of those two files has two links (but not necessarily to each other), and that they are the same size and created at the same time (to the nearest second). To check that two files are in fact linked, it is necessary to ask what their inodes actually are, and you should use ls -i as discussed earlier. The options -l and -i can be combined, giving

```
$ ls -il
```

but you may find the output becomes wider than the width of your terminal. Try it!

Similar to chgrp is chown ('change owner'), which has similar syntax, but can be used to change the actual owner of a file. This is an operation you are unlikely to wish to perform, and most systems restrict the command so that only the super-user may use it.

The most frequent change you are likely to make to a file, apart from its actual contents, is to the access privileges; chmod ('change mode') is used for this change. The syntax is chmod followed by a specification of changes to the access permission, followed by a file (or files) the change is to be applied to.

The specification can be done two ways — either the privileges for the user/group/other sets of users can be *set*, or they can be *changed*. A character known as a **who symbol**, which is one of u (user), g (group), o (other) or a (all), or a sequence of who symbols, denotes those users to whom the specification will apply. For instance, go refers to the group and others, but not to the file's owner. The symbol a is a synonym for ugo — this synonym is simply shorthand, as ugo is a very frequently used sequence of *who symbols*.

Following the sequence of who symbols comes one of +, - or =, followed by zero or more **perm symbols** (r, w, x or -), which represent permissions to be set or changed for the users specified by the previous *who symbols*. A + indicates *add* the permissions, - indicates *remove* those permissions, and = means *set* them. For example,

```
$ chmod go-w myfile
```

denies write permission to group and to others,

```
$ chmod u+x myfile
```

gives execute permission to the owner, and

```
$ chmod g=r-x myfile
```

sets group access to r-x, so that users in the file's group are able to read and to execute file myfile, but not write to it.

When a file is created, it has default access privileges that would be set by the system administrator. These can be changed by the user by means of the command umask ('user mask') followed by a string with the same information as for chmod above. For example,

```
$ umask u=rwx,g=r,o=
```

will cause all new files created to have read, write and execute privileges for the owner, but to deny write and execute privileges for the group, and to deny all privileges for others. This state of affairs will continue during the current session until umask is again invoked.

Worked example 5.4

Create a file that no-one can read, and confirm that you yourself cannot read it.
Solution: First of all, choose a name for the file (myfile, say) and use cat or vi to create the file. In order to deny read access to everybody, the command is

```
$ chmod a-r myfile
```

with a for *all* users, r for *read*, and - to deny. To check that you can't read it, try examining the contents using `cat` and you should get an error message:

```
$ cat myfile
cat: myfile: Permission denied
```

5.5 File contents

Given that you know a file exists, an obvious question is: 'What does it contain?' A simple answer to this question might be that it contains a sequence of bytes — but this would not be very helpful. We need to know what those bytes represent. We could start off by examining the filename; some UNIX files are required to have a particular suffix, and this information could indicate their contents. However, we should note that, for instance, if a file is to contain a C program, its suffix must be `.c`, but the converse does not hold. If we encounter a file called `myfile.c` then this does not mean that the file must contain a C program (although it would be perverse if in fact it did not).

It is not possible to infer from a file's suffix (if indeed it has one) what the contents of the file represent. Indeed, UNIX makes no stipulation of any sort as to what may or may not be stored in a file — a file is merely a sequence of bytes.

However, all is not lost. It is possible to make an intelligent guess as to what a file contains by examining the format of the data inside it. For instance, if the file contains words that occur in the C language, one might reasonably guess that the file contains C source code. Many sorts of data can have their type inferred from their format, and the command `file` is provided to do this. For example:

```
$ file prog.c
prog.c:        c program text
$ file libc.a
libc.a:        archive random library
$ file story
story:         English text
```

Don't worry about `file` telling you that a particular file is of a weird type you've never heard of! It probably means it contains something you aren't interested in anyway. Unfortunately, `file` is not infallible, and it is possible to confuse it, but nonetheless it's a pretty reliable aid.

Worked example 5.5

What type of file is /usr?
Solution: Use `file`:

```
$ file /usr
/usr:           directory
```

thus /usr is a directory.

We should also ask whether the question 'What does file X contain?' is a useful question. It is possible to define in a precise way what a C program must look like, but not, for instance, the data for transactions pertaining to a bank account. Rather than asking what type of data is in a particular file, we should instead be creating files whose contents are in a specified format.

5.5.1 Text files

We now concentrate on a particular class of files, **text files**, which are files divided into **lines** separated by a *Newline* character. Such files, which would normally contain only printable characters, include text program source files, shell scripts, and in fact any files you would wish to use a text editor on. However, this is not a requirement, and what we discuss in this section will also hold true for files containing other characters. Most of the files we will use as examples in the rest of this book will be text files.

Suppose we have created a file called `story`, which contains English text. Having established that it is a text file (by means of `file` or otherwise), we may wish briefly to examine its contents. We could, of course, invoke an editor such as `vi` and use the commands within the editor to move through the file and look at various parts of it, or we could use a pager. However, there are easier methods.

Often you will simply want to look at the first few lines of a file (for instance to verify that it was indeed the file you expected it to be). In this case, `head` will print out the first five lines of the file. In a similar vein, `tail` will print out the last five. If you want to see the first (say) 10 lines, then the command would be

```
head -n 10
```

where n = 'number'.

Strictly speaking, `tail` copies its input to standard output *beginning at a designated place*, which is usually a number of lines from the end of the file. There are many options available to `tail` to allow you to specify what is meant by the designated place, and how many lines are output — refer to the manual page for further details.

As an example of simple use, suppose file `myfile` contains 100 lines, as follows:

```
line 1
line 2
...
line 100
```

Then we might have

```
$ head -n 2 myfile
line 1
line 2
$ tail -n 3 myfile
line 98
line 99
line 100
$
```

Worked example 5.6

> Find the most recently modified file (excluding 'dot' files) in the current directory.
>
> **Solution**: This has clearly somehow got to involve `ls`. With option `-l` we could examine by hand every file and see which one was last changed. That is not the UNIX way of doing things — by examining the manual page for `ls` we find an option `-t` ('time') which will sort the files it prints out so that the most recent is shown first. Option `-1` (1 is digit 'one') forces the output to be one filename per line. Thus `ls -t1` will produce a list of filenames with the desired one at the top — use `head` to isolate it by piping the output of `ls` to `head` thus:
>
> ```
> $ ls -t1 | head -n 1
> ```

There is only a limited amount of space on a machine, and it may be that each user has been restricted (by the system administrator) as to how much filespace they are allowed to use. A quick way to find out how big files are is to use `wc` ('wordcount'), which indicates (i) the number of *lines*, (ii) the number of *words* and (iii) the number of *characters* (bytes) in a file. The latter two are only meaningful if the file is a text file, though. For example,

```
$ wc myfile
27 124 664 myfile
```

indicates that file `myfile` has 27 *lines*, 124 *words* and 664 *bytes* (characters). With options `-c`, `-w` or `-l` respectively, only the *byte*, *word* or *line* count will be printed. Note that `wc` does not work on directories.

5.5.2 Comparing files

A situation that often arises is that you are examining a file, and you discover a very similar file, and need to know the differences between the two files. This can happen when a file has been edited several times, and you lose track of precisely what changes have been made. The command `diff` ('differences') will come to your aid. Use it followed by the names of two files and it will tell you the changes in the following manner. Suppose we have two files, `file1` and `file2`, where `file1` contains the following text:

```
A
test
file
```

and `file2` contains

```
A
testing
file
```

then we would have

```
$ diff file1 file2
2c2
< test
--
> testing
```

indicating that line 2 containing `myfile` has been removed from `file1` and replaced by a line containing `testing`.

Related to `diff` is `cmp` ('compare'). Sometimes, especially within shell scripts, the verbosity of `diff` is not required, and a terse indication of whether or not two files are identical is required — `cmp` will give a short message if its two arguments are different, otherwise it will stay silent. Also, `diff` can only compare text files — `cmp` will compare two files *of any type* and indicate whether or not their contents are the same.

5.5.3 Filtering files

Text files — especially ones containing 'raw data' — often contain repeated lines. It is sometimes useful to know either how often this occurs, or to filter out the repeated occurrences. The command `uniq` ('unique') is provided for this purpose. For instance, supposing file A contains

```
aaa
bbb
bbb
bbb
bbb
bbb
ccc
ccc
aaa
ddd
```

then the following dialogue might take place:

```
$ uniq A
aaa
bbb
ccc
aaa
ddd
$ uniq -c A
1 aaa
5 bbb
2 ccc
1 aaa
1 ddd
```

With no options, uniq simply filters out consecutive repeated lines; option -c ('count') prepends each line of output with a count of the number of times that line was repeated. Option -d ('duplicate') causes uniq only to write out lines that are repeated, and -u ('unique') only to write out lines that are not repeated consecutively. Thus:

```
$ uniq -d A
bbb
ccc
$ uniq -u A
aaa
aaa
ddd
```

Another common situation arises when you have two or more files, containing what can be thought of as columns in a table. You require corresponding lines from the files to be concatenated so as to actually produce a table. Using the command paste will achieve this —

corresponding lines of its arguments are joined together separated by a single *TAB* character. For example, suppose file **A** contains

```
hello
Chris
```

and file B contains

```
there
how are you?
```

then the following dialogue can take place:

```
$ paste A B
hello there
Chris how are you?
```

Both `paste` and `uniq`, though only of use in limited situations, save a great deal of time editing files when they can in fact be used.

Sometimes, when dealing with files that are presented in a rigid format, you may wish to select character columns from such a file. The utility `cut` is a very simple method for extracting columns. Suppose we have a file `myfile` containing the following data (dates of birth and names):

```
17.04.61 Smith Fred
22.01.63 Jones Susan
03.11.62 Bloggs Zach
```

We can choose the years from each line by selecting character columns 7 to 8, thus:

```
$ cut -c7-8 myfile
61
63
62
```
('column')

> **NOTE**
>
> *A line is thought of as divided into fields separated by a known delimiter*

This command can also distinguish between **fields**, and to select family names from `myfile` (Smith, Jones and Bloggs), we could use `cut -f2 -d' ' myfile`, which specifies that we select field number 2 where the **delimiter** (option `-d`) is the space character:

```
$ cut -f2 -d' ' myfile
Smith
Jones
Bloggs
```
('field')

Related to `cut` is `fold`; `cut` will assume that you want the same number of lines in the output as the input, but you wish to select part of those input lines. On the other hand, `fold` assumes that you want all of your input, but that your output needs to fit within some lines of maximum width — for example, if you had a file with some very long lines in it that you needed printing on a printer that was fairly narrow. The action performed by `fold` is to copy its standard input, or names mentioned as arguments, to standard output, but whenever a line of length greater than a certain number (default 80 characters) is met, then a *Newline* character is inserted at that point. With option `-w` ('width') followed by a number, that number is taken to be the maximum length of output lines rather than 80. Try the following:

```
$ fold -w 15 <<END
Let's start
with three
short lines
and finish with an extremely long one with lots of
words
END
```

For more sophisticated processing of files divided into records and fields we can use Awk (see Chapter 11).

Another exceptionally useful command is `sort`, which sorts its input into alphabetical order line-by-line. It has many options, and can sort on a specified field of the input rather than the first, or numerically (using option `-n`) ('numerical') rather than alphabetically. So using file `A` above, we could have:

```
$ sort A
aaa
aaa
bbb
bbb
bbb
bbb
bbb
ccc
ccc
ddd
```

A feature of `uniq` is that it will only filter out repeated lines if they are consecutive; if we wish to display each line that occurs in a file once and only once, we could first of all sort the file into an order and then use `uniq`:

```
$ sort A | uniq
aaa
bbb
ccc
ddd
```

This has the same effect as using `sort` with option -u, which we have already mentioned.

Worked example 5.7

> Find out how many separate inodes are represented by the files (excluding 'dot' files) in the current directory.
>
> **Solution**: Using `ls -il` we can list the files, one per line, preceded by their inode number. Piping the output into `cut` we can isolate the first six character columns, which contain the inode number, and `sort` with option -u, which will sort these into order and remove all duplicates. These can then be counted by counting the number of *lines* of output using `wc -l`:
>
> ```
> $ ls -il | cut -c1-6 | sort -u | wc -l
> ```

5.5.4 Non-text files

We must address the question of what a file contains if it is not a text file. Clearly we cannot use the text utilities described above — not only will the file not be neatly split up into lines, the characters contained within it will in general not be printable. The `file` command gives us a rough indication as to what sort of data a file (binary or text) contains, but no more. If we need to know exactly what characters are contained in a file that is not printable, because it is in, for example, binary format, `od` will give us precisely that information. Thinking of a file as a sequence of bytes, `od` lists each byte in a representation that can be printed. The name stands for **octal dump**, and by default it lists the bytes by their octal (base 8) codes word-by-word (a word being typically 4 bytes).

Since computers use binary code internally, when in the past it was necessary to examine data, it was often not possible to display that data in any way other than as a representation of binary numbers. One of the simplest ways of doing this was to group the bits (binary digits) together in sequences of 3, consider each 3-bit sequence as representing a digit in base 8, and print out the data as a string of octal digits. Hence we get the phrase *octal dump*.

A more useful way to generate output is with option -t c, (c = 'character', t = 'type') whereby each byte is either printed as a 3-digit octal number that is the code for that character, or the character itself (if

Learning UNIX and Linux

NOTE

The escape sequence for the newline character is \n

it is printable), or backslash followed by a character (if a standard **escape sequence** is known). For instance,

```
$ od -t c bintest
0000000 201 003  \n 013  \0 001 200  \0
0000010  \0  \0   @  \0  \0  \0 251 230
0000020  \0  \0  \0  \0  \0  \0
0000030  \0  \0  \0  \0  \0  \0  \0  \0
0000040 274 020      \0 320 003 240   @
0000050 222 003 240   D 225   *     002
0000060 224 002 240 004 224 002   @  \n
0000070 027  \0  \0   h 324   " 343 240
0000100 003  \0  \0  \b 302  \0   b  \b
...
```

We see that the first byte in the file has code 201 in octal (which is 129 in decimal). The third byte is a *Newline* character. Just for comparison, a file called `hellotest`, containing one line that is simply the word `Hello`, would be displayed thus:

```
$ od -t c hellotest
0000000 H e l l o \n
0000006
```

The command has several possible options, which we do not list here.

If you just want to examine a binary file quickly, and see what printable strings exist within it, use command `strings`. This can be useful if you have *compiled* a program, such as one written in C, and that program contains strings whose value is of interest to you (filenames, for instance). Going through the binary code with `od` would be tedious.

A useful command we introduce at this point is `touch`. This command has the effect of changing the date and time that its file arguments were last modified — they are altered to the current date and time. If the files that are its arguments do not currently exist, they are created with size 0; `touch` is useful to create a file if you haven't yet decided what to put in it, but want it to be there. This might happen during the development phase of a program. It is also useful to indicate that the file is in some sense 'up-to-date'.

5.6 Printing files

Although you will probably spend a lot of time sitting in front of a computer terminal, you will from time to time need to get 'hard copy' of documents; that is, you will need to print them onto paper. To do this, type `lp` ('lineprinter') followed by the name of the file or files you wish to

be printed. If you omit filenames, the standard input will be printed, so
that can have data piped into it. It is important that you only attempt
to print text files. Most modern printers will be sensible if you send them
unprintable files, and simply refuse to print them, but a few will go
haywire.

Your machine will be set up with a 'default' printer, and your system
administrator should have told you which this is and where it is located.
If you give to lp the option -d ('destination') followed by the name of
another printer, that printer will be used instead. The option -n
('numerical') followed by a number will cause that number of copies of the
document to be printed (use with care!). For instance, to print two copies
of file myfile on the printer named def:

```
$ lp -n 2 -d def myfile
```

It is a fact of life that documents stored on a machine are changed
frequently. When a file is sent to a printer, it is often useful for an
indication to be given as to when the file was printed (so the reader will
be reminded how out-of-date it may be). It is also useful, when the
document is long, for each page to be printed together with a header
containing useful information such as the page number. When a file is
printed with lp, that file is printed completely naked; nothing except the
characters in the file appear on paper. The command pr is designed to
remedy this situation; it has numerous options, which allow you to tailor
your files to particular printers. pr divides the input into *pages*, each
commencing with a header naming the file and the date and time, and
ending with a trailer of blank lines. The size (number of columns and
width) of each page and the size of the header and trailer can be changed,
output can be multi-column, and various other attributes of the output
can be altered. The output of pr is sent to standard output, and so must
be piped to lp. For example, the following command will print file abc on
the printer named def, two columns per page (option -2, 50 lines per
page (using option -l):

```
$ pr -2 -l 50 abc | lp -d def
```

To use pr effectively, you must know the characteristics of the printer (or
printers) to which you have access; your system administrator should
provide you with that information.

It is common nowadays for laser printers to be available. Rather than
having a fixed set of characters like a line printer, or a coarse selection of
symbols that can be created by an artistic user such as in a dot-matrix
printer, a laser printer is suitable for intricate graphical printing. In order
to use such facilities, files for a laser printer must be in a special code. It

is worth mentioning that most laser printers will accept text input just like other printers.

5.7 File archives and file compression

It will often be necessary to take a copy of a complete directory, either for the purpose of storing it in a safe place in case the computer system 'crashes', or to send it to a different computer system. There are two particular problems that utilities such as cp are unable to address. First, different machines and operating systems store data in different formats, and it may be necessary to convert the format in which the files in the directory are stored. Second, cp does not handle links.

There have historically been two commands, tar ('tape archive') and cpio ('copy in out'), that have been used. Both work by copying all the files in the directory, together with data describing the structure of the directory, into a single file known as an **archive**. Unfortunately, both tar and cpio work differently and produce archives in different formats. Although tar was used much more extensively than cpio, it was felt necessary to create a completely new command that would perform the functions of both rather than try to update tar so that it would also do everything cpio would do.

Neither tar nor cpio became part of POSIX, but a new command pax ('portable archive exchange') has been written. We give a couple of examples illustrating both pax and tar.

To create a new archive, give pax the argument -w ('write') or tar the argument -c ('create'). The archive file will be sent to standard output. So to archive the contents of the current directory to the tape drive /dev/rst8, either of the following will work:

```
$ tar -c . >/dev/rst8
$ pax -w . >/dev/rst8
```

Alternatively, you can redirect the output to a file. To extract the contents of an archive, the standard input to pax or tar should be redirected from the archive; pax requires argument -r ('read') and tar argument -x ('extract'). Naturally, when unpacking an archive, you don't want to overwrite any files or directories that you have already created. It is a good idea to check the contents of an archive by means of the -t option to both tar and pax, which simply causes the names of the files in the archive to be listed.

Having multiple copies of directories — whether 'real' or archived — is bound to take up space. If you have created an archive — mydir.pax, say — you can **compress** the file and reduce its size, by means of the command compress. This creates a file mydir.pax.Z (note the .Z suffix) and deletes mydir.pax; the file mydir.pax.Z will have a smaller size than

NOTE

Typically a factor of between 0.5 and 0.2

mydir.pax. The actual reduction in file size depends on what the file to be compressed contains. For example:

```
$ ls
mydir.pax
$ wc -c mydir.pax
206336
$ compress mydir.pax
$ ls
mydir.pax.Z
$ wc -c mydir.pax.Z
89473
```

To reverse the compression, use the command uncompress. If you have stored any large files that you do not use on a regular basis, you may wish to compress them.

Worked example 5.8

> Copy the contents of your current directory to /tmp/backup preserving all links.
> **Solution**: Using pax -w we can create a new archive; store this in a temporary file, create /tmp/backup, change directory to /tmp/backup, and read the archive.
>
> ```
> $ pax -w . >/tmp/backup.pax
> $ mkdir /tmp/backup
> $ cd /tmp/backup
> $ pax -r </tmp/backup.pax
> ```

5.8 Other relevant commands

Many files have names containing a **suffix**, or a sequence of characters at the end of the name and commencing with a dot. For example, if you have a program written in the language C, the file in which that program is stored should have a suffix .c of necessity. Let us suppose you have written a C program that is stored in file myfile.c in your home directory /cs/ugrad/chris. From the point of view of the UNIX kernel, it is irrelevant what name this file has. Only when you attempt to compile and run the program will the suffix become important, as the UNIX command for compiling a C program demands that the .c suffix be present, and indeed will create files with the same **base** myfile and different suffix. In this example, a file myfile.o would be created (the 'o' stands for 'object code', i.e. binary code for the processor). A standard

Files

POSIX command makes no demands on a file's suffix, although other utilities may well do so; the manual page for that command will tell you.

The command `dirname` takes as argument the name of a file and strips off the actual filename, leaving only the directories. Command `basename` also takes a filename as argument, but strips off the directory information, leaving only the filename relative to its parent directory. If `basename` is given two arguments, and the second argument is a suffix of the filename, that suffix is also removed. For instance:

```
$ dirname /cs/ugrad/chris/test.c
/cs/ugrad/chris
$ basename /cs/ugrad/chris/test.c
test.c
$ basename /cs/ugrad/chris/test.c .c
test
```

The benefit of these two commands will not be apparent at this stage, but later on, when writing shell scripts to manipulate files, they are exceptionally useful.

When the command `mv` is called, the directory in which its first argument is located is updated so that the file's absolute name is changed. The inode of the file is not changed if the new filename is on the same filesystem. This command name is somewhat misleading, since the file doesn't really move at all.

We also need to know the *total* amount of space taken up by our files. Here the command `du` ('disk usage') comes to our rescue. With an argument of the name of a directory (or the current directory, if no argument is given), `du` prints the total number of *kilo*bytes used to store the data in the files in that directory. For example,

```
$ du
12      ./dir1
7       ./dir2
27      .
```

indicates that directory `dir1` takes up 12k (kilobytes) and `dir2` takes 7k, whereas the total amount of storage used for the current directory is 27k (including `dir1` and `dir2`).

There are some other standard commands that are not required for simple use of UNIX. Nevertheless, they are included within the standard, and are included here for completeness.

Suppose you have distributed some text files to a colleague, and you then make minor alterations to them. You want your colleague to have updated copies of the files. One possibility is to send them all the files anew, but this has the disadvantage that a potentially large volume of data must be transmitted, which may well incur costs. An arguably preferable method would be to send your colleague a list of the changes to the files. These changes can be displayed using `diff`, but it would be unreasonable for your colleague to edit all the files by hand to make the changes. Fortunately, the command `patch` is provided to perform the task automatically. It takes a file containing the changes, as generated by `diff`, and the name of a file to which those changes are to be applied, and carries out the changes.

The commands we have introduced in this chapter will be seen to perform only simple manipulations of UNIX files, especially when examining the contents of files. Three programs — Grep, Sed and Awk — which we discuss later in the book — provide comprehensive facilities for processing file contents, and obviate the need for more 'simple' UNIX commands over and above those mentioned in this chapter.

CHAPTER SUMMARY

Table 5.2   Commands discussed in this chapter

`basename`	display non-directory part of filename
`cd`	change working directory
`chgrp`	change file group ownership
`chmod`	change file access privileges
`chown`	change file ownership
`cmp`	compare two files
`compress`	compress files
`cp`	copy files
`cpio`	copy files to and from archives
`cut`	select columns or fields from each line of a file
`df`	display free disk space
`diff`	show differences between two files
`dirname`	display directory part of a pathname
`du`	display file space usage
`file`	describe file contents
`fold`	fold lines
`head`	show the first few lines of a file
`id`	display information about a user's identity
`ln`	link files
`lp`	send files to a printer
`lpr`	send files to a printer
`mkdir`	create new directories
`mv`	move files
`newgrp`	change your current group-id

Table 5.2   (cont.)

`od`	dump files in various formats
`paste`	merge corresponding lines of text files
`patch`	apply changes to files
`pax`	file archiver and format translator
`pr`	a very basic formatter for text files
`pwd`	display working directory
`rmdir`	remove empty directories
`sort`	sort or merge text files
`strings`	display printable strings in a file
`tail`	show the last few lines of a file
`tar`	create tape archives, and add or extract files
`touch`	change last modification time of a file
`umask`	change access privileges when files are created
`uncompress`	uncompress files
`uniq`	filter out repeated lines
`wc`	word, line and byte count

EXERCISES

1 Write a script to list the three most recently altered files (including 'dot' files) in the current directory.

2 What type of file is `/bin/id`?

3 List the files (excluding 'dot' files) in the current directory, together with their inodes, in numerical order of the inodes.

4 How many subdirectories are there in `/usr`?

5 Write a script to display the owner of the current directory *only*.

6 Write a script to display the names of files in `/bin` and `/usr/bin` that have the same name.

7 Write a script to list the files in the current directory (excluding 'dot' files) in 'long' format (that is, including the information that `ls` provides with option `-l`), and in increasing order of size (*difficult*).

8 List (without duplication) the groups that own the files in the current directory.

Processes and devices

In this chapter you will learn about

▶ processes, jobs and the execution environment; and

▶ UNIX handling of input and output devices.

The basic program unit apparent to a programmer working in a UNIX environment is the 'process'. An understanding of how processes are handled is fundamental to the effective use of UNIX.

6.1 Processes

So far we have considered a dialogue with a UNIX system as being a sequence of *commands* entered by the user, and the system taking *action* at each command. We now explore the mechanisms with which UNIX implements commands.

When describing an operating system, we need to remember that the computer system on which it is running contains electronics that run *only* machine code. Any command that a user types in is either translated into machine code directly by **compilation**, or **interpreted** by another program that is already in machine code. A machine code program is known as a **process**. Every command given to a UNIX system, and every program run on a UNIX machine, relates to a process — either it creates one or more processes, or it is interpreted by one that is already running. A UNIX shell has a mechanism for controlling processes that appears to the user to be independent of the electronics inside the machine.

6.1.1 Process status

Within a UNIX system there are one or more processing elements (which we will refer to as **processors**) that can only run a single process at any one time. At any instant, that process can be described completely by a sequence of bytes — some representing the memory contained within the processor, some describing the precise current state of the computation. It is possible to copy these bytes to memory, and replace them by a sequence of bytes from elsewhere in memory. Thus a partially completed process can be temporarily **suspended** (or **stopped**), and completed at a later time, and in the meantime another process can be run on that processor.

The kernel manages a large 'pool' of processes, most of which are not running at any specific instant, and moves them to and from the processor (or processors) as required. Much of this movement is automatic and hidden from users — for instance, when there are several users on the machine each with a program which is running, the relevant processes are moved in and out of the processor so that each is allocated a fair percentage of the time. However, users do have a certain degree of control over their own processes.

A process can be in a number of states, normally either **running** (currently being worked on by a processor), or **stopped** (not being processed, but available to continue evaluation when instructed). When a process completes its execution; it is removed from the system entirely and **killed**. Not all processes will have been invoked by a user — some are so-called *system* processes, and are constantly running while the system is operational.

When you initially log in, you invoke a program that is a copy of the shell, and known as your **login shell**. This program forms a process which must be present during the whole time you are logged in. Any subsequent process that is created by you is **controlled** from the terminal (or window) in which you were typing the command that created it.

If you type in a command to a shell, it can be of two possible types. Either it is a 'built-in' shell command, which is interpreted by the shell process directly, or a new process is created for it. In the latter case the binary code for it is copied from storage, and forms the process to execute that command. The process that is the current shell is suspended and the process for the new command is run. After that process has finished running, it is destroyed, and the shell process is resumed.

You can find out which processes you have, either running or stopped, by means of the command **ps**. This displays a list of your processes, by default in a format similar to the following:

```
$ ps
PID    TTY      TIME COMMAND
10312  p7    00:02:23 sh
14277  p7    00:00:00 ps
```

Each process is given a unique identification number, its **process-id** or **PID**, which is indicated in the first column of the output from **ps**. The second column displays the name of the terminal from which that process is being controlled (normally your own terminal or one of your windows).

NOTE

Known as 'time-sharing'

NOTE

POSIX does not specify the default format of the output

NOTE

All time when a process has been suspended, or has otherwise been moved out of any processor, is excluded from the figures

The column headed TIME is the amount of processor time the process has so far consumed while actually running, a measure of how much work the computer has so far done for that process. In the final column, the name of the command that the process is running is given. In the above example, the user has two processes running, the login shell sh, and the ps command that is being used to display the list of processes. The login shell (PID 10312) has already consumed 2 minutes and 23 seconds of processor time, whereas ps (PID 14277) has used less than 1 second (rounded down to 0 in the output from ps). The PID number is used internally by the kernel, and is not normally needed by the user.

Another very useful utility is top, which will display _in order_ the processes (including other users') which are taking up the most system resources. This can be useful if your machine appears to be slowing down, and you need to diagnose the problem. It is an interactive utility (press q to terminate it) which combines most of the functionality of ps and kill (see below). In the following sample output, the main system user is Sam, with a program gen taking up 249M of RAM, which has been running for over 18 hours. Chris also has two small programs running which have been active for several days. For the moment you do not need to be concerned with the details of the output of top.

```
 5:21pm  up 1 day, 23:02,  2 users, load av: 1.00, 1.00, 1.00
150 processes: 146 sleeping, 1 running, 3 zombie, 0 stopped
CPU states:  0.1% user,  0.7% system,  0.0% nice, 99.0% idle
Mem:  128808K av, 120728K used,   8080K free,  37432K buff
Swap: 152248K av,   9812K used, 142436K free  618980K cached

    PID USER     PRI  NI  SIZE  RSS STAT %CPU %MEM   TIME COMMAND
  10545 sam       16   0  249M 106M R    24.2 17.1  18.5H gen
  14250 chris      9   0    92   80 S    23.4 11.0  74.3H S5Ba
  14271 chris      9   0     0    0 SW   23.5 11.0  74.4H S5Bb
  28095 sam        9   0     0    0 SW    0.7  0.1   0:00 wget
  25716 root      19  19     0    0 SWN   0.0  0.0   0:00 init
     11 root       9   0     0    0 SW    0.0  0.0   0:00 khubd
    372 root       9   0   676  640 S     0.0  0.0   0:00 dhcpcd
    631 root       9   0   892  852 S     0.0  0.0   0:00 sshd
    646 root       9   0   692  688 S     0.0  0.0   0:00 syslogd
    649 root       9   0  1056 1048 S     0.0  0.1   0:00 klogd
```

6.1.2 Foreground and background

When running a command interactively — that is, when you type in a command and wait for the system to respond — the command is being run **in the foreground**. You can instruct UNIX to run a program **in the background** instead. This means that the program will begin to run but you will be prompted by the shell for the next command without waiting for the program to complete — your login shell and the background program are effectively running simultaneously. In order to instruct UNIX to run a command in the background, follow the command with an ampersand (&) — try the following:

```
$ date &
```

NOTE

The exact meanings of the messages will be clarified later on in this chapter

A line will be printed confirming that the command has been sent to the background, and then you will be prompted for your next command with $. Meanwhile, date is executing, and shortly after its output is displayed you will be informed that date has completed running:

```
[1] 7293
$ Fri Dec 7 18:29:04 GMT 2001
[1]+ Exit 0 date
```

6.1.3 Process control

To illustrate how we can control processes, we use as an example the command sleep. Followed by an integer, sleep *suspends* execution of the current shell for that number of seconds, so:

```
$ date
Fri Dec 7 17:22:21 GMT 2001
$ sleep 15
```
(there is a delay of 15 seconds at this point)
```
$ date
Fri Dec 7 17:22:36 GMT 2001
```

So sleep is a command that essentially does nothing, but a process is created for it nonetheless. So we might have:

```
$ sleep 100 &
[1] 16403
$ ps
PID   TTY      TIME COMMAND
10312 p7    00:02:25 sh
16403 p7    00:00:00 sleep 100
16425 p7    00:00:00 ps
```

NOTE

Jobs are discussed later on in this chapter

After 100 seconds process number 16403 will terminate. The system confirms that the command has been sent to run in the background by printing a line containing **jobnumber** (enclosed in square brackets), and the process ID number (16403) of the command.

6.1.4 Signals

The kernel controls many processes, created by possibly many users, and including many that are 'system' processes, necessary for the system to function. The kernel allows these processes to communicate by sending 'messages' to each other. Any process in the system can send a message to any other process, and because there could be many processes and many messages being sent, UNIX restricts the messages to being very simple.

These messages are known as **signals**, and each takes the form of a single byte. They are instructions to processes, such as *kill* (cease running immediately) and *stop* (become a suspended process). Signals are concerned with the **scheduling** of processes, that is, *when* and *in which order* they are executed. The command `kill` is provided for a user to send a signal to a specific process. A detailed discussion of signals is beyond the scope of this chapter, but one particular signal is important at this stage.

The signal `SIGKILL`, when received by a process, causes it to be destroyed immediately. For example, to kill the `sleep` process above, you could type

```
$ kill -s KILL 16403
```

where `kill` with option `-s` ('signal') causes the signal named after `-s` to be sent to the process whose PID is given as the final argument to `kill`. Note that, although this signal is referred to as `SIGKILL`, only the word `KILL` is passed to the command `kill`. This is because all signals are called `SIG`*something*, so the `SIG` is redundant in any context where the name of a signal is expected. There are many other signals, such as `SIGHUP` and `SIGTTIN`, some of which will be discussed later on.

This raises the question of why you might ever wish to destroy a process. It sometimes happens that a process that is running in the background is left there by mistake, for instance if the software that created it was poorly written. It also happens sometimes that you send a program to run in the background when you think it will run for a long time, and later on discover that because of an error in the program it is failing to finish.

It is important to remember that UNIX uses processes as its most basic concept of a 'program'. Remembering PIDs can be tedious, however. A more 'user-friendly' method of handling processes, called **job control**, is available, which we now introduce.

6.2 Environment

Another communication mechanism employed by UNIX is that of the **environment**. If you are already familiar with a programming language, the environment is a collection of **variable** names together with an associated value for each one. Unlike most other languages, variables in

UNIX are usually regarded as character-strings, and only interpreted as numbers (or other data types) in specific circumstances.

6.2.1 Environment variables

A *variable* in UNIX is a name associated with a **value**. For instance, there is a name LOGNAME whose value is your own username. Variable names are by convention formed of upper-case letters, whereas names of files are normally lower-case. The value of a variable can be referred to by prefixing the name with a $:

```
$ echo LOGNAME
LOGNAME
$ echo $LOGNAME
chris
```

Some variable names are set by the UNIX system for you; other names you can set for yourself. The syntax for assigning a value to a name is *name = value*, for instance:

```
$ ADDRESS="1 High Street"
$ echo I live at $ADDRESS
I live at 1 High Street
```

If the value of a variable includes whitespace (*Space*s or *TAB*s) or symbols known to the shell (such as & and |), the value should be enclosed in single or double quotes. For the moment, just think of the value as being a string; if it contains numbers, they are still just sequences of characters, and you will not (yet) be able to do any arithmetic on it. Check the values of the predefined variables listed in Table 6.1 using echo as above.

Table 6.1   Some predefined variables

EDITOR	Your preferred editor
HOME	The absolute pathname of your home directory
LOGNAME	Your login name
PATH	The 'search path' for commands
PRINTER	The 'default' printer that lp uses
PS1	The shell prompt
PS2	The shell 'continuation' prompt
SHELL	The pathname of the shell you use
TERM	The type of terminal or window you are using
VISUAL	Your preferred *full-screen* editor (possibly same as EDITOR)

Of these, PATH and PS1 deserve further discussion. When a UNIX shell encounters a command that is not built in to the shell, it looks at the variable PATH — as you may have noticed, the value of this variable is a sequence of pathnames, known as **pathname components**, separated by colons. UNIX then examines each of these pathnames in order, assuming each to be a directory, to see whether there is an executable file whose name is the same as that of the command. If it finds one, it is executed, otherwise an error message is generated when all the directories in PATH have been examined. Typically, PATH will have been set up on your system so as to contain the directories the system administrator knows you will need; a typical example might be:

```
$ echo $PATH
/bin:/usr/bin:/usr/local/bin
```

For the moment, do not try to reset the value of PATH.

If you want a variable's value to *contain* the dollar symbol, prefix the dollar with a backslash, or enclose the value in **single quotes**:

```
$ X='This is a $'
$ echo $X
This is a $
```

The variable PS1 controls the prompt the shell gives you; you can safely play with this variable:

```
$ PS1="Type in a command: "
Type in a command: echo $PS1
Type in a command:
```

The concept of a variable is understood by any process; a variable can be assigned a value by other utilities, not just by the shell. However, the value of a variable is not automatically available to other processes.

You may ask 'What happens if I change the value of LOGNAME?'. Try it — the system will not prevent you from changing it. The only problem to arise is if you run a command that needs to know about LOGNAME, such as one you may have written yourself. The system knows who you are, and does not need to examine LOGNAME to find out — using LOGNAME is an aid to you when writing shell scripts.

You can list all the variables set for you by use of the command env ('environment') with no arguments, which we discuss in more detail later on. Try it — you may need to pipe the output through a pager, since your system may have set many variables for you:

```
$ env | more
```

Find out the name of the type of terminal you are using.
Solution: Examine the contents of the environment variable TERM:

```
$ echo $TERM
xterm
```

6.2.2 Global and local variables

Suppose a process assigns a value to a variable. The value cannot be passed to the parent process, but may be passed to child processes. To illustrate this, consider a variable called X, which we set to be the number 42. Then invoke a second copy of the shell using sh; you will get the usual prompt, but this prompt is from the new shell, not from your login shell. The new shell is a child of your login shell. Now check the value of X, and you will see that it is not assigned a value:

```
$ X=42
$ echo $X
42
$ sh
$ echo $X
(blank line)
$
```

The new value of X is not passed down to the child process. We say that the value of X is **local** to the process that assigned it the value, and no changes will be recognised by any child process. If you now cause the child shell to finish by typing *ctrl-D*, you will get the $ prompt again, this time from your login shell. Now, if you examine the value of X again, you will see that it is 42, as that was the value assigned to it in the login shell.

We can cause a variable instead to be **global** by means of the command export, which means that its value will be passed down to all the child processes, and their children, and so on. Do the same as in the example above, but immediately after setting X to 42, type a line exporting X:

```
$ export X
```

Worked example 6.2

> Change your prompt from $ to enter command:
> **Solution**: The variable PS1 contains the prompt; reset it and export its value:
>
> ```
> $ PS1="enter command: "
> enter command: export PS1
> ```

Another method for assigning a variable a value is by means of the command `read`. Followed by one or more variable names, this reads words from the standard input and assigns them to the successive variables. The following script requests the name of a user and sends them a greeting by mail:

```
echo "Whom do you wish to greet?"
read RECIPIENT
echo Hello | mailx -s Greeting $RECIPIENT
```

Generally you will read one variable at a time, but it is possible to read several at once from a single line of input. In this case you must be careful if the number of variables and the number of words on the input line are different. If there are fewer variables than words on the line, the initial variables will be assigned one word each, and the final one the rest of the line; if there are more variables than words on the line, the final variables will be assigned the null string. If script `testread` has the following contents:

```
read X Y Z
echo "X=$X Y=$Y Z=$Z"
```

then we might have the following:

```
$ sh testread
hello there chris
X=hello Y=there Z=chris
$ sh testread
hello
X=hello Y= Z=
$ sh testread
hello there chris jo and sam
X=hello Y=there Z=chris jo and sam
```

Worked example 6.3

> Write a script to prompt the user for the name of a file and then
> print the file on their terminal.
> **Solution**: Use echo to prompt the user, read to get a filename into a
> variable, and cat to display the file:
>
> ```
> echo Type in a filename
> read FILENAME
> cat $FILENAME
> ```

One use of read that is not apparent from the above discussion is that
it can be used to allow the user control over the speed with which a shell
script is executed. Try creating a file (say cat2files) containing the
following:

```
echo Type in 2 file names
read FILE1 FILE2
cat $FILE1
echo Press Return to continue
read X
cat $FILE2
```

Now execute that script — it will print out the first file on the screen,
then pause for you to press *Return* before displaying the second file. The
second read assigns a value to the variable X (which is not actually used
for anything else), but waits for you to type in something before moving
on to the next line.

Suppose file myprogram contains

```
echo The emperor is $MY_NAME
```

and you wish to run the commands in the file with MY_NAME set to a value.
You could set MY_NAME, then export it, then run the file, so:

```
$ MY_NAME="Julius Caesar"
$ export MY_NAME
$ sh myprogram
The emperor is Julius Caesar
```

There is a problem with this, namely that you have reset MY_NAME in the
current shell as well. You may not wish to do this. You may wish to test
myprogram with the variable MY_NAME assigned a different value. This
would be especially important if you were writing a script that used
system-defined variables, such as TERM or LOGNAME, where it would be
confusing if you were to reset them. You can use the following:

```
$ MY_NAME="Julius Caesar" sh myprogram
The emperor is Julius Caesar
```

This does not affect the current value of MY_NAME, but has the same effect as inserting the single line

```
MY_NAME="Julius Caesar"
```

at the start of the file myprogram. An equivalent effect can be achieved using the command env:

```
$ env MY_NAME="Julius Caesar" sh myprogram
The emperor is Julius Caesar
```

6.2.3 Executable scripts

Suppose you have written a script, called (say) myprogram. In order to execute the commands in this file, we have indicated that they must be passed to the shell. Now, using

```
$ sh myfile
```

a copy of the shell command interpreter is created for the sole purpose of executing the commands in myfile and, when it has finished with them, the new shell terminates. Typing sh each time can be tedious, especially if you have written many scripts; if you change the permissions on myfile so that you have *execute* permission for it, then it can be run as any other command:

```
$ chmod +x myfile
```

This is the same as

```
$ chmod a+x myfile
```

which gives execute permission to all users. You can now type just the name of the file and it will run:

```
$ /cs/ugrad/chris/myfile
```

For example, if you create a file called mydate and containing

```
echo The date and time is:
date
```

then you could run the script by

```
$ $HOME/mydate
```

Alternatively, give it the name relative to the current directory:

```
$ ./mydate
```

Finally, examine the value of your PATH:

```
$ echo $PATH
```

NOTE

. is the current directory

If there is a dot as one of the components of PATH the current directory will also be searched, and you can then simply type mydate

```
$ mydate
```

Worked example 6.4

> Update your PATH so that it includes the subdirectory bin of your home directory.
> **Solution**: We assume that you have created the subdirectory by moving to your home directory using cd and then typing mkdir bin. The value of $HOME is the name of your home directory, so the subdirectory bin can be referred to by $HOME/bin. The variable PATH contains the directories, separated by colons, that are searched for. You want to replace the value of PATH by a new value, which is the old value with a colon, and then $HOME/bin added on at the end. You will then need to export the value of PATH so that child processes will use the new one.
>
> ```
> $ PATH=$PATH:$HOME/bin
> $ export PATH
> ```
>
> Note that we have added $HOME/bin to the *end* of $PATH; it would be unwise to place it at the start, in case you accidentally include a command in $HOME/bin that has a name identical to another command on the system. If this happened, your command would be executed in preference to the other one, which might have unexpected consequences. Of course, you might wish to write your own version of a system command, in which case having $HOME/bin at the *start* of $PATH would be necessary, but you are strongly advised against rewriting system commands.

NOTE

Not to be confused with the directory .

There is a command . which, when followed by a file that is a shell script, will cause the commands in the script to be executed by the calling shell. A new shell is not created. For most purposes it does not matter whether or not you use sh or ., but if you use sh you should bear in mind that any environment variables defined in the calling shell must be exported to be recognised within the script. If you use . changes you make to the environment will alter the environment of the current shell.

Worked example 6.5

> Write a command `changeprompt` to request you to enter a new shell prompt and then reset it to its new value.
>
> **Solution**: The variable `PS1` has its value as your prompt. Create a file to reset its value. Execute the file using . (not `sh`) to run the commands in your interactive shell.
>
> ```
> echo Type in the new prompt:
> read PS1
> export PS1
> ```

6.3 Program control

A process can create other processes. Consider a shell script containing one line, which is `date`. When the script is executed, *two* processes will be created, one for the invocation of the shell, and one for the command `date`. The shell is referred to as the **parent** process, and `date` as a **child** process. Some UNIX commands that appear simple may create child processes, and it is seldom of interest to users how many are created, and how they relate to the original command — the user is only interested in the original command.

The shell allows us to control programs without needing to concern ourselves with the finer details of which process is involved in which activity. The concept of a **job**, and associated shell facilities, will be helpful.

6.3.1 Job control

A job is a collection of processes grouped together and identified by a small integer. In the example above, the job number for process `16403` was 1. When a UNIX command is sent to the background using `&`, a single job is created consisting of one or more processes. That job will initially be sent to the background, but can be moved into the foreground or destroyed in much the same way as an individual process. Consider the following pipe:

```
$ cat testfile | wc &
[2] 2374
```

A single job (number 2) has been created in the background, but two processes are required, one for `cat` and one for `wc`. The process number `2374` is that of the last command in the pipe, namely `wc`. You can destroy the job, and consequently both processes, with

```
$ kill -s KILL %2
```

(instead of giving the command `kill` the number of the process to send a signal to, we give it the number of the job preceded by a percent character).

Worked example 6.6

Arrange to be given an 'alarm call' after 2 minutes.
Solution: Create a script that uses `sleep` to cause it to suspend for 120 seconds, and then use `echo` to write a message to your screen. The script should be run in the background.

```
$ cat >myalarm
sleep 120
echo Your alarm call ...
ctrl-D
$ sh myalarm &
```

If you now typed `ps`, you would find (amongst others) two processes:

```
23624 p2 S 0:00 sh myalarm
23625 p2 S 0:00 sleep 120
```

indicating that both the script `myalarm` and the command `sleep` had been invoked.

You may have several jobs running at any one time, and the command `jobs` will list them. For example,

```
$ jobs
[1] Stopped testA
[2]- Running sh myalarm &
[3]+ Running testB &
```

NOTE

The word `Suspended` *is used on some systems instead of* `Stopped`

indicates that you have three jobs. Jobs 2 and 3 are running in the background, whereas number 1 has been **stopped**. This means that the system is not running that job at all; it is suspended pending reactivation. You can try creating a few jobs yourself — the script `myalarm` from the last worked example is suitable to experiment with. Take a copy of `myalarm`, call it (say) `newalarm`, and execute both in the background; you should get a dialogue similar to:

```
$ cp myalarm newalarm
$ sh myalarm &
```

```
[1]  25816
$ sh newalarm &
[2]  25820
$ jobs
[1]- Running sh myalarm &
[2]+ Running sh newalarm &
```

If you have jobs running or stopped, one of them will be the **default** job, and is indicated in the output from `jobs` by the symbol + after its number — in the above example this would be job 3. The default job is the job that was most recently created (or sent a signal by you). If you have two or more running, one will be indicated by a - symbol, which indicates that if the default job was to terminate, this one would then become the default. In the example above this would be job 2. The default job is also known as %%.

Any job that is in the background or is stopped can become the foreground job simply by giving the job number (preceded by %) as argument to the command `fg` ('foreground'). Similarly, any stopped job can be reactivated to run in the background by the command `bg` ('background'):

```
$ bg %1
[1]+ testA &
$ jobs
[1]  Running testA
[2]- Running sleep 120 &
[3]+ Running testB &
$ fg %%
```

The reason for having default jobs is that quite often, when you have sent a job into the background, you will either want it to be brought back to the foreground or perhaps `killed`. In practice, you tend to find that you have not created any new jobs in the meantime, and it is useful to have a shorthand for referring to the default job.

Any job sent to the background will still have its standard output and standard error streams set up as if the job were still in the foreground. What this means for the user is that if a background job wants to write to your terminal, it will do so (so you should not be surprised if, when running jobs in the background, messages do appear on your screen). Yet any input you type on your terminal will be sent to the current foreground process or to the shell — if you had many background processes running, the system couldn't be expected to decide which job your input was intended for, so can only send it to a foreground process.

A background job must therefore do something sensible if it requires input from the terminal. What happens in this case is that the background job automatically stops — a signal called SIGTTIN is sent to it when it attempts to read from the terminal, and this signal has the effect of stopping the job. Consider:

```
$ cat &
[1] 13249
$
[1]+ Stopped (SIGTTIN) cat
```

The command cat, in the absence of any arguments, reads from standard input; cat is run in the background, so immediately demands input, but since it is in the background it cannot receive it. It therefore becomes suspended and you are sent a message to tell you of this fact.

If you send a job to the background that requires input from your terminal, it will become stopped as soon as it requires that input, and you must bring it to the foreground if you wish it to complete executing. Try this with mailx:

```
$ mailx -s "Test" chris &
[1] 24545
[1]+ Stopped (SIGTTIN) mailx
$ fg %1
```
(you can type in your message now)

6.3.2 Command history list

UNIX keeps a record of the commands you have typed in to your shell. Each command is given a number, starting with 1, and using the command fc ('fix command') you can re-execute previous commands. To list the commands you have already run, use option -l ('list'):

```
$ fc -l
1       date
2       sh myalarm &
3       mailx sam
```

If you run fc with no arguments, the shell first of all creates a temporary file (you don't need to know its name) containing one line, namely the last command you ran. In the above example, this would be

```
mailx sam
```

The shell would then run Vi on that file without you having to type vi yourself. You can then edit that file, thinking of it as a script of commands to be run — you can change the last command you ran, or add extra commands to the file. When you leave Vi, whatever is in that temporary file will be treated as commands to the shell and run immediately. Note that if, when leaving the editor, there is more than one line in the temporary file, each line in the file will be executed separately and in turn. An `fc` command is not itself entered in the history list.

You can select a number of commands by specifying the first and last numbers of the commands you have already run — so to rerun commands 2 through 4 and edit them,

```
$ fc 2 4
```

will create a file containing three lines and then apply `vi` to that file.

Often you will simply wish to re-run commands you have previously typed in without editing. Using option `-s` ('string') this can be accomplished. In the above example, to re-run the alarm, you could just have

```
$ fc -s 3
```

6.3.3 Running a job at a specific time

During a session on your UNIX system, most of the programs you run will be executed immediately. Sometimes this will not be desirable. If a program is likely to take a long time to run, you may wish it to run overnight, since, if a machine tries to execute too many processes at once, it becomes slow, to the detriment of all logged-in users. The command `at` can be used to schedule a job for a specific time in the future.

In its simplest form, typing `at` followed by a time and/or date will cause the standard input to be read, and those commands entered as input to be executed at that time, thus:

```
$ at 1530
at> echo "It's half past three"
ctrl-D
job 81 at 2001-12-07 15:30
```

The number of the job, together with confirmation of the date and time it has been scheduled, will be printed on the terminal. The output (both standard output and standard error) will be mailed to you. Alternatively, you can create a file (`testfile`, say) containing commands you wish to be executed, and then you can use `at` with option `-f` ('file'):

```
$ at -f testfile 1530
job 81 at 2001-12-07 15:30
```

The formats allowed for you to specify the time are broad and easy to use, but rather complex to specify — look in the manual page for `at` to

NOTE

The results will still be sent to you via email

check the exact syntax allowed. The following examples will give the general idea:

```
1645
16:45
16:45 GMT tomorrow
noon
4am Jan 25 2001
11pm today
now + 30 minutes
now + 1 month
```

If you take care that your time/date specification is unambiguous, it will probably be acceptable to at.

When a job has been created using at, it is placed on a **queue**. At the specified time and date, or as soon thereafter as the load on the system permits, an invocation of the shell will execute the commands given to at. The jobs on the queue can be examined with option -l ('list') and jobs on the queue can be removed with option -r ('remove') by at:

```
$ at -l
81 2001-12-07 15:30 a chris
$ at -r 81
$ at -l
$
```

The fourth column of the listing of jobs contains an a indicating that the queue is named a ('at queue'). You should not normally need to be concerned about which queue a job has been placed on.

Similar to at is batch. This command is used when you do not wish to specify exactly when a job should run, merely that the system load should not be high when you do it. A job submitted with batch is dealt with by the system in exactly the same way as at, except that batch will instruct the time of running to be now and will place the job on a separate queue. Jobs submitted to this **batch queue** can be listed and removed using at:

```
$ batch <testfile
job 121 at 2001-12-07 15:45
$ at -l
121 2001-12-07 15:45 b chris
```

Notice that the name of the queue is b ('batch queue')

The 'jobs' described in connection with at and batch should not be confused with the 'jobs' in the section on job control. Jobs in an at-queue can only be created and removed by batch or at.

NOTE

batch *is the same as the* command
at -q b -m now

Worked example 6.7

> Write a script to list all the files in your filespace, and run that script in one minute's time.
>
> **Solution**: Using `man ls` you will discover that option `-R` ('recursive') to `ls` will list all files in the current directory and recursively through all subdirectories. So we can pass `ls -R` as the command to be processed by `at`. First of all, however, we must change directory to the home directory.
>
> ```
> $ at now + 1 minute
> cd
> ls -R
> ctrl-D
> ```

NOTE

The word `crontab` *is obscure, but probably means 'commands run over night table'*

6.3.4 Running programs periodically

There is also a facility to specify, for instance, 'run program X every morning at 2 am'. This is enabled by the command `crontab`. The mechanism used by `crontab` is different from that for `at` or `batch`.

For each user, a file is kept on the system to specify which commands are to be run periodically, and when. You can edit this file using `vi` by invoking `crontab` with option `-e` ('edit'). Each line of this file commences with five columns, representing respectively minutes (0–59), hours (0–23) day of month (1–31), month (1–12), and day of week (1–7); each of these columns contains either a number, a comma-separated list of numbers, or an asterisk. The rest of each line is a command to be executed repeatedly whenever the five columns match the current time and date. An asterisk means 'every'. For instance, if the `crontab` file contains

```
30 15 * * * ls -R
0 0 * * 1 X
0 0 * 6 * Y
0 0 1,8,15,22 * * Z
```

NOTE

Monday is day 1 in the week, Sunday day 7

---

then the command `ls -R` will be executed every day at 3:30 pm, command `X` will be run first thing every Monday, and command `Y` first thing every day in June. Command `Z` is run on days 1, 8, 15 and 22 of each month. If you try to create an entry in the `crontab` file that is inconsistent, such as specifying a non-existent date, you will be warned and the `crontab` file will not be changed.

To list the entries in your `crontab` file without using the editor type `crontab -l`.

Worked example 6.8

> Create an entry in your `crontab` file to send user `jo` a friendly message every Christmas morning.
>
> **Solution**: Using `crontab -e` create a line in the file that is
>
> ```
> 00 09 25 12 * echo Happy Xmas | mailx jo
> ```
>
> indicating that the message `Happy Xmas` will be piped to the mail program `mailx` at 0900 hours on the 25th of the 12th month each year. The day field is left as a * since having specified the date we do not need to worry about the day of the week as well.

Some sites will restrict the use of this command — if you find difficulties, check with your system administrator first.

6.3.5 Big programs

Some programs take a lot of processing time before they complete. If you are running such a program, and the results are not needed urgently, you would probably like it to be executing on a processor when the system is not busy, and for it to be suspended when the usage of the machine becomes high, in order not to slow down more urgent processes. The facility called **nice** exists to **prioritise** a job. If `mycommand` is a big program, then

```
$ nice mycommand &
```

will run `mycommand` in the background with low priority.

If a process is already running and you wish to reduce its priority, the command `renice` can be used, but we omit discussion of this command here — examine the manual page using `man` for further information.

When you finish your session on the system, a signal `SIGHUP` is sent to all the processes you created during the session. Most processes, when they receive this signal, will terminate. If you have a job you wish to continue running in the background after you have logged off — and this will probably be true for any big jobs you run — you must make the job immune to the signal `SIGHUP` by means of command `nohup`. The syntax is `nohup` followed by a command; you will probably also wish the command to run in the background:

```
$ nohup testfile &
```

You would only want to run a command via `nohup` in the *foreground* if you were connected to the system using a communication link that might disconnect you without warning in the middle of a session. Standard output and the standard error stream from a job running with `nohup` are redirected to a file called `nohup.out` instead of to your terminal, if they are not already redirected, and the priority of the job is low (as with `nice`). The difference between `nice` and `nohup` is principally that a job run with `nice` will terminate when the user who invoked the job logs off.

6.3.6 Timing a program

It's often useful to know how long it takes to run a command. Perhaps you need to compare the speeds of different machines (if you have access to more than one) in order to choose the fastest machine. Perhaps you need to know if a program takes a long time to run so that you can schedule it when you run it again at a quiet time of day. The command `time` provides this information. With no options, `time` followed by a *simple* command (that is, not a pipeline or other complex shell construct) displays some statistics on the standard error stream.

A more concise output can be obtained by running `time` with option `-p`. In this case, only three numbers will be given. First, the total **real** (or **elapsed**) time (in seconds) the command took to run is displayed and then the **processing** time spent by the user's command executing on the processor. Finally, the time spent by the **system** (for example, moving processes in and out of the processor) is displayed:

```
$ time date
```
```
Fri Dec  7 09:45:32 GMT 2001
real    0m0.063s
user    0m0.010s
sys     0m0.042s
```
```
$ time -p date
```
```
Fri Dec  7 09:47:02 GMT 2001
real 0.6
user 0.1
sys 0.4
```

If the system is busy, the real time will be larger, since there will be many users running processes, all of which demand their fair share of processor time. However, for a particular command (such as `date`) the user and the system times ought to remain fairly constant, since that command will do the same work each time it is run. Try timing the `sleep` command:

```
$ time sleep 5
real 5.7
user 0.3
sys 0.3
```

NOTE

The statistics generated by `time`, and the format, vary on different systems

---

NOTE

'System' time refers to time spent by the kernel

NOTE

p = 'POSIX'

You will see that the total time for the command to run was slightly over 5 seconds, but the amount of processing time — and thus the work the system had to do — was very small in comparison. This is to be expected, since `sleep` does nothing anyway.

The times for the *system* and *user* are the actual processing time, and exclude any idle time when the relevant processes are not running, so that the *real* time will always be *at least* the sum of the *user* and *system* time.

If you wish to time a complex command, which is not a single word with arguments, then a simple way to do it is to create a shell script containing the command and time the execution of that script.

6.3.7 Running programs in order

You may wish a program to run only when another has completed. If a large program (`myprogram`, say) is to be run, and you require to be mailed a message when it has finished, you could create a file containing

```
sh myprogram
echo "Program completed" | mailx chris
```

and then run the commands from that file in the background using `sh` and `&`. This is not always convenient, and once `myprogram` has begun to execute you cannot go back and edit the file. Another possibility is to use the command `wait`. In order to do this, you require the PID of the command you wish to wait for. As an example, create a file called `myprogram` containing

```
sleep 200
date
```

Run this in the background:

```
$ sh myprogram &
```

```
[1]+ 14523
```

and you will be informed of the PID of the process running `myprogram`, in this case 14523. Now, create another file (say `notify`):

```
$ cat >notify
wait 14523
echo "Program completed"
ctrl-D
```

The command `wait` is similar to `sleep`, except that instead of waiting a specified number of seconds, it waits until a process (which is its argument) terminates. If we now run `notify` in the background,

```
$ sh notify &
```

then as soon as `myprogram` has finished, `notify` will write `Program completed` on your terminal.

There are restrictions on the use of `wait` — you can only wait for a process to complete if that process has been *spawned* from the current shell. Thus you cannot wait for someone else's process to complete. If you call `wait` with no arguments, it will wait for all child processes to terminate — therefore, if you are running many jobs in the background `wait` will not complete until each of them has finished. Normally you would use `wait` with a PID as argument.

6.4 Quotes and escapes

NOTE

This section is rather important!

A number of characters are understood by the shell to have a special meaning, such as `$`, `>` and `<`, for example, which we have already used. The purpose of quotes and backslash is to enable characters that are part of the shell's reserved characters to be used in a context where they are not recognised as such. In this section we discuss the three characters `'` (**single quote**), `"` (**double quote**), and `\` (**backslash**). The following other characters are reserved for the shell:

```
< >  | & * @ # ? ! - $ ( ) [ ] { } ; = % ' '
```

If you wish to use any of these characters in any context other than the shell defines for them, they must be either quoted or escaped. In general, if it's a single character, preceding it with a backslash will indicate that its literal value is to be used. Alternatively, if there are several such characters, enclose the whole string in single quotes:

NOTE

A single quote refers to a 'close' single quote '

```
$ X='hello <$Chris>'
$ echo $X
hello <$Chris>
```

There are two important points here that you need to remember. First of all, the shell strips off pairs of quotes, and matches an opening quote with its nearest possible closing match, so:

```
$ X='abc >''>&def'
$ echo $X
abc >>&def
```

This implies that a single quote cannot occur within a quoted string that is quoted using single quotes. The second point is that quotes must come in pairs. Notice what happens if they don't:

```
$ X='abc
>
```

At the end of the first line the shell is looking for a single quote; not having found one, it assumes that the *Newline* character you entered when you typed *Return* is part of the string, that you intended a space instead, and that you wish to continue entering the rest of the string on the following line. The > is the **continuation prompt** (different from $) indicating an unfinished command. If we then complete the dialogue:

```
$ X='abc
> def'
$ echo $X
abc def
```

Double quotes can be used in the same way as single quotes, except that not all characters enclosed between them become literal. In particular, variable names preceded by $ are replaced by their values. Double quotes may be used to include a single quote in a string:

```
$ PS1="$LOGNAME's prompt "
chris's prompt
```

Without quotes, the shell would assign $LOGNAME to PS1 and then try to execute **prompt** as the next command.

Having set up variables, you may wish to protect some of them to avoid accidentally changing them. The command **readonly** will prohibit you changing the value of a variable:

```
$ X=42
$ readonly X
$ X=99
X: read-only variable
$ echo $X
42
```

If a read-only variable has been exported, it will not be read-only for any child processes — 'read-only-ness' is not exportable.

6.5 Devices

A **device** is any piece of equipment connected to a computer system which performs communication between 'the outside world' and the system, such as a printer or a terminal. Although normally hardware, a device might be software that behaves, from the perspective of UNIX, in the same way as hardware. When you have run commands that use input and output streams, their behaviour as 'streams of characters' does not depend upon where they originate from or are directed to. They are simply streams of characters. It does not matter whether input comes from a terminal or from a file, nor whether output is piped to a printer, sent to the terminal, or redirected to a file. In fact, UNIX treats devices *exactly* the same as files.

From the perspective of a UNIX programmer, every device *is* a file.

Type `tty` to discover what the name of your current terminal (or window) is (say, `ttyp9`). Now change directory to `/dev` ('device') and use `ls` to examine which files are in it. You will find a very large number of files. Look closely at file `ttyp9`:

```
$ ls -l ttyp9
crw--w--- 1 chris tty 20, 2 Mar 26 12:02 ttyp9
```

This looks very much like an ordinary file, except that the first character in the output of `ls -l` is the character `c`, indicating that the file is a **character special file**, the technical jargon used to describe a device such as a terminal. You own the file, and can write to it. Try:

```
$ date >ttyp9
```

and the date will appear on your screen just as if you had typed `date` on its own.

Every device has a filename in the directory `/dev`.

If you attempt to write to a device owned by another user, it won't work. If you have several windows on your terminal you will normally be allowed to write to other windows — use `tty` to discover their names, and then try the above example with one of them. There is also a file in `/dev` called `tty` which is always a synonym for the current terminal's filename — so

```
$ date >tty
```

would produce the same output as above.

Standard input is received from, and standard output and standard error are sent to, the file that is your terminal, unless you redirect them elsewhere. They are not files, they are simply concepts to enable redirection of streams to take place. At the ends of pipelines, unless these streams are redirected, they are automatically directed at `/dev/tty`. Thus

```
$ sh myprogram
```

is equivalent to

```
$ sh myprogram 0</dev/tty 1>/dev/tty 2>/dev/tty
```

Other devices you may encounter include /dev/audio, if your terminal has a loudspeaker and microphone, /dev/console if you are using a workstation, and devices with names similar to /dev/rst8 if you ever need to use a magnetic tape drive.

There is, however, one device you will need, and will have to use by name. Suppose you have written a program that outputs diagnostic messages as well as its output, and you wish to view only the output. You could send the standard error stream to a file:

```
$ sh myprogram 2>test.errors
```

but this would be wasteful of filespace. You can discard this stream by redirecting it to a file (device) known as /dev/null:

```
$ sh myprogram 2>/dev/null
```

This file behaves in the same way as any other file or device, but it simply junks any output sent to it, and if you try to read from it it is always at end-of-file. Use /dev/null with care, and only when you know that you want output discarded.

Worked example 6.9

> Write a script to read in the name of a file and display a message only if it cannot be read.
> **Solution**: Use cat to read the contents of the file. If cat fails, the file is unreadable, and the error message, sent to standard error, should be displayed. However, we do not actually wish to see the file's contents, so junk them by directing the standard output to /dev/null:
>
> ```
> echo Type the name of a file:
> read FILENAME
> cat $FILENAME >/dev/null
> ```

6.6 Backquotes

NOTE

Use the manual page to find out about formatted output from date

Sometimes, redirecting output from a command is not quite what you want to do. If you need to set the value of a variable to be the output of a command, the mechanisms we have already met will not work. As an example, suppose you wished to set a variable YEAR to the current year. We can easily find the current year using date. Either use the **formatting** argument +"%Y" to date, or pipe the output through cut.

```
$ date +"%Y"
 2001
$ date | cut -f7 -d' '
2001
```

However, printing the output of `date` on your terminal or sending it to a
file will not allow it to be on the right-hand side of the equals symbol in
an assignment. If you enclose a command in backquotes (`'`), or
alternatively enclose it in `$(` and `)`, it is executed and its standard output
becomes a string which is then passed to the shell in place of the original
command. This is known as **command substitution**:

```
$ YEAR=`date +"%Y"`
$ YEAR=$( date +"%Y" )
```

As for double quotes, variable names preceded by a `$` symbol will be
replaced by their values between backquotes.

Worked example 6.10

> Reset your shell prompt to the name of the shell followed by a `>`
> symbol.
> **Solution**: the variable SHELL holds the name of the shell as an
> absolute pathname:
>
> ```
> $ echo $SHELL
> /usr/local/bin/sh
> ```
>
> The command `basename` can be used to remove the directory portion
> of a path name, so `basename $SHELL` will extract the name of the
> shell you are using. Use backquotes to turn the output from
> `basename` into a string, and remember that `>` and the space, since
> they are special symbols, must be quoted:
>
> ```
> $ PS1=$( basename $SHELL )"> "
> sh>
> ```

114

CHAPTER SUMMARY

Table 6.2   Commands introduced in this chapter

`at`	execute commands at a specified time
`batch`	execute commands when system load permits
`bg`	run a job in the background
`crontab`	schedule periodic background work
`env`	set environment for a command
`export`	set export attribute for a variable
`fc`	process command history list
`fg`	run a job in the foreground
`jobs`	list the jobs in the current session
`kill`	send a signal to a process
`nice`	run a command with changed priority
`nohup`	run a command immune to hangups
`ps`	display information about processes
`read`	read a line from standard input
`readonly`	set read-only attribute for variables
`renice`	change the priority of a running process
`sleep`	suspend execution for a time interval
`time`	display execution time for a command
`wait`	suspend process until completion of another process

EXERCISES

1 Arrange for a 'Good Morning' message to be mailed to you at 8 am every Monday morning.

2 Arrange for a list of *all* your files (including 'dot' files) and directories to be mailed to you every weekday at 6 pm.

3 Arrange for an 'alarm call' message to be written on your terminal in one hour.

4 What is the Process-ID (PID) of your login shell?

5 Write a script to write your username, your home directory, the type of your terminal, and the printer that lp uses, so the output looks like:

```
Your username is chris
Home directory is /cs/ugrad/chris
You are using a terminal which is a vt100
The default lineprinter is cs/p1
```

6 Write a script to prompt you for the name of a directory and then list the files in it.

7 Set an environment variable called MY_NAME to be your name in the form *first name* followed by a space followed by *family name*.

Introduction to shells

CHAPTER OVERVIEW

This chapter

▶ explains why a shell is needed; and

▶ introduces simple syntax for the shell, including conditional statements and loops.

In previous chapters, we have considered UNIX *commands* together with related concepts such as *process* and *environment*. In this chapter we consider the shell — the command interpreter — in more detail, and introduce the constructs that are a part of the shell and make it a programming language in its own right.

7.1 Why do we need a shell?

This question may be on your mind. Most of the commands discussed so far are to be found in directories mentioned in your PATH. You can edit files, print files, and run programs. You can schedule commands. You have access to languages such as Pascal or C on your system, and they can be used for complex programming tasks. So what else does the shell have to offer?

The shell allows you to check on the *success* and *failure* of commands, on the *state* of the filesystem, and on the *values* of environment variables, and to process this knowledge. It is a programming language in the full sense — it has the power of other programming languages — but tailored for use in conjunction with an operating system. It contains built-in features that allow the user to get the maximum amount of information from the kernel in an easy manner. By writing shell scripts you can also create your own commands.

Although the shell is a powerful programming language, it is designed as a user interface to a UNIX machine, and is not an ideal language for doing complex numerical calculations. If you have a particular application that does not clearly have a need to be written in the shell, then it is good practice to write it in another language better suited, and then call that program from the shell.

It is not possible to give exact instructions as to where the boundary lies — when you should decide that the shell is unsuitable and use another language — but the examples in the following chapters will give you a feel as to what sorts of task are typically programmed in the shell. Some people use a UNIX system happily and hardly ever use any of the shell facilities, while others are quite at home with the most complex scripts.

7.2 Shell syntax

Any computer language has a **syntax** — that is, a set of rules defining what you can write in the language, and what you are forbidden to write. The shell uses symbols and words in a very precise way. We will not attempt to give a formal definition of the shell's syntax here, but we will describe most of its features.

Recall that a *script* is a file containing commands that the shell is able to interpret. If a script is two or three lines long, it is likely to be clear to anyone reading the file what the commands do, and therefore what the purpose of the script is. If a script is a hundred lines long, it will not be so easy to see what is happening. Not only will it be difficult for someone else reading your scripts, but if you make an error while writing it, you may yourself find trouble discovering exactly where the error has occurred.

It is good practice to include **comments** in your scripts. These are messages the shell *ignores* — they are there merely for the benefit of anyone reading the scripts.

If you write a script, and include a **#** ('hash') symbol, then the rest of that line (including the **#**) is ignored by the shell (unless that **#** appears within quotes or is within a word). For instance, the following script

> **NOTE**
>
> *Comments only work in scripts, and will not work interactively when you are giving the shell instructions from a terminal*

```
MESSAGE="Hello $LOGNAME"
echo $MESSAGE
```

causes a message to be displayed on the terminal screen. The next script does exactly the same thing, but has had comments included.

```
# This script prints a friendly message on standard output
# Written by Chris, 5 December 2001
#
# This script requires variable LOGNAME to be set

MESSAGE="Hello $LOGNAME" # Set MESSAGE to the message
echo $MESSAGE # ... and echo it to stdout
```

The sort of information that should appear in comments includes

▶ who wrote the script,

▶ what the script does,

▶ when it was written, and

▶ what the individual parts of the script do.

For very short scripts, this may appear rather trivial, but for longer scripts comments are essential, and you should get into the habit of commenting all your scripts. Try creating a file (`messagefile`, say) containing the above script, and run it using:

```
$ sh messagefile
```

When the shell reads input, it reads the input line-by-line looking for commands, and each line is first of all stripped of comments. A command is normally terminated by the end of the line on which it appears, with the exception that if the end of the line is premature, and the shell knows you haven't completed typing in the command, it will recognise this and expect you to continue the command on the next line. If the shell is interactive, it will prompt you with a > to continue with a command that was started on the previous line. For instance, if you tried to echo a string and typed only one quote the shell would infer that you had not finished typing in the string, and that you would continue on the next line. Try it:

```
$ echo "Hello
> Chris"
Hello
Chris
```

You can also try creating a file containing

```
echo "Hello
Chris"
```

and executing the file as a shell script. Remember that the only difference between a shell script (which is a file containing shell commands) and the commands you type in on your terminal, is where the input to the shell comes from. In the case of an interactive shell, such as your login shell, the shell commands are typed in by you at your terminal; when a script is run, the shell reads commands from the script file.

You can also terminate a command with the symbols & or ; so you can have several commands on a single line. If you separate them with semicolons they will run one after the other, as if you had written them on separate lines. If you separate them by ampersands, they will be sent to run in the background one after the other, and will therefore be executed concurrently. A semicolon terminates a command and causes it to be run in the *foreground*. Try the following:

```
$ date; sleep 5; date
$ date & uname & who &
```

A sequence of commands separated by semicolons or *Newline*s is called a **sequential list**, and a sequence separated by ampersands is an **asynchronous list**.

7.2.1   Types of shell command

We must now distinguish between two concepts — **utilities** and **commands**. A utility is the name of a program, such as `wc`, `date` or `uname`. A command is an instruction to the shell to perform a task. A very simple command may well just be the name of a utility, but in general is more complex. Consider

```
$ uname -a >outputfile
```

which will display the 'vital statistics' of the system you are running the command on, redirecting the output to file `outputfile`. The *command*

```
uname -a >outputfile
```

comprises *utility* `uname` with argument `-a`, and standard output redirected to `outputfile`.

In order to combine the utilities we have met, and the sorts of command we already know about, into more complex structures, we need to be very precise about what sorts of command are available. The shell allows five different types of command:

- ▶ **simple command**
- ▶ **pipeline**
- ▶ **list command**
- ▶ **function definition**
- ▶ **compound command**.

When we use the word *command*, we mean any of the above five types of command. We discuss all of the above in this chapter, with the exception of functions, which are found in Chapter 9. Of the five types of command, we will explicitly define the first four, and all other commands we introduce come under the heading of compound commands. Don't worry if these names look complex — we need them so that later on we can be completely unambiguous when we discuss shells, and you may then need to refer back to here. For now, you should remember simply that command types are neatly categorised.

7.2.2 Simple commands

A **simple command** is a name (understood to be a valid UNIX utility name) together with options and arguments, any input or output redirection, and possibly preceded by variable assignments. Examples we have met in previous chapters include the following.

```
date
```

This is just the name of a utility that displays the current time and date.

```
cat 0< inputfile 1> outputfile
```

This is a utility with input and output redirected — it copies `inputfile` to `outputfile`.

```
VAR=42 NAME=Chris mycommand argument1 argument2
```

This utility (`mycommand`) is run with two arguments and variables `VAR` and `NAME` set — see Chapter 6.

7.2.3 Pipelines

NOTE

The length of pipelines is subject to system dependent limits

A **pipeline** is a sequence of commands separated by the pipe symbol (|); a single command is also technically a pipeline. We can string any number of commands together to form a long pipeline. The following are valid pipelines:

```
date
```

This is a simple command that displays the time and date.

```
who | cut -c1-8 | sort
```

NOTE

This pipeline assumes that usernames are at most 8 characters long

This is a pipeline of three simple commands; it will list the users currently logged in in alphabetical order, without any of the extra information that `who` displays. The first command in the pipeline lists users together with more information, including the terminal they are using the system from, and the second — `cut` — extracts the first eight characters from each line of the output of `who`. These eight characters are precisely the character columns that contain the usernames. The output of `cut` is then piped to `sort` to place the usernames in alphabetical order.

```
ls -l /usr/local/bin 2> errorfile | wc -l > outputfile
```

This is a pipeline of two simple commands, each redirecting some of its output, which counts the number of files in `/usr/local/bin`. If directory

/usr/local/bin exists, the number of lines produced by ls -l — and hence the number of files in /usr/local/bin — will be counted by wc, and the result sent to outputfile. If /usr/local/bin does not exist, an error message will be sent to errorfile.

```
who | VAR=42 mycommand | VAR=99 mycommand
```

This is a pipeline of three simple commands, the latter two run with variable VAR set to a specific value; since mycommand is not a system utility — it is the name of a script which you will have written — the effect of this pipeline will depend on what you have written in that script.

7.2.4 Grouping commands

Occasionally it will be necessary to group commands together so that they appear to the shell as a single command. For instance, suppose you wish to print a text file (myfile, say) on the printer, and you wish to append lines both at the start and at the end of the file. If this is to be performed in a script, you cannot use vi, since vi does not use standard input and standard output in a simple manner. What you also cannot do is to send the standard output of the echo and cat commands to lp separately — you would then get the header and footer messages printed on separate pages. There are several solutions that you will already be able to use. The first involves creating a temporary file to store the output, and then using cat on that file:

NOTE

Use lpr if lp is not installed on your system

```
$ echo "This is the start" > temp
$ cat myfile >> temp
$ echo "This is the end" >> temp
$ cat temp | lp
```

This is inelegant and to be discouraged — proliferation of temporary files causes confusion and wastes storage space. The second involves creating a script to perform the task, so:

```
$ cat <<END >temp
echo "This is the start"
cat myfile
echo "This is the end"
END
$ sh temp | lp
```

This method also uses a temporary file, but we can substitute the occurrence of temp for standard output, and pipe it to sh:

```
$ cat <<END | sh - | lp
echo "This is the start"
cat myfile
echo "This is the end"
END
```

By using the latter method we have overcome the need for a temporary file by taking the commands for `sh` from standard input explicitly by using the hyphen. What we have done is to anonymise the temporary file. However, we can improve on the here-document method by means of a technique called **command grouping**.

By enclosing a list of commands in parentheses, a new invocation of the shell is formed to execute that list of commands, just as if you had placed those commands in a file and run that file as a separate shell script. The solution to the above problem then becomes:

```
$ ( echo "This is the start"
> cat myfile
> echo "This is the end" ) | lp
```

If a sequence of commands (which can be separated either by newlines or by semicolons) is enclosed in *parentheses*, then they will be executed in sequence, and their output streams will be concatenated together to form a single stream, which can itself then be redirected.

Worked example 7.1

> Without creating any temporary files, and using a single shell command, instruct your shell to display the names of files in the current directory, preceded by an explanatory message, and *paged* (in case you have a large number of them).
> **Solution**: Use `ls` to list the files, `echo` to produce a message, and `more` as the pager. Then use command grouping to join the outputs of `ls` and `echo` together:
>
> ```
> $ (echo "Your files are:"; ls) | more
> ```

7.2.5 Exit status

Every time a UNIX command terminates, it returns a number, called its **exit status**, to the shell that caused it to run. Depending on the number, the shell can then take appropriate action. By convention, the exit status of a command is 0 if the command is successful. If a command fails, for whatever reason, a value different from 0 is returned (and this is typically 1). We can find out the exit status of the previous command executed by means of the special parameter $?. Immediately after running a

NOTE

We discuss special parameters in detail later on in this chapter

command, type echo $? and the exit status of that command will be displayed. The exit status of a pipeline is the exit status of the last command in that pipeline.

As an example, create a file (testfile, say), protect it so that you cannot write to it using chmod and then try to write to it:

```
$ chmod -w testfile
$ cat >testfile
testfile: Permission denied.
$ echo $?
1
```

The 1 that is the value of $? indicates that the cat command failed.

Worked example 7.2

> What is the exit status of
> mv ~/X /
> **Solution**: We would expect this command to fail. If ~/X does not exist, it will return exit status 1 for that reason. If it does exist, you should not have write permission for the root directory, and the command will fail. Anyhow, check the exit status by typing the command and then echo $?:
>
> ```
> $ mv ~/X /
> an error message
> $ echo $?
> 1
> ```

7.2.6 List commands

NOTE

|| *is pronounced 'or'*

A simple use of exit status is when using a **list command**. A list command is a sequence of pipelines separated by either || or &&. In the case of an **or-list**

```
$ pipeline1 || pipeline2
```

pipeline1 is run, and if a non-zero exit status is returned *pipeline2* is run. If *pipeline1* returns 0, the exit status for this list command is 0, otherwise it is the status of *pipeline2*. Thus the or-list succeeds if either the first command or the second succeeds. In the case of an **and-list**

NOTE

&& *is pronounced 'and'*

```
$ pipeline1 && pipeline2
```

pipeline1 is run, and if a zero exit status is returned *pipeline2* is run. The exit status for this list command is that of *pipeline1*, if non-zero, otherwise

that of *pipeline2*. An and-list succeeds if both its first and its second
component succeed. Both or-lists and and-lists can be strung together,
and the pipelines separated by || and && are evaluated from left to right.

Simple examples for || and && would be to check whether a command
has in fact completed successfully:

```
$ mycommand || echo Cannot run mycommand
$ mycommand && echo mycommand ran OK
```

In the first line above, if mycommand fails — that is, returns exit status
not zero — the subsequent echo command is run and informs you that
mycommand failed. In the second, if mycommand succeeds the subsequent
echo command is run.

Worked example 7.3

Compare files named file1 and file2, and if they are different mail
yourself a message indicating the differences.
Solution: Use diff to compare the two files. We see from the manual
page for diff that an exit status of 0 is returned only when the two
arguments to diff are identical. You can therefore send the output
of diff to a file and then mail yourself the contents of that file. ||
can be used so that the mail will only be performed if the diff
returned non-zero exit status.

```
$ diff file1 file2 >diffout ||
> mailx -s "Output of diff" chris <diffout
```

Using && we can sequence commands so that subsequent commands
will only run if earlier ones have been completed successfully.

Worked example 7.4

Compare files named file1 and file2, and if they are identical
delete file2.
Solution: Since we do not require a *list* of any differences it will be
quicker to use cmp, which, like diff, returns 0 exit status if its
arguments have the same contents. Use && to perform rm upon
successful completion of cmp.

```
$ cmp file1 file2 && rm file2
```

Parentheses can also be used to **group** list commands so that, for
instance,

command1 || (*command2* && *command3*)

125

NOTE

There is also a command
: (colon), which has the
same effect as true

would cause *command1* to be run, and if it failed the and-list *command2*
&& *command3* would then be run.

Two other commands it is appropriate to introduce here are true and
false. Both these commands do nothing at all, but return exit status 0
and 1 respectively. We shall use them later on in this chapter.

7.3 Arithmetic

The shell itself does contain some rudimentary facilities to do arithmetic,
which we shall discuss later. However, it is not itself designed for doing
such calculations, unlike most high-level languages. It is recognised,
however, that non-trivial arithmetic will be required by some shell
programmers. The solution adopted is to introduce a utility known as bc
('basic calculator'), which is a sophisticated calculator. Use of this utility
deserves a chapter in its own right, and we shall merely touch on the
possibilities that bc offers. The characteristics of bc include

▶ arbitrary precision arithmetic,

▶ a complete programming language including *for* and *while* loops and
   variables, and

▶ ability to perform arithmetic in bases other than 10.

We omit here the complex structures in bc and concentrate on using bc to
perform simple calculations in decimal.

By default, bc takes input from standard input; commands are one per
line or separated by semicolons. Each command to bc is either an
expression, which it evaluates, or a statement that affects the subsequent
output. As a short example, consider the following dialogue:

```
$ bc
1+2
3
100/7
14
scale=5
100/7
14.28571
sqrt(2)
1.41421
```

Most of this dialogue is self-explanatory; scale=5 indicates that
subsequent calculations should be displayed correct to 5 decimal places,
and sqrt is a predefined **function** that calculates the square root of its
argument.

To use a function in bc, type the name of the function followed by its *argument* enclosed in parentheses. Thus to evaluate 'log base e of 10' the expression would be l(10) (lower-case 'ell').

Table 7.1   Operators used by bc

+	addition
–	subtraction
*	multiplication
/	division
%	integer remainder
^	power

Table 7.2   Functions used by bc

sqrt	square root
length	number of decimal digits
scale	scale
s	sine, requires option –l
c	cosine, requires option –l
a	inverse tangent, requires option –l
e	exponential, requires option –l
l	natural logarithm, requires option –l

The available operators and functions are summarised in Tables 7.1 and 7.2. If the 'scale' is set to 0, no calculations are performed on digits after the decimal point, and integer arithmetic is performed. In this case the operator % will yield integer remainder so that 11 % 3 would yield 2. Some of the operators require bc to be called with option –l ('library'), and these are indicated in Table 7.1. Trigonometric functions assume you are working with radians (and not degrees), and the exponential function e raises e (the base of natural logarithms, 2.718...) to the power of its argument. In bc you can use parentheses to group parts of an expression together, so the expression

```
10 * (3 + 4)
```

would evaluate to 70. You can use as many parenthesised expressions as you like, provided you ensure that each opening parenthesis is matched by a closing one — i.e. the usual conventions in a programming language apply. Note that *multiplication* and *division* take **precedence** over *addition* and *subtraction*, so that

```
1 + 3 * 4
```

NOTE

If in doubt about precedence, use parentheses

is equivalent to

```
1 + (3 * 4)
```

and not to

```
(1 + 3) * 4
```

Worked example 7.5

> Use bc to find the number of seconds in a day.
> **Solution**: The calculation we require is 24×60×60, and the dialogue
> that would follow is:
>
> ```
> $ bc
> 24 * 60 * 60
> 86400
> ctrl-D
> ```

Since bc takes input from standard input, to leave bc you type *ctrl-D*
on a line of its own. We can also pipe expressions into bc, and

```
$ echo "1 + 2" | bc
```

would be a valid way of using bc, since the pipe ensures that the standard
output of echo becomes the standard input to bc.

Worked example 7.6

> Write a script to read in two numbers and display their product.
> **Solution**: Use read to input the numbers, and then construct the
> expression that represents their product using the * operator in bc.
> This expression can then be passed to the standard input of bc using
> echo.
>
> ```
> echo Input two numbers:    # Prompt the user ...
> read N1 N2                  # read in two numbers ...
> echo "$N1 * $N2" | bc       # pass their product to bc
> ```

7.4 Making decisions

Consider the following problem: 'If file A is smaller than 100 lines then
display it on the terminal, otherwise tell me that it's bigger than 100
lines.' How would you set about programming that using the shell? We
can find out how many lines are in A using wc, we can print a file, and we
can display a message. However the only method we have so far met for

deciding to execute commands conditionally is to use || or && and the exit status of a command. We would ideally like a command A_is_small which succeeds (exit status 0) if A is smaller than 100 lines. Our script might then look like:

```
(A_is_small && more A) || echo A is too big
```

The fundamental method by which the shell allows you to make choices as to what to do next in a script is by use of the exit status of a command. We can't in general expect commands such as A_is_small to exist already — there must be a more general method of translating such statements into things the shell can understand, which will return an appropriate exit status. We need to be able to compare numbers (such as file sizes) and strings (values of environment variables), and to interrogate easily the existence and access permissions of files.

7.4.1 The 'test' statement

The command to accomplish this is test. Followed by arguments, test will give an exit status of 0 if the arguments *evaluate* to True. There are two ways of invoking test:

test *arguments*

[*arguments*]

and we shall use the latter for the rest of this book. To give you the flavour, the following checks whether file testfile exists and displays a suitable message if it does:

```
$ [ -e testfile ] && echo Testfile exists
```

Using the alternative syntax this would look like:

```
$ test -e testfile && echo Testfile exists
```

The *operator* -e, when presented as an argument to test, examines the following argument and, if that file *exists*, the command succeeds (exit status 0), otherwise it fails with exit status 1. Various options are available to test; those listed in Table 7.3 relate to files, and with the exception of -f are self-explanatory.

Worked example 7.7

Write a script which will read in the name of a file and print out a message indicating whether or not it is a directory.
Solution: Use `test` with option `-d` to check the file, and `||` and `&&` to control which message is output.

```
echo Input a file name:    # Prompt the user ...
read FILENAME              # input a file name ...
([ -d $FILENAME ] &&       # check it's a directory ...
                           # then confirm this if so
echo $FILENAME is a directory) ||
echo $FILENAME is not a directory
```

Table 7.3 File operators used by test

`-d` *filename*	True if *filename* exists and is a directory
`-e` *filename*	True if *filename* exists
`-f` *filename*	True if *filename* exists and is **regular**
`-r` *filename*	True if *filename* exists and is readable
`-s` *filename*	True if *filename* exists and has size non-zero
`-w` *filename*	True if *filename* exists and is writable
`-x` *filename*	True if *filename* exists and is executable

Table 7.4 String operators used by test

`-n` *string*	True if *string* has length non-zero
`-z` *string*	True if *string* has length zero
string	True if *string* is not null
s1 `=` *s2*	True if strings *s1* and *s2* are equal
s1 `!=` *s2*	True if strings *s1* and *s2* are not equal

The options given in Table 7.4 relate to strings. For instance, to check whether variable `NAME` has been set a value that is not the null string, we might have:

```
$ [ "$NAME" ] || echo NAME is unset
```

Note that we have enclosed `$NAME` in double quotes; `test` expects to get an argument, and if we did not enclose it in quotes, and `NAME` was unset (or contained only whitespace), the line would become

```
[ ] || echo NAME is unset
```

prior to execution, which would give an error, whereas

```
[ "" ] || echo NAME is unset
```

would be OK.

Worked example 7.8

> Write a script to greet the person running it if they are logged on as
> user `chris`.
> **Solution**: Use `logname` to check the user's name (not the variable
> `LOGNAME`, which might accidentally have been changed), and `test` to
> compare it with `chris`.
>
> ```
> [ "$( logname )" = chris ] && echo Hello Chris
> ```

*Table 7.5 Arithmetic
operators used by* test

n1 -eq *n2*	True if numbers *n1* and *n2* are equal
n1 -ne *n2*	True if numbers *n1* and *n2* are not equal
n1 -gt *n2*	True if *n1* is greater than *n2*
n1 -ge *n2*	True if *n1* is greater than or equal to *n2*
n1 -lt *n2*	True if *n1* is less than *n2*
n1 -le *n2*	True if *n1* is less than or equal to *n2*

NOTE

*We will not cover
floating-point aspects of*
bc *here*

The numerical checks listed in Table 7.5 that `test` can perform are the
principal way of doing numerical comparisons using the shell. They only
work with whole numbers, however, and if you wish to perform complex
tasks using floating-point numbers you are advised to use `bc`. As an
example, we code the solution to the question posed at the start of this
section, which was: 'If file A is smaller than 100 lines then display it on
the terminal, otherwise tell me that it's bigger than 100 lines.'

```
FILESIZE=$( wc -l A )    # Use wc -l to count the lines
([ "$FILESIZE" -gt 100 ] && echo File too big) || cat A
```

There is a difference between the operators = and -eq. For instance,

```
[ 0 -eq 00 ]
```

succeeds, as 0 and 00 are numerically equal, but

```
[ 0 = 00 ]
```

fails, as they are different strings of characters.

131

Worked example 7.9

Write a script to request you to type in a number, and then to guess its square; it should then either congratulate you or tell you the correct answer.

Solution: After reading in a number into variable NUMBER, construct an expression $NUMBER * $NUMBER to be piped to bc, assigning the output of the calculation to SQUARE. Then, after reading in the user's guess into variable GUESS, use test to check whether GUESS and SQUARE are the same.

   Notice the different 'style' of comments used here — each on a line of its own; this style is preferred with long command lines.

```
# Prompt the user and read in the number
echo Type in a number:
read NUMBER

# Evaluate the square of the number using bc
SQUARE=$( echo "$NUMBER * $NUMBER" | bc )

# Prompt the user and read in the guessed answer
echo Guess its square:
read GUESS

# If the guess is equal to the square, confirm ...
([ "$GUESS" -eq "$SQUARE" ] && echo Correct) ||
# otherwise display the correct answer
    echo The correct answer is $SQUARE
```

NOTE

WARNING!

   Since test requires arguments, you must separate those arguments from the word test by whitespace. Similarly, if you are using the square bracket notation for test, you should separate the square brackets from what is inside the brackets. Otherwise, the brackets themselves would become part of the strings which they should enclose. For instance,

```
[ hello = hello]
```

would attempt to compare string hello with string hello] and think that you had forgotten to provide the closing square bracket.

7.4.2 The 'if' statement

For making simple decisions based on a command's exit status, || and && are fine, but if many commands are involved it may become quite difficult to read. For this reason, another syntax for checking the exit status of a command is provided, taking the form of an if statement. To illustrate this, recall the example used to introduce || and &&:

```
$ mycommand || echo Cannot run mycommand
$ mycommand && echo mycommand ran OK
```

This could be rewritten using `if` as follows:

NOTE

The line that starts with else *is optional*

```
$ if mycommand
> then echo mycommand ran OK
> else echo Cannot run mycommand
> fi
```

NOTE

The keyword fi *denotes the end of the statement*

This mechanism is very similar to that used in Pascal or C. You may find it easier, or clearer, to use than || or &&. It should be stressed that an `if` statement fulfils exactly the same function as || and &&.

Worked example 7.10

> Write a script to inform you whether or not you have used more than 100k of disk space.
> **Solution:** Using `du` with option `-s` will give you a number that represents the number of kilobytes of storage you have used, and will also display the name of the directory for which it performed that calculation. You can use `cut` to extract the first field of that output, namely the number. Then `test` can check whether this number is greater than 100, returning an exit status of 0 if so, and `if` can check this exit status and run `echo` to display a message if it is indeed the case.
>
> ```
> # Evaluate the number of kilobytes of storage used
> KBYTES=$( du -s ~ | cut -f2 -d' ')
>
> # Check the value of KBYTES ..
> if   [ $KBYTES -gt 100 ]
> # and display message if >100
> then echo "You have used more than 100k"
> # and display message if <=100
> else echo "You have used less than 100k"
> fi
> ```
>
> Using || and &&, this could have been coded so:
>
> ```
> KBYTES=$( du -s ~ | cut -f2 -d' ')
> ( [ $KBYTES -gt 100 ] &&
>     echo "You have used more than 100k" ) ||
>   [ $KBYTES -gt 100 ] ||
>     echo "You have used less than 100k"
> ```

7.5 Loops

It is often necessary to execute part of a script multiple times. This can be done either a given number of times, or while a given condition is met. This construct is known as a **loop**, and exists in some form in all programming languages. There are two basic types of loop which the shell supports.

7.5.1 'For' loops

The for loop is a method of executing a section of a script for a specified (and fixed) number of times. For instance, to page, in sequence, each readable file in the current directory:

NOTE

r = 'readable'

```
$ for i in $( ls )
> do
>     [ -r $i ] && more $i
> done
```

The syntax for the for loop is

for *name* in *values*
do
commands
done

and this causes the variable *name* to be set in turn to each word in *values*, and *commands* executed with *name* set to that value. So, in the above example, $(ls) becomes a list of the files in the current directory, and variable i is set to each one in turn. The filename, which is the value of i, is tested to see if it is readable, and if so it is paged using more.

Worked example 7.11

> Send a personalised greeting (such as Hello jo) to each of the users jo, sam and george:
> **Solution**: You cannot simply use mailx jo sam george, as they would then each receive the same (unpersonalised) message. So you should instead use a for loop to create each message in turn and then mail it to the appropriate user.
>
> ```
> $ for user in jo sam george
> > do
> > echo "Hello $user" | mailx $user
> > done
> ```

7.5.2 'While' and 'until' loops

You may wish to execute a sequence of commands for a variable number of times while a certain specified condition holds. The `if` statement allows a single test to be carried out; multiple tests can be carried out using `while`. The syntax is

```
while   command1
do      command2
done
```

indicating that *command1* is executed repeatedly. Each time its exit status is checked, and if the exit status is zero, *command2* is executed. As soon as *command1* yields a non-zero exit status, the `while` loop ceases immediately. As a simple example of a while loop, the following will display `tick` on your terminal repeatedly once a second:

```
$ while true
> do
>     echo tick
>     sleep 1
> done
```

Worked example 7.12

Use a `while` loop to print out the 'twelve times table':

```
1 x 12 = 12
2 x 12 = 24
  ...
12 x 12 = 144
```

Solution: Use a `while` loop and `bc` to do the calculations. Set a variable i to start at 1 and then become in turn 2, 3, up to 12. While the value of i is less than or equal to 12 evaluate $i * 12 using `bc`, storing the answer in variable `result`, display the line of the table, and add one to i using `bc` again.

```
$ i=1
$ while [ $i -le 12 ]
> do
>     result=$( echo "$i * 12" | bc )
>     echo "$i x 12 = $result"
>     i=$( echo "$i + 1" | bc )
> done
```

Similar to `while` is `until`; the syntax is the same as `while`, but instead of the condition that *command1* must succeed for the loop to continue to execute, *command1* must fail, and the loop finishes when the condition gives non-zero exit status. So

```
until   command1
do      command2
done
```

indicates that *command1* is executed repeatedly. Each time its exit status is checked, and if the exit status is *not* zero, *command2* is executed. As soon as *command1* yields a zero exit status, the `until` loop ceases.

Worked example 7.13

> Write a script to repeatedly request names of files to be displayed, until you type in `QUIT` to stop.
>
> **Solution**: Use an `until` loop repeatedly to read in the name of a file, and then (after having checked that it can be read) display it. Note that we commence by setting the value of the filename, stored in the variable `FILENAME`, to `""` (i.e. the null string). This is advisable, just in case the user running the script has already set `FILENAME` to `QUIT` — in which case the script would stop immediately it had begun to run. This may appear highly unlikely, but you should always err on the side of caution.
>
> ```
> FILENAME=""                         # Initialise FILENAME
> until [ "$FILENAME" = "QUIT" ]  # Finish when value is QUIT
> do
>     echo "Name of file to print (or QUIT to finish):"
>     read FILENAME                   # Read in FILENAME
>     if   [ -r "$FILENAME" ]      # If it's readable ...
>     then lp "$FILENAME"             # print it
>     fi
> done
> ```

Two other commands are provided for use in `while`, `until` and `for` loops. The first one is `break`, which is a method of breaking out of a loop. If a `break` command is encountered the immediately enclosing loop will terminate immediately. The other command is `continue`; unlike `break`, instead of completely leaving the loop, control passes back to the beginning of the loop.

Worked example 7.14

A file called `core` is sometimes created when a program 'crashes' — it is very big, and you will often need to delete it. Write a script to check once a minute to see whether you have created a file called `core` in your home directory, and to terminate with a message on your terminal warning you of this fact.

Solution: There are several ways of approaching this, and we present two possible solutions. Both use loops, check the existence of the file `core` using the `test` command, and `sleep` for 60 seconds between tests. The first uses `until`:

```
until [ -f $HOME/core ]    # Stop when $HOME/core exists
do
    sleep 60               # Wait one minute
done
echo core file created     # Notify the user
```

The second solution involves looping forever. Within each loop it does the `test` and, if this detects the file, it uses `break` to leave the loop:

```
while true                 # Forever ...
do
    sleep 60               # Wait one minute ...
    if   [ -f $HOME/core ] # If $HOME/core exists ...
    then break             # leave the loop
    fi
done
echo core file created     # Notify the user
```

Try running one of these scripts in the background. You can create a file `core` yourself, using `touch`, say, to check that it does indeed work:

```
$ touch core
```

Instead of writing a shell script, you might have considered `crontab` for this task.

7.6 Searching for files

In spite of files being arranged in a directory structure, the complexity of the file structure is still high. Using `ls` may not be an easy way of finding some files — suppose, for instance, that you had a large number of files and many subdirectories, and that somewhere you had created a file `myfile`. How would you find it? In any event, searching for files other than by name is hit-and-miss using `ls` — how could you print out the names of all your executable files of size greater than 1k, for instance?

You would, at this stage, have to list all your files, send the output to a file, and edit that file.

There is a command `find` which can be used to examine all files within a directory (and all subdirectories of it) and select them according to criteria such as the *group* the file belongs to, the *time* of last modification, its *name*, its *access permissions*, its *size*, and so on. The syntax is `find`, followed by a pathname (which should normally be a directory), and then the criteria `find` is to use. For instance, to print the pathnames of all files in your home directory called `myfile`, you could have:

NOTE

`find` *will work if its argument is just a file*

```
$ find ~ -name myfile -print
```

This will search your home directory (`~`), looking for files whose name (`-name`) is `myfile`, and display (`-print`) the full pathname of each such file to standard output. Note that the criteria for `find` selecting files are real words, not single letters. Note also that in order for `find` actually to print out the names of the files found, you must explicitly state this by using `-print`. Instead of printing the names of the files found, you can tell UNIX to run any other command on those files. It is likely that you will normally only use `find` to display the names of files, but instead of simply displaying names, `find` can be instructed to perform other actions on files it has selected. The following instructs `find` to perform `wc` on all files in the current directory (and any subdirectories) owned by `chris`:

NOTE

The criteria for `find` *are simply arguments to* `find`, *not options*

```
$ find . -user chris -exec wc {} \;
```

The directory `find` is searching is `.` (the current directory), the criterion it uses to select files is `-user chris`, meaning files owned by `chris`. The action it takes when it has selected a file is to execute (`-exec`) the command `wc` on the file. The notation `{}` is shorthand for the name of that file. The semicolon terminates the action to be taken (otherwise the shell command used as the action for `find` would get confused with the `find` command itself), and must be escaped with a `\`.

The arguments to `find` are of three varieties: *options* which affect the command's behaviour, *tests* which specify which files are to be selected, and *actions* which specify what will be done with the selected files. Table 7.6 and 7.7 list useful tests and actions.

Worked example 7.15

Remove all files named `core` from your filespace.

Solution: Use `find` to locate the files, and then `-exec` to call `rm` to delete them:

```
$ find ~ -name core -exec rm {} \;
```

Table 7.6 Tests used by `find`	

`-empty`	file is empty, either a regular file or a directory
`-gid` *n*	file's group ID is *n*
`-group` *name*	file's group name is *name*
`-inum` *n*	file's inode is *n*
`-links` *n*	file has *n* hard links
`-name` *pattern*	filename matches *pattern*
`-perm` *mode*	file's permissions are (exactly) *mode*
`-size` *n*	file has size *n* blocks of 512 bytes
`-type` *c*	file's type is *c*
`-user` *name*	file's owner is *name*

Table 7.7 Actions used by `find`

`-exec` *command*	execute *command*
`-printf` *format*	display the filename

7.7 Formatted output

NOTE

The shell command `printf` *is very similar to* `printf()` *in the language C*

NOTE

Some shells do not yet support `printf`

To display messages on standard output we have so far used `echo`. This command can only write a single string on a single line. A command `printf` is provided to format a message any way you desire. Use of `printf` involves giving it a string, known as the *format*, as first argument, followed perhaps by subsequent arguments. The format string is copied to the standard output with certain changes made. A simple example is

```
$ printf "Hello"
 Hello$
```

Note that `Hello` is precisely what has been printed — no extra spaces and no *Newline* character after it, so that the next dollar prompt follows it immediately.

If a \ (backslash) is encountered, it is treated as an **escape character** with the following character examined, and the pair are replaced according to Table 7.8. Not all of these characters will be interpreted sensibly by all terminals, especially formfeed and vertical tab.

Table 7.8   Escape sequences

\\	\
\a	'alert' (bell)
\b	'backspace' (moves cursor left one space)
\f	'formfeed' (skips one 'page' if possible)
\n	'newline' sequence
\r	'carriage return' (moves cursor to start of current line)
\t	'tab'
\v	'vertical tab'

Perhaps the most common escape sequence you will meet is \n, to terminate a line:

```
$ printf "Hello\nthere\n"
Hello
there
```

When a % ('percent') is included, the following several characters represent a **conversion specification**, to instruct how one of the arguments is to be displayed. There should be the same number of conversion specifications as arguments following the format string, and they are paired up with the arguments in order. The next example illustrates the use of %d to insert a number into the output:

```
$ printf "%d is a square number\n" 64
64 is a square number
```

The string %% is not a specification, and is replaced by a single % in the output:

```
$ printf "%s is %d%%\n" "one half" 50
one half is 50%
```

Common specifications are given in Table 7.9. Between the % and the conversion character may come a number indicating the **field width** in which the argument should be printed, and preceding this number may come a - (hyphen) indicating that the argument should be displayed

Table 7.9   Conversion characters

d	integer (printed in decimal, base 10)
o	integer (printed in octal, base 8)
x	integer (printed in hexadecimal, base 16)
s	string
c	character

left-justified within the field (it would by default be right-justified). If the data is numeric, then following the % immediately with a + would cause the number always to be displayed with a leading + or − sign. Note that if you wish `printf` to terminate a line, you must do so yourself by including a \n within the format string. The following examples illustrate use of `printf`:

```
$ printf "Hello %s\n" $LOGNAME
Hello chris
```

The string value of `LOGNAME` is substituted for `%s`.

```
$ printf "The temperature is %+7d degrees\n" 21
The temperature is     +21 degrees
```

The number 21 is substituted for `%d`, preceded by a + sign, and padded out with blanks to fill seven character positions.

```
$ printf "You are %s\nyour home directory is: %s\n" \
$( logname ) $HOME
You are chris
your home directory is: /cs/ugrad/chris
```

The string that results from executing the command `logname`, and the value of the variable `HOME`, are substituted for the two `%s` specifications. Note the *Newline*s within the format string, and the use of a backslash to continue the statement onto another line when it becomes long.

Worked example 7.16

Write a script to read the standard input and display each word from the input right-justified in one column of width 30. A blank line (or end of file) will terminate the script.

Solution: This is concerned with formatting, so we need `printf`. Use a `while` loop to continually read in words until a 'null' one is read in (which happens with a blank line or end of file).

```
read X                  # Read first word
while [ "$X" ]          # while a "real" word ...
do
  printf "%30s\n" $X    # print it ...
  read X                # and read next one
done
```

7.8 Passing information to scripts

A script can be passed data by many methods, such as input streams, and the values of environment variables. We look now at this in more detail.

7.8.1 Scripts with arguments

Just as a UNIX command can take arguments, so can a script. After all, a script is a command written by a user. The first argument of a script is referred to within the script as $1, the second by $2, and so on. These are known as **positional parameters**. They can be manipulated like any other variables, except that they cannot be reset using =. Create a file (argfile, say) containing one line:

```
echo $1 $2
```

Now run that script, but give it two arguments:

```
$ sh argfile hello 99
hello 99
```

There are some other 'variable names' that have special meanings when used within a script. The name of the script (i.e. the name of the file containing the script) is denoted by $0, and the number of positional parameters by $#. Suppose the following script, called showargs, is invoked:

NOTE

In this context # does not introduce a comment

```
This script is $0, and it has $# arguments
First argument is $1
```

NOTE

Note that $0 uses the name of the script that has been called

The output we would get would be:

```
$ sh ./showargs foo bar
This script is ./showargs, and it has 2 arguments
First argument is foo
$ sh showargs "foo bar"
This script is showargs, and it has 1 arguments
First argument is foo bar
```

In the second invocation, the first argument of showargs is the string "foo bar", not foo — the quotes around it cause it to be considered as a single word.

When a script is given many arguments, accessing them one-by-one using positional parameters is often awkward. We can use $* to refer to them all at once. In other words, the value of $* is the *single* string "$1 $2 $3 ...". In order to experiment with these parameters, create a script containing

```
for i in $*
do
echo $i
done
```

and call it `testfile`. When it is run, the `$*` will be replaced by the arguments of the script; thus calling `testfile` with arguments `jo`, `sam` and `george`, so

$ testfile jo sam george

would be equivalent to running a script containing:

```
for i in jo sam george
do
echo $i
done
```

We must be careful, though; the shell will strip out quotes before passing arguments to a command, and we need to be able to handle

$ sh testfile jo "Sue Smith" sam

in a sensible manner. To this end we can use `$@`, which is similar to `$*`. Edit `testfile` to replace `$*` by `$@`. In both cases the result is the same, namely

$ sh testfile jo "Sue Smith" sam
```
jo
Sue
Smith
sam
```

indicating that the quotes have been stripped before the arguments have been passed to `testfile`. If, instead, the first line of the script is

for i in "$*"

the quotes are stripped from the arguments, which are then enclosed by a new pair of quotes. Thus the string `jo Sue Smith sam` is the expansion of `$*`, which is then quoted within the script indicating a single string, and the output is:

$ sh testfile jo "Sue Smith" sam
```
jo Sue Smith sam
```

If, however, `"$@"` is used, the arguments to the script are passed without modification, including quotes, to replace `"$@"`, and the quotes are then interpreted within the script:

```
$ sh testfile jo "Sue Smith" sam
jo
Sue Smith
sam
```

If a script requires an indeterminate number of arguments, you may wish to discard the earlier ones — for instance, if they are options and you have finished processing all the options. The command `shift` will remove $1 from the positional parameters, $2 will become $1 (etc.), and $*, $@ and $# will all be changed accordingly.

Worked example 7.17

> Write a script called `mypager` to take arguments that are files and page each of them in turn using `more`. Additionally, `mypager` may take a single argument, `-i`, which will cause a message to be displayed on the screen before each file is paged, giving the name of the file, and requiring the user to press *Return* to continue.
> **Solution:**
>
> ```
> IFLAG=no
> if [ "$#" -gt 0 ]           # Make sure there are some files
> then    if [ "$1" = "-i" ]  # Check if the option is called
>         then IFLAG=yes       # If so, reset the flag ...
>              shift           # and delete the argument
>         fi
> fi
>
> for i in "$@"               # Go through each file in turn
> do
>     if   [ "$IFLAG" = "yes" ]   # If "-i" ...
>     then echo "Paging $i"       # output message ...
>          echo "Press Return to continue"
>          read j                 # wait for Return
>     fi
>     more "$i"              # Page the file
> done
> ```

7.8.2 Parameter expansion

We have already considered assigning values to variables in the previous chapter. In this section, we look at the shell's features that allow it to examine in detail whether variables have been set values and what form those values take.

Often you will write scripts where you will use variables that you assume will have certain values. They may be variables you have created yourself for your own benefit, or they may be 'system' variables, such as `PATH`, which have been set for you. However, there is always a possibility that such a variable has not been assigned a value. A case in point is the variable `NAME`, which is not mentioned in the POSIX standard, and commonly contains the user's real name. Many shells and utilities (especially mailers) use it, and it's quite reasonable to assume that it has been set a value. Unfortunately, this is not guaranteed.

It is thus good practice, whenever writing a script that relies on a variable not defined as necessarily existing in POSIX, to check that it has in fact been assigned a value, and that that value is of the correct format. **Parameter expansion** is the mechanism usually employed.

Consider `NAME`, and suppose a particular script requires it; we could include the following code to check whether it indeed does have a value, and if not we could give it a *default* value:

```
if [ -z "$NAME" ]
then NAME="A.N. Other"
fi
```

This will work. It is also verbose — a script that uses many variables would be tedious to write if you include checks for all the variables in the script. It should be emphasised that it is a very good idea to check that variables have in fact been assigned values before you attempt to use those variables. Parameter expansion will not do anything that cannot already be done using `test`, but it provides a concise and easy to read notation that avoids saturating scripts with `test`s.

At this point we need to discuss an apparently minor — but nonetheless important — feature of variables. If a variable has not got a value, this can be for two reasons. Either it has not been mentioned at all before, in which case it is **unset**, or it has been set but has the null string as its value, so

```
$ NAME=""
```

or, alternatively, since it would not be ambiguous:

```
$ NAME=
```

For most purposes the two situations have the same result. If you wish to unset a variable rather than just set its value to null, use **unset**:

```
$ unset NAME
```

145

To ensure that a variable is set, the form is

${*variable*:-*default*}

which expands to the value of *variable*, if that variable has been set or is null, otherwise to *default*. For instance, instead of the `test` example above, the first time you use `NAME`, replace `$NAME` by

```
${NAME:-"A.N. Other"}
```

The following script will check to see if variable `NAME` has been set; if not it will be replaced by the value of `LOGNAME`, and display a welcome message:

```
$ echo Hello ${NAME:-$LOGNAME}
```

Try this, first of all without `NAME` set, and then after you have given it a value.

The form of *default* can be anything that returns a value — the above could be accomplished equally well using:

```
$ echo Hello ${NAME:-$(logname)}
```

Worked example 7.18

> Create a welcome message to initially check variable `NAME` to find out your name; if it is unset, it checks `LOGNAME`, and if `LOGNAME` is unset it uses command `logname` as a last resort.
> **Solution**: As in the example above, if `NAME` is unset we fall back on the value of `LOGNAME`, but then we also have to check that `LOGNAME` has been assigned a value. So we can replace `$LOGNAME` by the result of running the command `logname`.
>
> ```
> $ echo Hello ${NAME:-${LOGNAME:-$(logname)}}
> ```

If a variable is unset, the `:-` mechanism will not assign the default value to it — that default is merely substituted for the expression at that single instance. If you also wish the variable to be set to the default, use `:=` instead of `:-`, so:

```
$ unset NAME
$ echo Hello ${NAME:=$LOGNAME}
Hello chris
$ echo $NAME
chris
```

Another behaviour that might be desirable is for the shell to give you an error message if a variable is unset — this is especially useful if there is no sensible default value you can substitute for the variable. Replace `:-` with `:?` so:

```
$ unset NAME
$ echo Hello ${NAME:?}
NAME: parameter null or not set
```

If you follow the ? with a string, that message will be displayed instead of `parameter null or not set`:

```
$ echo Hello ${NAME:?"who are you?"}
NAME: who are you?
```

Worked example 7.19

> Ensure that `PATH` is set; if it is not, reset it to `/bin:/usr/bin`, and inform the user of its value.
> **Solution**: Use positional parameters
>
> ```
> $ echo The PATH is ${PATH:="/bin:/usr/bin"}
> ```

When using `:-` the default value is substituted if the variable is null or unset. If you use `:+` the reverse happens — the default value is substituted only if the variable is set and not null:

```
$ unset NAME
$ echo ${NAME:+Chris}
(blank line)
$ echo ${LOGNAME:+Chris}
Chris
```

We can discover the **length** (i.e. the numbers of characters) of a string:

```
$ echo $LOGNAME
chris
$ echo ${#LOGNAME}
5
```

Worked example 7.20

Use a loop to print out a line of 50 pluses so:

++

Solution: Use an `until` loop, and store the plusses in a variable, `LINE` (say). Start off by setting `LINE` to null, and repeatedly add a single `+` to it until its length has become 50.

```
LINE=""                       # Set LINE to null
until [ ${#LINE} -eq 50 ]     # Until its length is 50 ...
do
  LINE=$LINE+                 # add another "+" to it ...
done
echo $LINE                    # and finally display the line
```

CHAPTER SUMMARY

Table 7.10
Commands introduced
in this chapter

bc	calculator
break	exit from `for`, `while` or `until` loop
continue	continue `for`, `while` or `until` loop
false	returns 'false' value, exit status 1
find	find files
printf	write formatted output
shift	shift positional parameters
test	evaluate expression
true	returns 'true' value, exit status 0

EXERCISES

1 List all regular files in your home directory whose size is less than 512 bytes.

2 What is the maximum length of a line in /usr/dict/words?

3 Write a script called mcat which will be identical to cat with the following difference: if any file argument given to mcat either does not exist or is unreadable, mcat will not send *any* output to the standard output. The behaviour of cat is such that all its readable arguments are copied to standard output.

4 List the name of each regular file in the current directory (or any subdirectory of it), together with the first line of the file.

5 List all users currently logged in to the system, in 4 columns of width 10 characters, so:

```
chris       jo       sam    george
pete        sue      dave   jane
emma        bill
```

6 Write a script to prompt the user for two numbers, representing the width and height of a rectangle in *cm*, and display the area of the rectangle both in square *metres* and in square *inches* (1 *inch* = 2.54 *cm*).

7 Write a script to take text input from standard input, and copy it to standard output with each line preceded by a line number in the same manner as cat -n. Do not use the command cat.

More on shells

CHAPTER OVERVIEW

This chapter covers

▶ arithmetic expansion, pattern matching and 'case' statements;

▶ scripts that require options; and

▶ file system conventions.

In this chapter we examine shells in more depth. Much of this chapter is dependent on you being comfortable with the previous chapter, and if you have not yet familiarised yourself with the material in that chapter you are strongly encouraged to return to it.

8.1 Simple arithmetic

8.1.1 Arithmetic expansion

The utility bc was discussed in the previous chapter, and will perform any calculations required, to any accuracy, just as if you had a pocket calculator available. Although bc does have all the facilities required, it is in many circumstances 'overkill' — the overheads of calling and executing a utility such as bc are high. It is therefore desirable to have another method of doing simple arithmetic tasks as a part of the shell, thus obviating the need to call a utility like bc. The mechanism is known as **arithmetic expansion** and takes the form of

$((expression))

where *expression* is a valid arithmetic expression, using only integers (no floating point arithmetic), and the operators described below. Boolean expressions are represented by 1 for True and 0 for False. The operators, which are listed in Table 8.1, are a subset of those available in the C programming language, and parentheses may be used to group subexpressions. Thus the following dialogue could take place:

```
$ echo $(( 1 + 2 + (3 * 4) ))
15
$ echo $(( 1 > 2 ))
0
$ echo $(( 1 < 2 ))
1
```

Table 8.1   Operators for arithmetic expansion

+	plus
*	times
/	integer division
%	integer remainder
==	equal to
!=	not equal to
>	greater than
>=	greater than or equal to
<	less than
<=	less than or equal to

NOTE

One stone = 14 pounds

As an example, the following script will read in a number, assumed to represent pounds weight, and write to the standard output a message translating that to stones and pounds:

```
echo Type in a whole number representing pounds weight:
read POUNDS
STONES=$(( $POUNDS / 14 ))
SMALLPOUNDS=$(( $POUNDS % 14 ))
echo $POUNDS pounds is $STONES and $SMALLPOUNDS pounds
```

Worked example 8.1

Write a script `convertsec` to read in a number, thought of as representing seconds, and print out the number of hours, minutes and seconds it represents, so:

```
$ convertsec
Enter a number of seconds:
12345
12345 seconds is 3:25:45
```

Solution: First of all, check that the number is not less than zero, and then do the calculation, which is self-explanatory.

```
# Prompt the user and read in number of seconds
echo Enter a number of seconds:
read SECONDS

if   [ $SECONDS -lt 0 ]              # Check it's positive
then echo Number must be positive
else MINUTES=$(( $SECONDS / 60 ))   # Total minutes
     RSECONDS=$(( $SECONDS % 60 ))  # Residual seconds
     HOURS=$(( $MINUTES / 60 ))     # Total hours
     MINUTES=$(( $MINUTES % 60 ))   # Residual minutes
     printf "%d seconds is %d:%02d:%02d\n" $SECONDS \
                       $HOURS $MINUTES $RSECONDS
fi
```

You may wish to compare arithmetic expansion with using bc. The example in the previous chapter, which displays the '12 times table' would be coded as a script using arithmetic expansion as follows:

```
i=1
while [ $i -le 12 ]
do
   result=$(( $i * 12 ))
   echo "$i x 12 = $result"
   i=$(( $i + 1 ))
done
```

Try out both — you will find that when you use arithmetic expansion it is much faster. Where possible, you should use arithmetic expansion in preference to bc, but if you are in any doubt as to whether arithmetic expansion can give you sufficient precision, you should play safe and use bc.

8.1.2 The 'expr' command

The command expr ('expression') performs a similar function to arithmetic expansion. In fact, it can be considered just a different syntax — just as [*expression*] can be replaced by test *expression*, so $((*expression*)) can be replaced by expr *expression*. Non-POSIX shells will probably only support expr.

NOTE

We do not explore non-arithmetic capabilities of expr *here*

There is, unfortunately, a catch. You can also use expr to perform more functions than just arithmetic — it is also capable of rudimentary operations on strings. If you give expr an argument that is not a 'sum', it will assume it is a string and print it:

```
$ expr hello
```

```
hello
```

Between $((and)), the shell knows it is expecting an arithmetic expression. Following expr the shell does not know that what follows will be such an expression — it might be simply a string. For instance,

```
$ expr 1+2
1+2
```

In this example, 1+2 was not recognised by expr as '1 + 2'. In order for expr to work correctly with arithmetic, each 'token' — that is, number/operator — must be separated by whitespace:

```
$ expr 1 + 2
3
```

Since expr is simply a command like any other, any characters within the expression that are special to the shell (such as *) must be escaped, for instance:

```
$ expr 6 \* 7
42
```

NOTE

For historical reasons, expr *uses* =

If you had not escaped * in this example it would have been replaced by the names of all the files in the current directory. Another difference between arithmetic expansion and expr is that the equality operator for expr is =, not ==.

Worked example 8.2

Write a script to read in a number and decide whether or not that number is prime.

Solution: This calculation is one you would typically code in another programming language — it is not too complex to use the shell for, although efficiency considerations would discourage it. Using a variable I to iterate from 2 to half the possibly prime number N, keep checking whether or not I divides N exactly. If a divisor is found, set RESULT to 1. If we used bc for this, it would be extremely slow.

```
echo "Type in a number"
read N
RESULT=0
I=2
HALFN=$(( $N / 2 ))              # HALFN is N/2
while [ $I -le $HALFN ]         # Stop when I equals N/2
do
   if [ $(( $N % $I )) -eq 0 ]  # If I divides N exactly
```

```
    then RESULT=1                      # ... RESULT is 1
        break                          # ... and leave the loop
    fi
    I=$(( $I + 1 ))                    # Increment I
done
if [ $RESULT -eq 0 ]                   # If no divisor found
then echo "$N is prime"
else echo "$N is composite"
fi
```

A better algorithm would have been to iterate to $\sqrt{N}$ rather than N/2, but arithmetic expansion doesn't allow for the square root function. Try this example using `expr` instead of arithmetic expansion.

8.2 Pattern matching

8.2.1 Patterns

Using a notation known as **pattern matching**, we can consider concepts such as 'all files with suffix `.c`', or 'all arguments to the command that are three characters long and commence with a digit'. Pattern matching is used in several situations by the shell, and we shall introduce those particular instances as we meet them. If the shell encounters a word containing any of the following symbols (unless they are 'escaped' by being preceded by a backslash or contained within (single) quotes)

>   ? * [

then it will attempt to match that word with filenames, either in the current directory, or absolute pathnames (if they commence with /). A ? matches any *single* character, * matches *anything at all*, and [introduces a list of characters it matches. If the word commences with a * or a ?, it will only match filenames in the current directory not commencing with a dot. When the shell has worked out which filenames the word matches, it will replace the word by all those names. Try:

NOTE

echo * won't format filenames into neat columns, and the output might be longer than your terminal is wide

```
$ echo *
```

Since * matches anything, it will match any files in the current directory, and the resulting output will be similar to that from `ls`. Suppose you have a file `mycommand`; then try

```
$ echo m*
```

Since m* matches all filenames in the current directory commencing with m, all those filenames will be displayed, including `mycommand`.

Worked example 8.3

> Use `ls -ld` to list all 'dot' files in your home directory.
> **Solution**: Use `ls -ld`, but instead of giving it argument `~` or `$HOME`
> to list files in your home directory, you must isolate only those whose
> names commence with a dot. The 'dot' files in your home directory
> will each be matched with either `~/.*` or `$HOME/.*` and one solution
> is therefore:
>
> `$ ls -ld $HOME/.*`

A `*` will match any number of characters, a `?` will match one single
character, but is otherwise used in exactly the same way as `*`, so

`$ echo ????`

will display all filenames in the current directory that have four characters
in their names (but do not commence with a dot). Pattern matching does
not extend to subdirectories of the current directory, and `???` would not
match `a/b`.

Worked example 8.4

> How many directories or files located in the root directory have
> names three characters long?
> **Solution**: Use pattern matching and `ls` to select the files and `wc -w`
> to count them.
>
> `$ ls /??? | wc -w`

Many files on a UNIX system come equipped with a specified **suffix** —
that is, a sequence of characters at the end of the filename. Some also
give meaning to other parts of their filenames — look at the files in `/lib`,
for instance, which contains files of the form `lib`*something*`.a` and are
library files used by the C compiler. Pattern matching is useful for
isolating files whose names you know to be of a specific 'shape'.

Worked example 8.5

> Display detailed information on all files in the current directory with
> the `.c` suffix.
> **Solution**: Using `ls -l`, we need to give it as arguments those files
> with suffix `.c`, and the pattern `*.c` will match precisely those files:
>
> `$ ls -l *.c`

Between symbols [and] comes either a list of characters, or one or more *ranges* of expressions, possibly preceded by the ! (exclamation mark) character. A range, which is denoted by two characters separated by a hyphen, means all those characters that are lexically between (and including) those two characters. Thus [m-q] matches any lower-case letter between m and q inclusive. Note that the character to the left of the hyphen in a range must lexically precede the character to the right or the range matches nothing. The ! indicates that the word will match any single character not specified between the brackets. Table 8.2 gives some examples of simple patterns.

Table 8.2   Some patterns

[abc]	matches a or b or c
[l-z]	matches all lower-case letters l to z inclusive
[A-Cb-k]	matches upper-case letters A to C and lower-case b to k
[XYa-z]	matches X and Y and any lower-case letter
[-a-z]	matches any lower-case letter or a hyphen
[!0-9]	matches any character that is not a digit

Worked example 8.6

> List all commands stored in /bin whose names consist of two characters, the second one being a vowel.
> **Solution**: Use ls with an argument which will match this pattern. ? matches a single character, and [aeiouAEIOU] matches any vowel, thus:
>
> ```
> $ ls /bin/?[aeiouAEIOU]
> ```

NOTE

*WARNING: rm * deletes all files in your current directory — be careful using patterns with rm*

We shall use pattern matching later on in this chapter in the context of case statements, and you should remember that it is a much more powerful tool than simply for checking filenames. In the meantime, using ls followed by a pattern is an excellent method of getting used to pattern matching. Remember that *, ?, [and] all involve patterns, and that if you use them in a script and don't want them to relate to patterns, they must be escaped using \ or single quotes. In later chapters we shall introduce a similar concept to pattern matching, known as **regular expressions**.

Worked example 8.7

> Create a script to remove all files with suffix .o in the current directory, prompting you for each one as to whether you do in fact wish to delete it, and confirming whether or not it has been removed.

> **Solution**: These files are matched by *.o, and we can pass the files one-by-one to rm -i using a for loop. rm yields exit status 1 if it fails to remove its argument.
>
> ```
> for i in *.o                     # Loop through files
> do
>   if   rm -i $i                   # If deleted ...
>   then echo File $i deleted       # confirm this ...
>   else echo File $i not deleted   # otherwise not
>   fi
> done
> ```
>
> We could not simply have used
>
> ```
> rm -i *.o
> ```
>
> since we would then have been unable to generate the 'confirmation' message.

8.2.2 The case statement

A statement that involves pattern matching is case. It works by starting off with

```
case expression in
```

where *expression* has a value (and would typically be a variable preceded by $). Following that, there is a sequence of

pattern) *command-list* ;;

NOTE

Double semicolons are required, because a single semicolon is used to separate multiple commands occurring on a single line

and the case statement is terminated with esac. The value of *expression* is evaluated, and the first of the patterns that matches it has the following *command-list* executed. For example, a very simple version of the command file, which only examines the suffix of its first argument, might look like:

```
case $1 in
  *.c)      printf "%s:    %s\n" "$1" "c program text" ;;
  *.a)      printf "%s:    %s\n" "$1" "archive library" ;;
  *.o)      printf "%s:    %s\n" "$1" "object file" ;;
  *)        printf "%s:    %s\n" "$1" "unknown type" ;;
esac
```

Where patterns appear in a case statement they are matched with the expression at the start of the case statement, and not with any filenames. If a pattern appears within a command-list in a case statement, however, the pattern is matched to filenames as before. The following script lists the files in the current directory, but asks you whether you wish to list the 'dot' files:

```
echo "List dot files as well? "   # Prompt user
read YESORNO                      # Read reply

case "$YESORNO" in                # Check reply
   [Yy]*)    ls * .* ;;           # Commence with a Y?
   [Nn]*)    ls * ;;              # Commence with an N?
   *)        echo "Sorry, don't understand";;
esac
```

NOTE

The names for the compilers may be different on your system, and are not specified in POSIX

Note the technique used here for asking the user a yes/no question — the answer is assumed to commence with a Y or an N, in upper or lower case, and that is sufficient. This script would happily accept input Yqwerty as a positive response. If you required the user to type in exactly the word YES, the pattern, instead of [Yy]*, would be [Yy][Ee][Ss].

Worked example 8.8

Write a script named compile to take a single argument representing the name of a program written in a high-level language, and then compile that program using one of cc (for C), pc (for Pascal) or f77 (for FORTRAN). File suffixes .c, .p and .f respectively are assumed to indicate the language type.

Solution: We need to check the file suffix using a case statement.

```
# First, check we do have a single argument
case $# in
   1)  ;;
   *) echo "$0: Incorrect number of arguments";;
esac

# Now examine the suffix of argument 1
case $1 in
   *.c) cc $1 ;;
   *.p) pc $1 ;;
   *.f) f77 $1 ;;
   *)    echo "Unknown language";;
esac
```

Where the same command is required for two separate patterns, rather than duplicating the line (or lines) of commands, you can combine the two (or more) patterns. So the pattern

```
sam|chris
```

would match *either* sam *or* chris.

Worked example 8.9

> Write a script to read in a string representing a telephone number as
> dialled from the UK, and indicate whether it is an overseas number
> (commencing 00 or 010), a *value added* number (commencing 0898 or
> 0891), a freephone number (commencing 0800), a *service number*
> (three digits commencing with a 1) or a *national* code (ten digits
> commencing 0 or eleven digits commencing 01).
>
> **Solution**: We could use many if statements, but the script would be
> very messy. This is the sort of problem for which a **case** statement is
> ideal.
>
> ```
> # Prompt user and read in the number
> printf "Input phone number: "
> read N
>
> # Examine the various patterns that might match N
> case $N in
>   00*|010*)    echo "International" ;;
>   0898*|0891*) echo "Value added" ;;
>   0800*)       echo "Freephone" ;;
>   1??)         echo "Service number" ;;
>   0????????)   echo "National code (pre 1995)" ;;
>   01?????????) echo "National code (after 1995)" ;;
>   *)           echo "Unknown code" ;;
> esac
> ```

8.3 Entering and leaving the shell

In this section we look at the command sh — the shell. As we have
discussed, the shell is a program. It is treated just as any other utility,
and as such can take arguments. If it takes one filename as its argument,
the action taken is to take its input (the commands for that shell) from
that file, which is called a **shell script**. With no arguments, the shell reads
its commands from the standard input. When a shell terminates, just like
any other command it returns an exit status, which is normally the status
of the last command executed by that shell.

Create a file (mycommand, say), containing a single line which is the
shell command false. Run the command and check its exit status using
$?:

```
$ sh mycommand
$ echo $?
1
```

Add an extra line, which is the shell command **true**, to the end of **mycommand** (using **vi** or **>>**) which is the shell command **true**; run the command again and check the exit status. This time it will be 0.

A shell can be forced to terminate with a specific exit status by means of command **exit**. Add the following line to the end of **mycommand**, run it again and see what exit status you then get:

```
exit 42
```

Any commands that might be executed after an **exit** command are discarded; **exit** kills the shell immediately. The same is true of an interactive shell.

Type **sh** to start a new interactive shell, and reset the prompt (so you know which is the new shell, and which the previous one) then type **exit** followed by a number. You will see that the new shell terminates (since you are back to the original prompt), and **$?** confirms that the new shell did indeed return an exit status to the original shell.

```
$ sh
$ PS1="--> "
--> exit 99
$ echo $?
99
```

Worked example 8.10

Write a script called **morning** to exit with exit status 0 (if it is run before noon) and status 1 (if run after noon).
Solution: Use **date** to check the time, then **test** to check whether the time is am or pm.

```
HOUR=$( date +"%H" )    # HOUR is a number between 0 and 23
if   [ $HOUR -le 11 ]   # Check HOUR is AM
then exit 0             # ... then exit with status 0
else exit 1             # ... otherwise status 1
fi
```

This command can then be used, for instance, in the following manner:

```
$ if sh morning
> then echo "Good morning"
> else echo "Good afternoon"
> fi
```

> You could have piped the output from `date` to `cut` instead of using the formatting option to `date`, as in previous worked examples. By now, however, you should be getting into the habit of using `man` to find out more information on commands.

The shell supports various **options**, just like other commands. A very useful option is `-x` ('eXpand'), which instructs the shell that, each time it is about to execute a command, it should display on the standard error stream the name of that command. This is performed after all variable names have been replaced by their values, and other substitutions done; it is thus a very good method of **debugging** shell scripts in the event of them not working as planned. For instance, supposing file `badcommand` contains

```
date            # This is OK ...
cat $LOGNAME    # but file chris doesn't exist
```

We could then run this with option `-x` set:

```
$ sh -x badcommand
+ date
Mon Dec 10 17:39:52 GMT 2001
+ cat chris
cat: chris: No such file or directory
```

Shell options can be set during a shell session by means of the command `set`:

```
$ set -x
```

NOTE

Not unset

and can be **unset** as follows:

```
$ set +x
```

Within a script — or indeed when using an interactive shell — you can set the positional parameters $1, $2, etc., without passing them as arguments to the script. This uses `set`, and in the same way as before. Suppose we have a file `testfile`, which contains a script. Having `set -x` at the start of the file and executing the file using `sh` would be equivalent to not having `set -x` in the script, and running the script with `sh -x testfile`. If we wanted to pass other arguments to `testfile`, we could either have:

```
$ sh testfile arg1 arg2 arg3
```

or we could `set` the extra arguments at the start of the script with

```
set arg1 arg2 arg3
```

in which case $1 would become arg1, $2 would become arg2, $3 would become arg3 and $# would become 3. This is handy when debugging scripts that use positional parameters. After setting positional parameters, you can list what they are, together with the values of all other environment variables, by just typing `set`. You can unset all of them with:

```
$ set --
```

Try the following:

```
$ set --
$ set Chris
$ echo Hello $1
Hello Chris
$ set Sam
$ echo Hello $1
Hello Sam
```

The line `set Sam` has reset the value of the first positional parameter $1 to Sam.

8.4 More about scripts with options

Writing a script with arguments is straightforward — you just need to examine $1, $2, etc. — but what about options? Suppose you wanted to write a command `mycommand` which, if given option `-h`, would print a 'help' message rather than executing:

```
$ mycommand -h
Usage: mycommand [-h]
```

You could check whether $1 is equal to '`-h`', but if you had several possible options, not just one, the number of permutations would make this a very messy programming exercise. If `mycommand` took option `-a` in addition to `-h`, you would have to check for:

```
mycommand -h
mycommand -a
mycommand -ah
mycommand -ha
mycommand -a -h
mycommand -h -a
```

in addition to any invalid options it might be presented with. The utility `getopts` is provided to assist in writing shells that have options. Consider the instance above — we could have as the contents of `mycommand`:

```
while getopts h OPTIONNAME
do
    case $OPTIONNAME in
          h)   echo 'Usage: mycommand [-h]' ;;
          ?)   echo 'Bad option to mycommand'
               exit 1 ;;
    esac
done
echo "Arguments were $@"
```

The action that `getopts` performs is to look at `getopts`' first argument, which should be a list of letters — representing the valid options allowed by the script — and possibly colons (see below). It then looks at the next argument to the script in which it occurs. If the argument to a script is an option (i.e. preceded by a minus sign), `getopts` checks to see whether the option is in the list of valid options. If not, an error message is displayed. The second argument to `getopts` is a variable name, which is set to the option that `getopts` has discovered. Only one option at a time will be checked, so you need to enclose `getopts` in a `while` loop. Let's see what happens when `mycommand` is called:

NOTE

Options must precede all other arguments that are not options

```
$ mycommand -h hello
Usage: mycommand [-h]
Arguments were -h hello
$ mycommand -x hello
mycommand: illegal option -- x
Bad option to mycommand
$ mycommand hello there
Arguments were hello there
$ mycommand hello -h
Arguments were hello -h
```

NOTE

In the case of `mycommand hello -h`, *the argument* `-h` *is not an option*

NOTE

If you intend to write scripts which require options, then using `getopts` *is the preferred method*

Some commands take options that require arguments — such as `lp`, whose option `-d` must be followed by the name of the destination printer. This is handled in `getopts` by using colons.

If an option requires an argument, then a colon should follow the option name in the list of allowed options to `getopts`. When that option is encountered, the value of its argument will be stored in the system variable `OPTARG`. For instance, suppose a script called `mymessage` takes one option `-m`, followed by a string, and displays that string. With no arguments, `mymessage` displays `Hello`. The string would be an argument to the `-m` option. This script might be coded thus:

```
MESSAGE=Hello                    # Variable to store message
if getopts m: OPTIONNAME         # If an option found
then
   case $OPTIONNAME in           # Check which option found
       m)   MESSAGE=$OPTARG;;
       ?)   exit 1;;             # Exit if not -m
   esac
fi

echo $MESSAGE                    # Output the message
```

The number of the next argument to be processed by `getopts` is stored in `OPTIND`, so that by using `shift` you can strip off the options from the command and leave the rest of the arguments for processing later.

Worked example 8.11

Write a script `mymail` to call `mailx` to send messages. The script should take an optional argument `-s` (to specify the subject) and one or more other arguments to specify the recipients (just like `mailx`). No other options apart from `-s` should be allowed. If `mymail` is called without option `-s` it should prompt the user for a subject.

```
$ mymail -s "Test message" sam
(message)
$ mymail sam
Subject: Test message
(message)
```

Solution: Use `getopts` to process the command line the script is invoked from:

```
SUBJECT=""
if getopts s: OPTNAME            # Valid option is 's'
then                             # which takes an argument
   case $OPTNAME in
      s) SUBJECT="$OPTARG";;     # The argument to 's' is
                                 # SUBJECT
      ?) echo "Usage: $0 [-s subject] users"
         exit 1;;                # Exit if invalid option
   esac
fi

shift $(($OPTIND - 1))           # Remove the options
USERS="$*"                       # The rest of the line
                                 # is the recipients
```

```
if      [ -z "$USERS" ]            # ... which is compulsory
then    echo "Must specify recipients"
        exit 1                     # Exit if no recipients
fi
while   [ -z "$SUBJECT" ]          # Loop until subject
do                                 # is not null
        printf "Subject (no quotes): "
        read SUBJECT
done

mailx -s "$SUBJECT" $USERS"
```

8.5 Symbolic links

In Chapter 5 we introduced *links*. Recall that a file is represented by a name and by an inode, and that a single inode can have several names. We use a *link* to create an extra name for an inode using the command ln, so

$ ln fileA fileB

will cause fileA and fileB to be two names for the same file. If you delete one of them, the other continues to exist, and the file only disappears when both are removed. They share the same inode.

These *hard* links can only be used within a single filesystem. Hard links can also only be used on *ordinary* files, and not on directories. If you try, for instance,

$ ln / rootdirectory

NOTE

Not POSIX

you will get an error message.

There is another type of link referred to as a **symbolic link**, or **soft link** which can get around these problems.

A hard link is an entry in a directory associating a filename with an inode. A soft link is an entry in a directory associating a filename with another filename. This is an important distinction — hard links are names for inodes, soft links are names for other filenames. To create a soft link, use ln with option -s ('symbolic'). Consider:

$ ln -s fileA fileB

which will create a symbolic link, called fileB, to a file fileA, which should already exist. Examining your files with ls -l would give something like

```
lrw-r--r--  1 chris ugrads 122 May 21 18:40 fileB -> fileA
```

indicating that `fileB` is a symbolic link (`l` in column 1), and that it points to (`->`) `fileA`. Whenever you use `fileB`, UNIX will assume you want to access `fileA` and treat `fileB` accordingly. If `fileA` does not exist, and you try to access `fileB`, you will get an error message telling you `fileB` does not exist.

You can make a symbolic link to any file, provided that the file already exists. The advantage of symbolic links is that you do not have to worry about the filesystems the system's storage is divided into. There is a danger, though: if the file pointed to by a symbolic link is deleted, the link remains in place. Try:

```
$ ln -s fileA fileB
$ rm fileA
$ cat fileB
cat: fileB: No such file or directory
```

Thus you must be careful when deleting files which are pointed to by symbolic links.

Worked example 8.12

> In your home directory create a symbolic link called `systmp` which is linked to `/tmp`.
> **Solution**: Use `ln -s`, as just described. You cannot use a hard link, since `/tmp` will (almost certainly) be on a different filesystem.
>
> ```
> $ ln -s /tmp $HOME/systmp
> ```
>
> Now try the following to confirm it works:
>
> ```
> $ ls $HOME/systmp
> $ ls /tmp
> ```

8.6 Setting up terminals

With a bit of luck, you'll never have to worry about the 'characteristics' of your own terminal, but it is possible that you may have to hook up a terminal to the system and then find it's not quite in order. The command `tput` is provided to help you check basic characteristics of your terminal, using knowledge provided by the environment variable `TERM`. It can perform operations such as 'resetting' or 'initialising' your terminal (if either is possible) and cause your screen to 'clear'. The usability of this command depends entirely on the type of terminal you are using, and only three actions are specified by POSIX. To clear the terminal screen, invoke `tput` with argument `clear`:

```
$ tput clear
```

The reset and initialise procedures require arguments `reset` and `init` respectively, and their actions depend on the system you are using. Typically you may need `tput reset` if your terminal starts to respond unexpectedly, which is sometimes due to having received spurious data it has interpreted. This can sometimes happen if you `cat` a binary file by mistake. Check the manual page for `tput` to find out precisely what effect binary files will have on your system.

The *TAB* key provides a *TAB* character as input to the system. For most purposes a *TAB* can be treated as a *Space*, and both are sometimes collectively described as **whitespace**. The effect of touching a *TAB* key is to move the cursor to the next **tab position**. You can reset the tab positions on your terminal (just for the duration of your current session) using the command `tabs`. Followed by a comma-separated list of numbers, `tabs` will reset the tab positions to those column numbers. So, to set the tab positions to columns 5, 10 and 15, you would type:

> **NOTE**
>
> *The* **tabs** *command only works on some terminals*

```
$ tabs 5,10,15
```

Tabs are useful in text files if you want to line up columns, and don't wish to involve yourself in any complex text formatting programs. It is a good idea when writing shell scripts to 'line up' the first character of each command to clearly identify commands inside a loop. For instance, in the following script, the 'body' of the `for` loop is made up of two commands that have been indented by several spaces.

```
for i in *
do
    printf "File %s has size " $i
    wc -c $i
    printf "\n"
done
```

Rather than count the number of spaces each time, you may find it easier to insert a *TAB* character instead:

```
for i in *
do
TABprintf "File %s has size " $i
TABwc -c $i
TABprintf "\n"
done
```

8.7 Conventions used in UNIX file systems

In Chapter 5 we introduced the hierarchy of UNIX directories and files. In this section we look in more detail at *which files* are stored *where*. Although your home directory will be located at least one level down the hierarchy, and whatever subdirectories you create are your own business, there are some conventions it would be unwise to ignore. Conventions are not always followed, however, even in parts of the file hierarchy that contain system files, and there is no requirement for them in the standards.

Executable files, whether they are binary files or executable shell scripts, are usually held in directories called `bin`, or with `bin` as part of their name. For instance:

```
/cs/ugrad/chris/bin
/cs/ugrad/chris/import/bin
/cs/ugrad/chris/bin/star4
/cs/ugrad/chris/bin/scripts
```

> **NOTE**
>
> *'Imported' is used to indicate commands that have come from other systems*

> **NOTE**
>
> *Recall that binary code is machine-specific*

> **NOTE**
>
> `var` = *'variable size'*

If `bin` is the *last* component of the pathname, the previous components would typically indicate some property of the commands held in the directory. The directory `/cs/ugrad/chris/import/bin` might well hold commands `chris` has been mailed by colleagues. If `bin` is not the last component, subsequent names in the pathname might indicate the type of machine the commands can run on. Commands in `/cs/ugrad/chris/bin/star4` might be binary commands that will only run on a Star4 system, and `/cs/ugrad/chris/bin/scripts` might contain shell scripts.

Devices are contained in directories called `dev`; most systems will simply have `/dev` as the only such directory, since they cannot be created by users at will. Manual pages are always contained in a hierarchy with `man` as the last component. Source code (such as C or Pascal programs) is often held in directories called `src`. Files that must be stored temporarily while being sent to a printer or waiting to be sent off by the electronic mail program, are held in directories called `spool`. Files and directories whose size is known to vary considerably are often held in a directory called `var`. It would not be uncommon for `chris`'s **mailbox** — the file in which incoming mail is stored before being read — to be the file `/var/spool/mail/chris`. Libraries — that is, sets of data required by specific utilities such as the C compiler — are held in directories called `lib`, and 'include' files — also required by the C compiler — are held in directories called `include`. Have a look at the root directory, and you will see several of these directories.

There is a wide variety of practice across manufacturers and institutions, but these conventions are broadly adhered to, even if minor variations are added; if you find a directory called 4lib you would be fairly safe guessing it to be a 'library' directory.

The last directory name that interests us here is tmp. This directory is used for **temporary files**. Many commands — including several of the scripts in this book — use temporary files that are only required while the command is running, and the existence of these files is of no interest to the user running the command. Instead of using the current directory to store the temporary files, it is good practice to use a completely different directory. There are two principal reasons for this. First, it avoids the problem of the current directory filling up with unwanted files (should they accidentally not be deleted) and secondly, it prevents existing files being overwritten (should their names happen to coincide with that of the temporary file). There is also an advantage from the viewpoint of the system administrator — provided that the locations of the tmp directories are known, they can periodically have their contents removed, so that unwanted temporary files do not waste storage space.

You can expect to find a directory called /tmp, and you can choose names for temporary files to place in that directory by using $$ as part of the filename.

NOTE

$$ *is the current process number*

Worked example 8.13

> Write a script to repeatedly request you to type in the names of files, and to concatenate them and display on the terminal the resulting file after all the concatenation has taken place. The script should terminate when you enter a blank line in response to the request for a filename.
>
> **Solution**: We need to concatenate the files to a temporary file, cat that file, then delete it.
>
> ```
> # Start by choosing a unique name for the temporary file
> TMPFILE=/tmp/$LOGNAME.$$
>
> # Double check that it doesn't exist - just in case
> if   [ -f $TMPFILE ]
> then echo "Temporary file exists"
>      exit 1      # The command fails ...
> fi
>
> while true      # Forever ...
> do   printf "New file (Return to finish): "
>      read NEXTFILE
>      if   [ -z "$NEXTFILE" ]
>      then break # Leave the while loop
>      fi
>      cat $NEXTFILE >>$TMPFILE
> ```

```
done

cat $TMPFILE        # Print the temporary file
rm $TMPFILE         # Remove the temporary file
exit 0              # Exit cleanly
```

First of all, a filename is chosen to store the concatenated text as it is produced; a check is made to ensure that it does not in fact exist. This is necessary — in the unlikely event that another user had chosen the same temporary filename, and you did not make this check, the results of running the script would at best be unpredictable. A more sophisticated solution would try generating other filenames until it found one that did not exist. The script then loops continuously, requesting the user to enter a filename, reading that name from standard input, and storing it in the variable NEXTFILE. If NEXTFILE has zero length (i.e. the user has typed in a blank line) the loop is exited using break, otherwise the named file is appended to the end of the temporary file. Finally, after the loop has been exited, the temporary file is sent to standard output and then removed.

CHAPTER SUMMARY

Table 8.3   Commands introduced in this chapter

exit	cause the shell to exit
expr	evaluate an expression
getopts	parse options for a utility
set	set options and positional parameters
tabs	reset the tab positions
tput	change terminal characteristics
unset	unset options and positional parameters

EXERCISES

1 Write a script cm2ftin which uses arithmetic expansion to convert from centimetres to feet and inches, rounded down to the nearest whole number of inches. Input should be a whole number of centimetres, and you may assume 1 foot is 30 cm.

```
$ cm2ftin
Enter cm: 42
42 cm is 1 foot 5 inches
```

2 Repeat exercise 1 using `expr` instead of arithmetic expansion.

3 Write a script to read a single argument, representing the name of a text file, and display the average number of characters per line (excluding *Newline* characters) to two decimal places. Make sure that the script can handle the cases when it is called with the wrong number of arguments and when it cannot access the required file. *Hint:* use `read` and `wc`.

4 Write a script called `area` to take two numerical arguments, representing the base length and height of a right-angled triangle, plus one or two options −a and −h (meaning *area* and *help*). With option −a, the area of the triangle should be displayed on standard output preceded by the message `Area is`, and with option −h a short help message should be displayed. With no options, there should be no output; any other option should be ignored, except that a warning message should be output on standard error.

5 Write a script called `hello` to display one of `Good morning`, `Good afternoon` or `Good evening` depending on the time of day. You should use the output of `date` and pattern matching.

6 Write a script called `saytime` to display the current time in words.

7 Write a script called `drawsquare` to take as argument a single number, between 3 and 15 inclusive, and draw on the standard output a square, using the symbols + (plus), − (hyphen) and | (vertical bar), so:

```
$ drawsquare 4
+--+
|  |
|  |
+--+
```

If `drawsquare` is presented without arguments, with more than 1 argument, or with a single argument that is not a number between 3 and 15, it should display an error message and exit with status 1.

8 Write a script called `drawcube` to take as argument a single number, between 3 and 15 inclusive, and draw on the standard output a cube, using the symbols + (plus), − (hyphen), / (slash) and | (vertical bar), so:

```
$ drawcube 4
    +--+
   /  /|
  /  / |
+--+  +
|  | /
|  |/
+--+
```

If drawcube is presented without arguments, with more than 1 argument, or with a single argument that is not a number between 3 and 15, it should output an error message and exit with status 1.

9 Write a script called eurhello to display a greeting in one of several languages. With option -e, or with no options, eurhello should use the greeting Hello, with option -f it should use the French Bonjour, and with option -g it should use the German Guten Tag. It should also allow an option -G, which takes an argument, allowing an arbitrary greeting. Following any options, an argument, which is a string representing the name of the person to whom the greeting is addressed, is required:

```
$ eurhello Chris
Hello Chris
$ eurhello -f "Monsieur le President"
Bonjour Monsieur le President
$ eurhello -G "Hi there" Sam
Hi there Sam
```

If several of the three possible options are given as arguments to the script, the last (rightmost) one takes precedence.

Advanced shell programming

This chapter covers

▶ trapping signals;

▶ shell functions;

▶ the 'exec' and 'eval' mechanisms;

▶ mailing files which are not text files; and

▶ other POSIX utilities not discussed elsewhere in this book.

In this chapter we examine briefly those aspects of shells that are not required later in this book, and which may be considered as 'advanced' in comparison with those topics already covered. The other chapters in the book will enable you to use the shell quite adequately, and the contents of this chapter are by no means necessary for you to be a competent shell programmer. However, even if you do not at this stage make use of the facilities discussed in this chapter, knowledge of their existence is important should you in the future decide to study shell programming in greater detail. Also, if you read shell scripts written by other people, and if you encounter unfamiliar utilities, you will at least recognise the facilities they may use.

9.1 Sending and trapping signals

In some circumstances you will wish that accidentally typing *ctrl-C* will not kill the current process. This would be true, for example, in the execution of a complex script that makes non-trivial changes to files, where your filespace would be left in a mess if the script died when only half-completed. There is a mechanism, known as **trapping signals**, whereby a shell takes an action specified by you when it receives a signal, rather than taking the default action. The command used to intercept a signal is **trap**, and it is used in the following manner:

trap *'action' signal*

The *action* is either null or a string containing a command, and the *signal* is one of the signal names. Create a script **interrupts** containing:

```
trap 'echo Ouch' INT
echo Beginning
sleep 10  .
echo ten seconds
sleep 10
echo twenty seconds
sleep 10
echo thirty seconds and ended
```

and execute it using **sh**. Try to interrupt it by typing *ctrl-C* at your terminal a couple of times and see what happens. You should see

```
$ sh interrupts
Beginning
```
ctrl-C
```
Ouch
ten seconds
```
ctrl-C
```
Ouch
twenty seconds
```
ctrl-C
```
Ouch
thirty seconds and ended
```

Similar to **SIGINT** is **SIGQUIT**. This signal can usually be generated from your terminal by typing **ctrl-**. The difference between the two is that **SIGQUIT** will on many systems generate a **coredump**, that is a file named **core** which contains information about the interrupted command when it received the signal. The file **core** can be used to examine the state of the program when the signal was received. A **core** file can be interrogated by an experienced UNIX programmer using utilities such as **dbx**, but at this stage you will not be interested in its contents. A coredump is usually a big file and should be removed unless you intend to use it. Try the following:

```
$ sleep 1000 &
[1] 17465
$ kill -s QUIT %1
[1]+ Quit (core dumped) sleep 1000
```

Check which files you have using `ls` and you should find that one named `core` has now been created.

When a shell script exits, a signal is sent to it called `EXIT`, which can be trapped. To see which signals you have trapped, use `trap` with no arguments. Be careful which signals you trap — in particular, don't try `KILL` (or you would have difficulty using `kill` to destroy the process) or `HUP` (or unpredictable things would happen if you tried to suspend the process). If you have set a trap on a signal, you can remove it by giving it the action `-` (minus symbol), so:

```
trap - INT
```

will restore *ctrl-C* to its normal function.

NOTE

You will not be allowed to trap KILL

Worked example 9.1

> By setting a trap on your login shell, arrange to be given the message Goodbye when you logout.
> **Solution**: The signal `EXIT` is sent to your login shell when you logout, so use `trap` to perform an `echo` when this signal is intercepted:
>
> ```
> $ trap 'echo Goodbye' EXIT
> ```

There are various other signals — the main standard ones are listed in Table 9.1, although most UNIX systems support many more.

Table 9.1   Signal names

SIGEXIT	trapped by all shells immediately before exit
SIGHUP	hangup — sent to child process when parent dies
SIGINT	Sent by *ctrl-C*
SIGQUIT	Sent by *ctrl-* and may coredump
SIGKILL	'Sure kill' signal — cannot be `trapped`
SIGALRM	'Alarm' — used by e.g. `sleep`
SIGTERM	The 'default' signal used by `kill`

9.2 Functions

The shell supports **functions**, which are a way of grouping commands together in a non-trivial manner without needing to write a new shell script. In complexity, functions lie between a straightforward pipe (or similar shell command) and a script.

To create a function, you first of all choose a name for a function, then enter that name, followed by (), followed by a shell command enclosed in braces. For example, a simple function `myls`, which performs `ls -l $HOME`, might be **defined** thus:

NOTE

Separate the braces from the function definition by blanks

```
$ myls() { ls -l $HOME }
```

To execute a function, simply type its name:

```
$ myls
```

A function can only be used by the shell in which it has been defined, and subshells or child processes cannot use it. A function will use the environment of the current shell (so that you need not `export` variables that the function may use).

Worked example 9.2

> Write a function `myusage` to display the total disk space used by your home directory, preceded by a message reminding you of that directory's pathname.
>
> **Solution**: Standard syntax for defining a function is followed. To find the disk usage, `du` is used; the output from `du` with option `-s` consists of two fields: the size of the directory that is its argument, and the name of the directory. Use `cut` to isolate the size. The output from `du` thus piped to `cut` will print the size of your home directory on standard output.
>
> ```
> $ myusage() {
> > printf "Directory %s uses " $HOME
> > du -s $HOME | cut -f 1
> > }
> ```

You may be wondering why functions are needed — at first sight, they may appear an added complication to the shell, and duplicate the purpose of executable shell scripts. However, there are some operations which *cannot* be performed by a script. Consider writing a command to alter the value of a variable in the current shell. If it is implemented as a shell script, running the command involves creating a child process whose parent is the current shell. Any change in that variable's value will be done by the child process. However, there is no way that the child process can communicate the new value back to its parent, and the variable's value in the current shell thus remains unchanged. A function, however, would be executed by the current shell without sparking a child process, and could therefore be used successfully.

Having defined one or more functions, you may wish to run a command without looking up the function definitions. You may, for instance, have a shell script that runs a command called `myls`. You would not wish the command run by the shell script that was called `myls` to be confused with the *function* called `myls`. Since a function is not the name of a file, you cannot use the value of `PATH` to perform the disambiguation.

As a simple example, supposing you had called the function above `ls` instead of `myls`. Then, to run the original utility called `ls`, simply prefix the command with `command`:

```
$ command ls
```

The effect of `command` is identical to typing a command not preceded by `command`, except that user-defined functions are not looked up.

Functions can be defined interactively or within a script, in which case they can be used from within that script only, unless the script is run using **dot** (`.`) (see Chapter 6).

Another reason for using functions is efficiency. Executing a function involves the shell in less work because it does not have to create a new process. It can also be argued that functions are easier to understand than shell scripts. One common function that many users define, in order to speed up their sessions, is `ll`:

```
$ ll() { ls -l }
```

If you wish to exit from a function before the end you should use `return` — this is equivalent to the use of `exit` to leave a shell script early.

9.3 Aliases

Functions are general-purpose, and can be arbitrarily long. A mechanism similar to functions, but suitable for naming short commands only, is that of **aliasing**. The format is

`alias` *alias-name=string*

and whenever the alias-name is encountered it is replaced by the string, whose value is then executed as a command. For instance, instead of naming `ll` above using functions, we could have

```
$ alias ll='ls -l'
```

The command `alias`, with no arguments, lists all the aliases you have set up, and `alias` followed by a name (assumed to be the name of an alias)

will display the string that alias represents. To remove an alias definition, the command `unalias` can be used.

When the shell encounters a name, it first of all checks to see whether it is an alias; if not, the shell sees if there is a function definition for it. If both of these fail, it examines the `PATH` to find an executable command by that name.

9.4 The 'exec' mechanism

When you execute a script, a copy of the shell is created. Thus when that script itself executes a command, a process is created for that command as well as the process for the calling shell. This is potentially inefficient, especially if the script is relatively simple, but essentially unavoidable.

In a few instances, however, the calling shell is redundant, in particular if a utility is executed as the last command in the shell. The shell will terminate precisely when the utility has terminated. During the time that the utility is running, the shell's process continues to run, but is simply waiting for the utility to finish — nothing more. This is inefficient because the kernel still needs to manage the shell process, and the shell is a 'big' program. The command `exec` is provided to reduce this redundancy.

Using `exec` the final command can be executed by the same process as the calling shell. UNIX accomplishes this by replacing the machine code that the shell process contains with the machine code for the command, and the shell cannot therefore execute any later commands. Suppose file `sleepfile` contains one line, `sleep 100`:

```
$ sh sleepfile &
[1] 28409
$ ps
  PID TT STAT  TIME COMMAND
15826 p4 S     0:21 sh
28409 p4 S     0:00 sh sleepfile
28410 p4 S     0:00 sleep 100
28417 p4 R     0:00 ps
```

There are four processes: your login shell 15826, the `ps` process, process 28409 for the shell that interprets the script, and the process 28410 for the command in the script. Now, replace the first line of the file by `exec sleep 100`, and we get:

```
$ sh sleepfile &
[1] 28547
$ ps
```

```
PID TT STAT  TIME COMMAND
15826 p4 S    0:22 sh
28547 p4 S    0:00 sleep 100
28551 p4 R    0:00 ps
```

The shell script was created with PID 28547. When we look at the processes, we have the login shell and the `ps` process as before, but process 28547 is the `sleep` command, not a shell.

Worked example 9.3

Write a script to take one argument, assumed to be a filename, and run `vi` on that file using `exec`. If no arguments are given, the script should exit with return status 1.
Solution:

```
# Check number of arguments
if [ $# -ne 1 ]

# If too few arguments, warn user
then  echo $0 requires exactly 1 argument
      # and exit with status 1
      exit 1
# otherwise run vi
else  exec vi $1
fi
```

9.5 The 'eval' mechanism

Suppose you are using variables that contain values representing the names of other variables. For instance, you wish to check the values of variables X1 through X100, and you need a loop to perform this task. You cannot choose another variable N, loop the value of N from 1 to 100 using `expr`, and examine the value of X$N. It simply won't work. Nor does the shell allow *indexed* variables, such as arrays, as in Pascal or C. You must use `eval` instead; `eval` will examine its arguments, and concatenate them to form a command it then executes. The arguments to `eval` are examined and any environment variables are replaced by their values. This forms the command that is then executed. So to print out the values of PS1, PS2 and HOME, we might have:

```
for i in HOME PS1 PS2
do
    eval echo The value of $i is '$'$i
done
```

For the first iteration of the loop, the value of i is HOME; the command

```
eval echo The value of $i is '$'$i
```

is then executed. The first thing that eval does is to replace $i by HOME and remove the quotes, and then the remainder of the line after eval is executed as a command itself:

```
echo The value of HOME is $HOME
```

This process is then repeated with i set to PS1 and then to PS2.

Worked example 9.4

Create a script to read in a single-line command and execute it.
Solution: Use read to read the command into a variable (say CMD) and eval to execute that command.

```
echo "Type a command:"     # Prompt the user ...
read CMD                    # read in the command ...
eval $CMD                   # and run it
```

Note that the last line of the script must not be simply $CMD — see what happens if you change that line to $CMD and then enter ls $HOME as the command. You will get a message

```
ls: $HOME: No such file or directory
```

indicating that it was trying to find a file whose actual name is $HOME.

If you find yourself needing to specify an array of variables while shell programming, then using eval is the only method available to you. Your problem is likely to be solved more effectively using another utility, and Awk — which is introduced in Chapter 11 — is recommended.

9.6 Sending data across networks

9.6.1 Sending printable characters

If you send electronic mail to someone, the message you send must consist only of printable characters. If you wish to send other data you must encode it into a form containing only ordinary text. The reason for this is that some networks interpret some non-printing characters as instructions, which could cause messages to go astray or their contents to be changed. The command uuencode takes a file and writes to standard output a representation of that file containing only ASCII characters; the command uudecode takes a file and performs the reverse operation. Either one or two arguments are needed by uuencode — the second one is the name of the file as it will be known when decoded (which is not necessarily the same as the name of the file you are encoding). The first argument, if there are two, is the file to be encoded (standard input is encoded if there is only one argument). The format of the file after encoding is a sequence of lines commencing with a *header line* and terminating with **end** on a line of its own. The header line consists of three fields — the word **begin**, the access permissions the file should have after it is decoded, and the name of the file after decoding. For example, suppose we have a file **A** containing an 'alert' character (*ctrl-G*), and we wish to mail it to **sam**, and to be received with name **chris_file**. We can check what the file contains using **od**, which will confirm that \a (i.e. *ctrl-G*) is indeed included in **chris_file**

NOTE

od *is discussed in* Chapter 5

```
$ od -t c A
0000000   h   e   l   l   o  \a  \n
0000007
```

This file can now be coded using **uuencode**. Note that the output is sent to standard output:

```
$ uuencode A chris_file
begin u=rw,go= chris_file
':&5L;&\'"@CP
```
(line containing a single blank space)
```
end
```

So, to send the encoded file to **sam**, we merely pipe the output to **mailx**:

```
$ uuencode A chris_file | mailx -s "Binary file" sam
```

The resulting file can then be recreated by **sam** storing the mail message in (say) **mailfile** and typing:

```
$ uudecode mailfile
```

Any lines before **begin** and after **end** are ignored by **uudecode**, so you don't need to worry about any extra header lines the mailer inserts into your message. Try this yourself — choose a file, **uuencode** it, mail it to a friend, and get them to **uudecode** it. Have a look at the encoded version, and the final decoded file, and convince yourself that it does in fact work.

Try now encoding a large file, say /usr/dict/words:

```
$ uuencode /usr/dict/words tmpfile
```

Look at the output — it consists of lines of fixed width (61 characters) commencing with the letter M.

```
  ...
M=&4*87)B;E86P*87)B;W)E='5M"F%R8G5T=7,*87)C"F%R8V%%D90I!<F-A
M9&EA"F%R8N80IA<F-A;F4*87)C8V8]S"F%R8V-0<VEN90IA<F-H"F%R8VAA
M9OIA<F-H8C"F%R8VAA:7-M"F%R8VA!;F=E;(IA<F-H8FES:&]P"F%R8VAD
  ...
```

9.6.2 Splitting files

It is possible to write scripts to read in a file containing several encoded files and automatically separate them.

NOTE

Often restricted to 64k bytes

Some mailers and networks restrict the size of messages they can send so that if you wish to mail a large file you cannot send it in a single message. You could, of course, edit the message into several smaller files and send each one in turn, but that would be tedious. The command `split` will split a file automatically for you into similar sized pieces. For instance, try

```
$ split /usr/dict/words
```

and you will find that a large collection of files have been created in the current directory with names `xaa`, `xab`, `xac`, etc., all of which (with the exception of the last one) are 1000 lines long (test this with `wc`). With option `-l` ('lines') followed by a number, `split` will chop a file into a collection of files each of that number of lines. The reason for having 1000 lines as the default size of the file is not only that 1000 is a 'nice round number', but also that 1000 lines of text with 61 characters per line (`uuencode` outputs lines which are 61 characters wide) comprise just less than the 64k limit that some mailers impose on files.

Worked example 9.5

You have a long file called `bigdata`, which contains control characters, and you wish `sam` to have a copy of it. Arrange to send `sam` a copy via electronic mail.

Solution: First of all, `bigdata` must be encoded and then split into small enough chunks to pass through the mailer. Each of those chunks must be individually mailed to `sam`.

```
$ uuencode bigdata bigdata | split
$ for i in x??
> do
> mailx -s "File $i" sam <$i
> done
```

You must ensure that you have no files whose names are of three letters commencing with an x before attempting this exercise. The

> xaa files will be overwritten by split if files of the same name already exist in your current directory. The files sam receives can be joined together and then uudecoded to recreate the original file bigdata. Although uudecode will strip away headers and footers from a *single* file, it will not cope with extra lines inserted in the middle of a file. The recreated file will have to be edited to remove all headers and footers introduced by the mailer.

It is to be hoped that sending data across a network will result in the message received being identical to that sent. Regrettably, this is not always the case. If the communications medium is prone to interference (such as a crackly telephone line) it sometimes happens that data becomes corrupted. The command cksum can be used to identify quickly whether this has happened. Followed by a filename, cksum will print a large number, known as a **checksum**, based on the contents of the file, together with the number of characters in that file. If anything is altered in the file, the number created will be very different, as in the flowing example in which the capital 'T' becomes a lower-case 't':

On some non-POSIX systems the command sum *is provided instead of* cksum

```
$ echo "To be or not to be" | cksum
3740407258      19
$ echo "to be or not to be" | cksum
1143317160      19
```

If the sender and the recipient of data both run cksum on the message, and this yields the same number, then they can both be confident that the message has not been corrupted during transmission. To try out cksum, create two files (say data1 and data2) using vi, and containing the same piece of text (a short poem would be suitable). Then see what happens if you first of all use cksum to check whether they are the same, and then try diff.

9.7 Makefiles

Note the suffix .c *for C files*

Program links are not related to file links

When developing software you will frequently create files that depend on the existence and/or state of other files. Consider the situation where you have a C program, and which you wish to call myprogram, which is stored in two files, prog1.c and prog2.c. In order to compile the program you would compile each of the two source code files, creating files prog1.o and prog2.o respectively which contain object code (binary code). Those two files would then be **linked** to create the final file myprogram. That is, the binary code in prog1.o and prog2.o will be joined together to produce a single binary file — this is in fact not a trivial operation. We therefore have the dependencies:

▶ prog1.o depends on prog1.c

▶ prog2.o depends on prog2.c

▶ myprogram depends on both prog1.o and prog2.o.

In order to compile this C program using the command cc, you would have three commands to perform:

```
$ cc -c prog1.c
$ cc -c prog2.c
$ cc -o myprogram prog1.o prog2.o
```

The first two lines, which translate the two source files to object code, can be performed in either order. The final command, which links two object code files together, must wait until the first two have been completed.

If you were to type in these commands each time, there would be a danger of making an error and accidentally forgetting to recompile one of the source files after editing it. Alternatively, you could place all three commands into a file and then execute that file as a shell script. This would have the disadvantage that if you edited (say) prog1.c you would also have to recompile prog2.c even though this was not necessary.

In this small example, this might seem a minor problem, but when performing serious system development it is not unusual to have large volumes of code that take a long time to compile. In such a case, it is sensible to minimise the amount of work that has to be done when small changes to the code are made.

A tool that makes use of file dependencies is known as make. This works in the following way: a file, called a **makefile**, is created (usually in the same directory containing the software being developed), and a program called make reads that file. The makefile contains information indicating

▶ which file depends on which other file(s), and

▶ what commands must be performed to bring a file 'up-to-date'.

The above example could have as the contents of its makefile:

```
myprogram: prog1.o prog2.o
        cc -o myprogram prog1.o prog2.o

prog1.o: prog1.c
        cc -c prog1.c

prog2.o: prog2.c
        cc -c prog2.c
```

You will notice two types of line in this file. There are lines that are not indented — they take the form of a word (known as the **target**) followed by a colon, and then followed by some other words, where the words would usually be names of files. These lines indicate that the word (file) on the left of the colon is dependent on the filenames on the right of the semicolon. Thus `myprogram` depends on both `prog1.o` and `prog2.o`, etc.

The indented lines (which must be indented with a single *TAB*, not with *Space*s) indicate the action to be taken if the dependency (which would be shown on the previous line) is not up-to-date. So, if `myprogram` was older than either `prog1.o` or `prog2.o`, the command `cc -o myprogram prog1.o prog2.o` would be executed.

In order to use makefiles, data in the format discussed above should be stored in a file with name either `Makefile` or `makefile`. Then, to bring the software up-to-date, simply type `make` followed by the target which you need updated:

```
$ make myprogram
```

If you invoke `make` without any arguments, it will assume that the target is the first target mentioned in the makefile. If you run `make` with option `-n` it will display the commands that it would execute, but will not actually run them. If you are unsure of the correctness of your makefile, it is wise to run `make` with the `-n` option initially simply to ensure that the actions it performs are in fact the actions you expect. For instance, taking the above example would give:

```
$ make -n
cc -c prog1.c
cc -c prog2.c
cc -o myprogram prog1.o prog2.o
```

If, while running `make`, one of the commands fails (for example, you had not created `prog1.c` at all, or there was an error in that C program), then `make` would terminate at that point.

This utility has many other features, and can handle much more complex dependencies than the simple ones indicated here. If you are creating programs as part of a course in Pascal or C (say), then a simple makefile such as this one will be adequate. Only when you move on to more complex programming tasks will you need to examine `make` in greater detail.

Two other standard commands, which are principally used within makefiles, are worth mentioning briefly. Command `ar` is used to maintain 'archives' of files, and is used principally for maintaining libraries of object code. When an executable file consisting of binary code is produced, it contains information used by debugging utilities, but not required simply to execute it. This redundancy can be eliminated from such a file by means of the command `strip`.

NOTE

Object code is usualy produced by a compiled language such as C

9.8 Safe programming

To write a script that always works as you want it to, it is good practice
to perform as many checks as you can. Whenever you try to use a file,
make sure that a suitable action is taken if you cannot access that file.
Whenever you write a script called with options or arguments, make sure
that the first few lines check that it has been called with sensible options
and arguments.

So far we have met ways of checking access to individual files, and have
remarked that names of files may be subject to certain limits. A utility
called `pathchk` is available which will give more information than `test`.
When followed by the name of a path, `pathchk` will check that it does not
breach any of those limits, by (for example) being simply too long. It will
also check that no component of the pathname cannot be searched
because it does not have *execute* permission. With option `-p` ('portable')
it will also indicate any potential problems where the name may be
acceptable for the current system, but breaches certain minimum limits
defined by POSIX, and might thus present problems if the name were to
be used on a different system.

Worked example 9.6

> Is it sensible to write a script to create and use a file called
> `instrumentation` and expect this script to work on all systems?
> **Solution**: This is a problem that concerns the portability of a
> filename; use `pathchk` with option `-p`:
>
> ```
> $ pathchk -p instrumentation
> pathchk: name 'instrumentation' has length 15; exceeds
> limit of 14
> ```
>
> This message indicates that any filename of length above 14 may not
> be allowed on every system, so the answer is 'no'.

If, during the course of a session logged on to a UNIX system, you
have reset a number of variables, it may be that you accidentally change
the value of a system variable that was defined when you logged in. You
can find what the values of the system-defined variables are with
command `getconf` ('get configuration'). This can also be useful in a shell
script if you wish to check that such variables have the required values.
Perhaps the clearest example of where this would be useful would be in
the case of `PATH`. It is common to reset the value of `PATH`, as we have
already discussed, so that it includes directories within your own file
space. If you were to make an error while doing this and left out one of
the system directories, you might be unable to proceed, as some
commands you needed to use would be denied you. By using

NOTE

PATH *is discussed in*
Chapter 6

```
$ getconf PATH
```

the default value would be printed out and you could reset PATH to a
sensible value, which would allow you to continue.

There are a number of variables which are not 'environment' variables
(and cannot be changed) but indicate the system limits (such as the
maximum length of a filename allowed, and the maximum number of
processes you can have running at any one time). These values can only
be accessed using getconf.

9.9 Setting up a terminal

We have assumed that your system administrator has set up your terminal
and the system so that the terminal will work. This is a very reasonable
expectation, but sometimes you may need to communicate with a UNIX
machine from an unusual terminal that has not been set up for you. If you
have a problem with your terminal, then in the normal course of events it
can be corrected using tput; this will not help though if the system does
not already have all the information it needs about the terminal.

The command stty is used to specify to the UNIX system the
characteristics both of the terminal and of the communication device
linking the terminal and the system. Clearly, if you cannot communicate
at all with the UNIX system, stty is of no use to you. If you can get the
system as far as reading a line containing stty, you are then in a position
to correct such things as the size of terminal screen that UNIX thinks you
have, which control characters are matched to which keys, and so on. Try
this command with option -a to display the current settings for your
terminal. You will get several lines of output, which will look something
like:

```
$ stty -a
speed 9600 baud; rows 25; columns 80; line = 2; intr = ^C;
...
-parenb -parodd cs8 -hupcl -cstopb cread -clocal -crtscts
...
```

In this instance, the terminal has 25 rows and 80 columns and
communicates with the processors at 9600 **baud**. The keystroke necessary
to send an interrupt signal SIGINT is *ctrl-C*. Look at the manual page for
stty to discover the meaning of the other information it displays. In
order to change any of the settings, follow stty by the setting you wish to
change and its new value. For example, to cause your terminal to have a
width of only 30 character columns, you should type:

```
$ stty columns 30
```

> **NOTE**
>
> tput *is discussed in Chapter 8*

> **NOTE**
>
> *WARNING! Be careful using* stty — *mistakes may be difficult to correct*

> **NOTE**
>
> *baud is 'bits per second'*

If you try this example, remember to reset the terminal to its original settings afterwards.

9.10 More on files

UNIX supports **named pipes**, also known as **FIFO** files ('first in first out'). A named pipe is like an ordinary pipe, except that it has a name by which it can be referred to from within a program (normally pipes are anonymous). In order to implement a named pipe, UNIX creates a file as the named pipe, whose name is the name of the named pipe. The command `mkfifo` is available to create such a file. The use of such a file is that many processes can write to it at once, the file will temporarily store the data it receives, and when the contents are requested by another process the contents of the file will be 'flushed'. Try the following:

```
$ mkfifo pfile
$ ls -l
total 0 prw-------   1 chris       general     0 Dec  3 15:08
pfile
$ echo Hello >pfile &
[1] 2230
$ echo There >pfile &
[2] 2231
$ cat pfile
There
Hello
[1]- Done      echo Hello >pfile
[2]+ Done      echo There >pfile
```

You will notice that the `ls -l` indicates that `pfile` exists as a file in the current directory, but the character in the first column is a p indicating that it is a named pipe. Once a named pipe is 'opened', when you start to write something to it or read something from it, you can write to it from several processes (such as the two `echo` processes in the above example) — the pipe can therefore have several input streams. The input streams are then merged and the result can be read by reading the named pipe just like any other file.

As soon as all the processes writing to the named pipe have terminated, the named pipe closes and any processes attempting to read it receive the end-of-file character. The named pipe acts as a 'buffer', temporarily storing characters sent to it from its input streams, and after sending these characters to the standard output they are deleted.

There is one 'feature' of named pipes — all processes that read from, or write to, a given named pipe must be running on the same processor as that which created the pipe in the first place. If your UNIX system contains many processors you must take care. We do not discuss named pipes further here, save to indicate that if you are familiar with programming in C you may wish to investigate them in greater detail.

If you create a binary file using (say) C, that file will contain **symbols**: that is to say, it will contain the names used within that file for data that may need to be communicated to and from the file. Although discussion of the format of object files is outside the scope of this book, the command nm is provided to list names in such a file, and will be of interest to a C programmer. To see how nm works, look in directory /usr/lib, see what files there are in that directory with suffix .a and choose one of them (say libc.a). A large volume of output will be produced, so you will probably wish to pipe it through more:

```
$ nm /usr/lib/libc.a | more
```

A similar task can be accomplished on the *source code* files written in C or FORTRAN using ctags, which will create a file called tags listing the named functions defined in those files given to ctags as arguments.

When creating text files that include *TAB*s, it is sometimes inconvenient to have those *TAB*s there — or vice versa, you may wish a file to include *TAB*s where otherwise it might not. Situations where this may be important include preparing input for utilities such as Awk or make. *TAB*s are sometimes included in text files automatically, especially by some editors, in order to utilise space more efficiently. The command expand takes input containing *TAB*s and produces standard output which is the same as the input but with the *TAB*s replaced by the appropriate number of spaces. The command unexpand does the reverse — a file containing spaces will have some (or all) of the spaces replaced by *TAB*s, where tab stops are assumed to occur at every eighth column. See also the command tabs discussed previously.

If you have two text files whose lines have been sorted into order, the utilities comm and join may be of use. To select those lines common to both files, or which occur in only one of them, use comm. This command is complementary to diff and to uniq. The output of comm, when given two arguments representing filenames, is a sequence of lines containing three tab-separated columns. The first column contains the lines unique to the first file, the second column the lines unique to the second, and the third column those lines common to both. For instance, if file A contains

```
apple
orange
pear
pomegranate
strawberry
```

NOTE

To list all .a files, type
ls /usr/lib/*.a

NOTE

ctags can also be used
on some other language
constructs

NOTE

diff, uniq and paste are
discussed in Chapter 5

and file B contains

```
apple
peach
pomegranate
raspberry
```

then the output from

```
$ comm A B
```

would be

```
                apple
orange
        peach
pear
                pomegranate
        raspberry
strawberry
```

To join lines containing a common **field** from the two files, use `join` — this command is complementary to `paste`. The two files are considered to contain a number of blank-separated columns. Lines with an identical first column cause a line to be displayed that is the first field followed by the other fields from the line in the first file, then the other fields from the second. To illustrate this command, suppose A and B contain lists of fruits together with other data; then `join` will output a sequence of lines that commence with the fruit names and then include the extra data from A and B. Suppose A is

```
apple 2 kilos Monday
orange 4 kilos from Jones' shop
pear none
pomegranate 3 kilos Tuesday
strawberry 2 boxes
```

and file B contains

```
apple 1 kilo Wednesday
peach none
pomegranate 1 kilo Thursday
raspberry none
```

then the effect of `join` would be

```
$ join A B
apple 2 kilos Monday 1 kilo Wednesday
pomegranate 3 kilos Tuesday 1 kilo Thursday
```

9.11 Miscellaneous utilities

Although the structure of files on a UNIX machine is uncomplicated, other operating systems may impose a more complex structure on how their files are represented. If you need to convert a file, either to export it to, or to import it from, a non-UNIX system, use dd ('disk-to-disk'). For example, some systems require that files be structured as having a sequence of fixed-size **blocks**, or might use a different character set from ASCII. This command can also perform simple translation of characters — for instance, if you received a file funny, which contains only upper-case letters, then dd can create a file with lower-case letters in place of the upper-case ones:

NOTE

conv = 'convert'
lcase = 'lower case'

```
$ dd conv=lcase < funny
```

You can try this. More seriously, if you do need to read from or write to a file to be used on a non-UNIX system, you should examine the manual page for dd carefully.

Suppose you wished to run a utility with the arguments to that utility piped to it. This might be the case if the arguments were to be split over several lines. A simple example might be if you had a file list containing filenames, and you wished to ls -l each of them. Using the mechanisms so far discussed, the resultant script would be inelegant:

```
$ X=$( cat list ); eval ls -l $X
```

By use of the $(...) mechanism, we have concatenated all the lines of list into a single string, and have passed that string to ls -l. The utility xargs can help: it takes as its arguments a command, and then reading from its standard input appends options to that command, and then runs it. The above example would then become:

```
$ xargs ls -l <list
```

NOTE

find was introduced in
Chapter 7

A more serious, and frequently quoted, example of the use of xargs is in conjunction with find, where with the -exec argument find might create a large number of processes. Suppose your home directory contains a large number of subdirectories, and you wished to perform ls -ld on each of them. One possibility would be:

```
$ find ~ -type d -exec ls -ld {} \;
```

but this would create as many processes as directories — it is inefficient. More effective — and quicker — would be:

```
$ find ~ -type d -print | xargs ls -ld
```

The final three commands that are mentioned in this chapter are introduced for completeness; they are included in the POSIX standard, and you should know of their existence.

There is a command `logger` ('log error message') which can be used to save a message for reading later on by the system administrator. It might be used (say) to inform the administrator if a batch job failed to read a system file correctly; the user would not be in a position to forward the message easily, and the action to be taken would definitely be for the administrator to perform.

Although you are likely to be using UNIX where English is a normal medium of communication, the concept of **locale** is supported whereby both messages from commands and the character set used can be customised to other languages. The command `locale` allows you to examine the current locale, and `localedef` to define a new locale.

NOTE

Unless your administrator has given you specific instructions on how it should be used, you are probably advised not to use `logger`

CHAPTER SUMMARY

Table 9.2   Summary of utilities

`alias`	define or display aliases
`ar`	maintain a library archive
`cksum`	file checksum utility
`comm`	select/reject lines common to two files
`command`	execute a simple command
`ctags`	create a 'tags' file
`dd`	convert file format
`eval`	construct command by concatenating arguments
`exec`	execute command by replacing shell process
`expand`	replace tabs by spaces
`getconf`	get configuration variables
`join`	relational database operator
`locale`	display information about the 'locale'
`localedef`	define the 'locale'
`logger`	log message for the system administrator
`make`	maintain and update groups of programs
`mkfifo`	create a FIFO file
`nm`	display name list of an object file
`pathchk`	check pathname is valid
`return`	return from a function
`split`	split a file into pieces
`strip`	remove unnecessary data from executable files

Table 9.2   (cont.)

`stty`	set terminal options
`trap`	intercept a signal
`unalias`	remove alias definition
`unexpand`	replace spaces by tabs
`uudecode`	decode a file which was coded with `uuencode`
`uuencode`	encode a binary file
`xargs`	construct argument list and execute command

EXERCISES

1 Write a *function* `thisyear` to cause the message `This year is` to be displayed followed by the current year.

2 Write a *function* `changedir` to prompt you for a directory name and `cd` to that directory. Why must you use a function, and not a script?

3 Write a *function* called `addtopath` to request you to type the name of a directory, and if that directory exists and you can read it, to add it to the end of your `PATH`.

4 Write a script to prompt you for the name of a directory, and the email address of a user, and to mail the contents of that directory to that user.

5 Define an alias `debugsh` to have the effect of `sh` with option `-x`.

6 Write a script which will, every minute, display the date and time, but when run in the foreground will terminate if it receives *ctrl-C* three times.

7 Write a script to request you to type in the name of a shell environment variable, and display its value.

Regular expressions and filters

This chapter covers

► regular expressions; and

► simple use of the utilities Grep, Sed and `tr`.

The purpose of this chapter is to consider in detail three powerful UNIX utilities which are usually used as filters (components of a pipeline).

10.1 Using filters

Any command that reads data from standard input and writes data to the standard output stream, is known as a **filter**. Most UNIX utilities are filters, or can be used as such. Most utilities are also simple in their functionality.

Much UNIX programming involves transforming input, of a known form, to output, also of a known form. This output depends on the input in a specified manner, and often involves creating a pipeline. In order to use UNIX effectively, you must develop the skill of being able to choose utilities to pipe together. It is not always obvious why the filters that are 'standard' for UNIX have been developed, but they have been found to be very powerful 'building blocks'. We now examine three filters, all significantly more complex than those we have met before, but whose relevance will be striking.

The editor Vi is an interactive tool, and is one of the few UNIX utilities that cannot be used as a filter. The commands we now look at perform tasks you might consider suitable for an editor such as Vi, but are designed so that they can work as filters.

You may be wondering why, having discussed detailed syntax for the shell, we now need to introduce further commands. After all, we did claim that the shell was a 'full programming language'. In UNIX there are rarely unique solutions to problems, although some techniques are arguably 'better' than others. Most tasks have many possible ways in which a UNIX programmer can solve them, but an experienced programmer will be able to chose a solution that can be implemented fast and efficiently. The purpose of commands such as `grep`, `sed`, `tr` and `awk` is to provide speedy solutions for tasks that are frequently encountered and difficult to program using the shell alone.

Whenever you write a shell script that takes more than a few lines, stand back from the problem for a moment and ask yourself whether some utility will do the job for you. Maybe there isn't, but often you will be able to save yourself time and trouble by recalling a utility you'd almost forgotten about. When you have finished reading this book, go back to the earlier chapters and remind yourself of the commands — such as `comm` and `uniq` — whose usefulness may not then have been apparent.

10.1.1 Collating sequence

Before considering these filters we must digress with some remarks about *characters*. Specifically, we must ask the question: 'how are they ordered?' We have already remarked that to each character is assigned a *code* (normally the ASCII representation), and the ordering of characters corresponds with the numerical order of the codes. So, for instance, the code for `b` is one greater than the code for `a`. There are two possible problems with this: first, it is not necessarily the case that ASCII is being used, and secondly, the code representation — and ordering of characters — is different depending on which native language you speak. Although most UNIX systems use standard English/American, and a standard keyboard, POSIX allows for user interfaces consistent with other languages and equipment. Where, for instance, do accented letters fit in the alphabet, or completely different letters such as Greek? We therefore have a concept called a **collating sequence** which is a specification of the *logical* ordering for the character set you are using. In practice, this ordering applies just to letters and to digits, although it is defined for the whole character set. The collating sequence can be changed in POSIX by amending the **locale**.

In the following discussion we will refer to **ranges**, which are collections of characters that are consecutive within the collating sequence. A range is specified by a *first* and by a *last* character, separated by a hyphen. For instance,

```
b-z
```

refers to the characters between `b` and `z`, inclusive, in the current collating sequence.

NOTE

awk *is discussed in the next chapter*

NOTE

Locale was mentioned in Chapter 7

Characters come in various familiar flavours: there are letters, numbers, punctuation marks, and so on. These are **character classes**, and there is a notation for referring to these classes that is used by some utilities. The form this takes is a name of a class enclosed between [: and :] as shown in Table 10.1

Table 10.1 Character classes

[:alnum:]	letters and digits
[:alpha:]	letters
[:blank:]	usually *Space* and *TAB*
[:cntrl:]	all control characters
[:digit:]	digits
[:graph:]	printable characters excluding *Space*
[:lower:]	lower-case letters
[:print:]	all printable characters
[:punct:]	punctuation marks
[:space:]	whitespace characters
[:upper:]	upper-case letters
[:xdigit:]	hexadecimal digits (0-9A-Fa-f)

10.2 Character-to-character transformation

Translating a file so that specific characters are replaced by others can be accomplished with `tr`. This command takes as arguments two strings, which may consist of any number of individual characters, ranges and character classes. If both strings are the same length, instances of characters in the first string are replaced by the corresponding character in the second. For example, to capitalise all the lower-case letters in the input we would have:

> **NOTE**
>
> *The command* tr *can only be used as a pipe — it cannot take a filename as an argument*

```
tr "a-z" "A-Z"
```

or alternatively

```
tr "[:lower:]" "[:upper:]"
```

Try this out using just standard input and standard output. To capitalise all the words in /usr/dict/words you would have:

```
tr "[:lower:]" "[:upper:]" < /usr/dict/words
```

Worked example 10.1

Write a filter to replace all digits by blank spaces.
Solution: Use [:digit:] to represent digits as first argument to `tr`.

```
tr "[:digit:]" "          "
```

The second argument to `tr` must not be shorter than the first. If the second argument is longer than the first, the excess characters in the second argument disregarded, so that in the pipe

```
tr "a-z" "A-Z123"
```

the characters 1, 2 and 3 are unaffected.

The two arguments to `tr` are strings; as usual, if the strings contain whitespace they must be quoted, and the standard conventions for quoted strings are used. So for a filter to replace all blanks in the input with a B, you could have:

NOTE

At this point you may wish to re-read the section of Chapter 4 that deals with quotes

```
tr ' ' 'B'
```

Remember that between double quotes the characters $, * and @ have special meanings and that certain characters must be escaped. If neither string argument to `tr` includes characters requiring quoting, then the quotes are not needed. The following three filters are equivalent:

```
tr a-z A-Z
tr "a-z" "A-Z"
tr 'a-z' 'A-Z'
```

Although the strings that `tr` is given as arguments do not always require quoting, when the strings contain no characters that are interpreted by the shell in an undesired fashion, it may be helpful to quote them anyway, and from now on we will always quote strings. This has two benefits — firstly, it reminds you to be careful that some characters may need to be escaped in the strings, and secondly it may make it easier to see where the two strings start and finish.

Worked example 10.2

> Write a filter to replace all double quotes by single quotes.
> **Solution**: The tricky part of this example is to specify the strings correctly. The first string is a double quote, but in order for it not to be interpreted by the shell, it must either be preceded by a \ or enclosed by single quotes. The second must also either be escaped with a \ or enclosed in *double* quotes. Either of the following two filters will solve the problem.
>
> ```
> tr '"' "'"
> tr \" \'
> ```

NOTE

This notation is used by `tr` *only*

We can specify a string comprising a number of instances of a single character: `"[X*5]"` is the same as `"XXXXX"`. The notation `"[X*]"` yields a string containing sufficient numbers of the character X so that if used as a component of the second string, the second string is long enough to match the first one. For instance, to replace all digits with a question mark, you could use either of the following:

```
tr "0-9" "[?*10]"
tr "0-9" "[?*]"
```

Worked example 10.3

> Write a filter to replace all letters in the first half of the alphabet by A and all in the second half by Z.
> **Solution**: Use `tr`, and note that there are 13 letters in the first half of the alphabet, each having an upper-case and a lower-case character. Thus the first half of the alphabet is represented by a set of 26 characters.
>
> ```
> tr "A-Ma-mN-Zn-z" "[A*26][Z*26]"
> ```

There are also options available to `tr`; with option `-d` ('delete') and only one string as argument, all occurrences of characters specified by that string are deleted. With option `-c` ('complement') as well as `-d` all characters not occurring within the string are deleted.

Worked example 10.4

> Write a filter to delete all non-letter characters from the input.
> **Solution**: Use `tr` with option `-c` to specify all *non*-alphabetic characters, and `-d` to delete them.
>
> ```
> tr -cd "A-Za-z"
> ```
>
> Alternatively, use character classes:
>
> ```
> tr -cd "[:alpha:]"
> ```

After all other changes have been performed, repeated instances of a character specified in the final string argument can be replaced by single instances of the same character using option `-s` ('squash'). In this case, the string passed to `tr` represents those characters on which this operation is performed. So to replace multiple spaces by single ones:

```
$ echo "hello    there    Chris" | tr -s " "
hello there Chris
```

10.3 Selecting lines by content

10.3.1 Regular expressions

The *pattern matching* described in Chapter 6 is a very simple means of associating many strings which have a common pattern with a single string that describes that pattern. It is fine for matching filenames, and for the use of a `case` statement. However, a more powerful mechanism, known as **regular expressions** or **RE**s, is available for use in certain UNIX utilities.

There are different types of regular expression, and regular expressions can be defined in a variety of ways. UNIX specifies two sorts — a **basic regular expression** (or **BRE**), and an **extended regular expression** (or **ERE**). We start by defining a basic regular expression.

10.3.2 Basic regular expressions

The general idea is just like pattern matching — a BRE consists of a sequence of characters, some of which have a special meaning. The BRE is said to **match** a string if

▶ each part of the BRE with special meaning corresponds to a part of the other string, and

▶ the other individual characters in the BRE and the string correspond.

In order to check whether a BRE matches a string, the two strings are examined working from left to right. Each time a match is found, the corresponding parts of the BRE and the string are discarded and the process continues immediately after.

First of all, we consider how to specify a match for a *single character*. For this we use a BRE called a a **bracket expression**, which is an expression enclosed in square brackets (`[]`). The expression enclosed by the brackets is either a **matching list** or a **nonmatching list**. A matching list consists of a sequence of:

▶ single characters (escaped, if necessary),

▶ ranges (as described above for `tr`),

▶ character classes (as for `tr`)

and a character matches a matching list if it matches any of the patterns that make up that sequence. The following BRE matches the letters a, x, y, z and any digit.

NOTE

`^` *corresponds to* `!` *in pattern matching*

```
[ax-z[:digit:]]
```

If a matching list is preceded by a circumflex (`^`) it becomes a nonmatching list, and matches any character not specified in that list.

```
[^[:upper:]#]
```

will match any character that is neither an upper-case letter nor the symbol `#`. If you wish to specify the hyphen character in a range, you must have it as either the first or the last character in the bracket expression, so that

```
[-xyz]
```

199

will match x, y, z or -. A dot (.), when not enclosed in square brackets, matches any single character. To match a string containing more than one character, you can concatenate characters which you wish to match, dots and bracket expressions. So,

```
[Cc]hris
```

will match Chris or chris, and no other string;

```
[[:alpha:]]..
```

will match any three-character string commencing with a letter. More generally, if you follow a bracket expression (or a single character or a dot) with an asterisk (*), that expression together with the * will match zero or more consecutive occurrences of the expression. So

```
[[:digit:]][[:digit:]][[:digit:]]*
```

will match any string consisting of two or more digits. The two characters ^ and $ are used to indicate the start and end of a string respectively, so

```
^A.*E$
```

will match any string commencing with A and terminating with E, including ANGLE and AbbreviatE, but not DALE or Alpha.

Worked example 10.5

What BRE will match a string that is just a sequence of digits?
Solution: One digit is matched by [[:digit:]], zero or more digits are matched by [[:digit:]]*, and so [[:digit:]][[:digit:]]* will match one or more. The BRE will commence with ^ and end with $, to indicate that this is *exactly* what the string will contain, and will not have other characters at the start or at the end. The answer is therefore

```
^[[:digit:]][[:digit:]]*$
```

10.3.3 Extended regular expressions

Basic regular expressions are sufficient for most purposes, but a more sophisticated form of regular expression is available known as an **extended regular expression** or **ERE**. There are a couple of principal extra features available using EREs that are unavailable to BREs.

The symbol +, following a bracket expression (or single character or dot) indicates one or more consecutive occurrences of the expression, in the same way that * indicates zero or more. The symbol ?, in the same context, indicates zero or one occurrences of that expression, so

```
[[:alpha:]]+[[:digit:]]?
```

NOTE

The ? is not to be confused with the ? in pattern matching

matches any string commencing with a letter, consisting only of letters, and terminated optionally by a single digit.

If two EREs are separated by a | (vertical bar), the result matches either of those two EREs. Parentheses may be used to group subexpressions together:

```
(xyz|ab)\.c
```

will match either `xyz.c` or `ab.c`, and no other string. If you need a parenthesis to be a matched character in an ERE you must escape it.

Worked example 10.6

> Write an ERE to match any string consisting either of only upper-case letters or only lower-case letters.
>
> **Solution**: As in the previous worked example, the expression will commence with ^ and end with $. By taking advantage of the symbol + a match for upper-case letters would be `[[:upper:]]+` and `[[:lower:]]+` for lower-case letters. A sequence of letters of the same case will be matched by `([[:upper:]]+|[[:lower:]]+))`, and a solution is therefore:
>
> ```
> ^[[:lower:]]+|[[:upper:]]+$
> ```

ACRONYM

Grep refers to the ex
command g/*RE*/p

10.3.4 Grep

We have defined regular expressions; in order to use them, we begin with a utility called Grep. The function of Grep is to select lines from its input (either standard input or named files given as arguments) that match a BRE normally given as first argument to `grep`. The BRE is known as a **script**. Those lines of input that match the BRE are then copied to standard output. For instance, to print out all words ending in `ise` or `ize` from `/usr/dict/words`, you could have:

NOTE

Single quotes needed here as $ *is in the BRE*

```
$ grep 'i[sz]e$' /usr/dict/words
```

With option `-E`, grep will use EREs instead of BREs. With option `-F`, grep uses only *fixed* strings — there are no regular expressions, the string given as argument to `grep` is matched against the input exactly as it appears. With option `-c`, instead of copying matched lines to standard output, a count of the number of matched lines is displayed instead.

Worked example 10.7

> How many words in `/usr/dict/words` begin with a vowel?
> **Solution**: Use `grep` with option `-c` to select and then count lines beginning with upper-case or lower-case vowels. The BRE contains a

list of all such vowels, preceded with a ˆ to indicate that the vowel must be at the start of each word:

```
$ grep -c 'ˆ[AEIOUaeiou]' /usr/dict/words
```

NOTE

On some non-POSIX systems separate commands egrep *('Extended GREP') and* fgrep *('Fixed GREP') are used instead of* grep -E *and* grep -F

Option -i ('insensitive') causes grep to ignore the case of letters when checking for matches, and overrides any explicit specification regarding upper-case and lower-case letters in the regular expression. Thus a solution to the previous worked example could be:

```
$ grep -ci 'ˆ[aeiou]' /usr/dict/words
```

With option -f ('file') followed by a filename, regular expressions contained in that file are used instead of being given as an argument to grep. If the file contains more than one regular expression, then Grep selects lines that match any of the REs in the file. This is the preferred method by which Grep can select lines where there is a choice of matching specifications.

The 'reverse behaviour' — namely displaying those lines not matching the RE specified — can be enabled with option -v ('inVert'). This is often simpler than constructing a new regular expression. An example of this being useful might be to a FORTRAN programmer. A program written in the computer language FORTRAN treats any line starting with a C as a comment; if you were examining such a program, and wished to search for lines of code containing some identifier, and were not interested in the lines of comments, you might wish to use

```
grep -v 'ˆC'
```

to strip out the comments to begin with.

If grep is given several files as arguments, option -l ('list') displays a list of those files containing a matching line, rather than those lines themselves.

Worked example 10.8

Suppose you have saved many mail messages in files in the current directory, and you want to check which file or files contain messages whose subject is something to do with 'examinations'. Each mail message contains a line beginning with the string Subject: followed by the subject of the message (if any).

Solution: We require grep -l followed by a BRE followed by * to list the filenames. The following lines might occur as the 'subject' lines of the messages:

```
Subject: Examinations
```

```
Subject: examinations
Subject: NEXT MONTH'S EXAMS
Subject: Exams
```

These all have a common string, namely exam, in upper-case or lower-case (or a mixture of cases). So, to match these lines, a BRE is required to recognise Subject: at the start of the line, followed by some characters (possibly none), followed by exam in any mixture of cases. The Subject: at the start of the line is matched by ^Subject and .* matches the characters between that and exam. In order to ensure that the cases of the letters in exam do not matter, you can either explicitly match them with [Ee][Xx][Aa][Mm], or you can instruct grep to be 'case-insensitive' with option -i. The following two solutions would be acceptable:

```
grep -l '^Subject: .*[Ee][Xx][Aa][Mm]' *
grep -li '^Subject: .*exam' *
```

Note that this is not an infallible solution. It will also select files with subjects related to counterexamples and hexameters, and will not find a file with subject examinations. When using UNIX tools to process data from electronic mail or other documents containing English text, you must be conscious of human fallibility. Some solutions will of necessity be approximate.

10.4 Stream editor

ACRONYM

Sed = 'Stream EDitor'

Whereas Grep selects lines from input and copies those lines to standard output, Sed will in addition change those lines if required. Just as with Grep, Sed takes a **script** either as an argument, or from a file by using option -f, and filters its input according to the instructions in that script. For Grep, the script consists simply of one or more BREs, and the output is formed of those lines of input matching one or more of those BREs. For Sed, the behaviour is more complex. Each Sed instruction is of the form

address command arguments

NOTE

You may wish to re-read this paragraph after you have completed this section

where *address* and/or *arguments* are optional. The *address* indicates which lines of the input *command* is to be performed on.

Actually, we need to be slightly more precise than this. Each time a line of input is read, it is first of all stored in an area called the **pattern space**. The instructions forming the script are then examined one-by-one, in order, and each instruction whose *address* matches the address of the input line has its command applied to whatever is currently in the pattern space. When all the instructions in the script have been examined, the contents of the pattern space are copied to the standard output, and the pattern space emptied ready for the next input line. This is repeated for the next line of input until the input is exhausted.

The simplest Sed script is the script containing nothing; since there are no instructions, an input line is copied to the pattern space which is then immediately copied to the standard output. Try it:

```
$ sed ''
```

Addresses for Sed come in several forms, as itemised in Table 10.2.

Table 10.2   Sed addresses

empty	matches *all* lines
number	matches input line *number*
number1,number2	matches all lines in the range from *number1* to *number2* inclusive
$	matches the *last* input line, and can also be used in place of *number2* in the previous type of address
/*BRE*/	matches any line matched by BRE

Both ^ and $ can be used. To try some of these addresses, the easiest command we can use is probably d to *delete* the contents of the pattern space. So

```
sed '1,4d'
```

deletes lines 1 to 4 inclusive from the input. Try the following using the standard input:

```
sed 'd'       deletes all the input
sed '3d'      deletes line 3 only
sed '2,$d'    deletes all lines except the first
sed '/^A/d'   deletes all lines commencing A
```

An often used command is s ('substitute'), which is used to exchange part of a line (specified by a BRE) with another string. This command is used as follows:

s/*BRE*/*replacement*/

The pattern space is searched from left to right to find an instance of the BRE. If none is found, no change is made, otherwise the string that matches the BRE is replaced by the *replacement*. Normally only the first occurrence of the BRE is altered, but if you follow the command with g ('global') then *all* matches for the BRE in the pattern space are changed. Note that after the change, the altered string stays in the pattern space and can then be changed by later Sed commands in the same script. So, for example,

```
$ sed 's/Chris/Sam/g'
```

changes all occurrences of Chris to Sam,

```
$ sed 's/^= /?/'
```

changes each equals symbol at the start of a line to a question-mark, and

```
$ sed 's/[:punct:]//g'
```

removes all punctuation (equivalent to tr -d "[:punct:]").

Worked example 10.9

> Write a Sed command to remove all whitespace that terminates lines.
> **Solution**: The BRE [:blank:] matches a single whitespace
> character, [:blank:]* matches any number of them, and
> [:blank:]*$ when they occur at the end of a line. To delete them
> we replace them by nothing.
>
> ```
> sed 's/[:blank:]*$//'
> ```

Although it is most common for simple Sed commands to be applied to all lines of the input, you should also be familiar with being able to specify addresses of lines. Sometimes an editing problem can be solved either by a complex edit on every line of input or by a simple edit on only some of the input lines — the latter approach is preferable.

Worked example 10.10

> Write a filter to precede each word in /usr/dict/words containing a
> capital letter by an asterisk.
> **Solution**: Using Sed we can match lines containing such words by the
> BRE [A-Z]. Using this BRE to specify addresses, on those lines we
> can use s to substitute the start of each line (^) by a *:
>
> ```
> $ sed '/[A-Z]/s/^/*/' </usr/dict/words
> ```
>
> It is usual for Sed to be an element of a pipeline but, unlike tr, Sed
> can take a filename as argument, in which case the input will come
> from that file. So another solution would be:
>
> ```
> $ sed '/[A-Z]/s/^/*/' /usr/dict/words
> ```

If an ampersand (&) is met as part of the replacement string, it is replaced by the string that has been matched; the following will enclose each capital letter in the input by square brackets:

```
$ sed 's/[A-Z]/[&]/g'
```

If you want an actual ampersand to occur in the replacement string, it must be escaped by preceding it with a backslash.

If you give sed option -n ('noprint') then the pattern space will not automatically be sent to standard output; so sed -n '' will not give any output at all. We can use command p ('print') to copy the pattern space explicitly to standard output; so the following two commands are equivalent:

```
sed ''
sed -n 'p'
```

See what happens if you have just:

```
sed 'p'
```

We can use p to good effect if we wish to select only part of the input, so

```
sed '15p'
```

will display line 15 of the input only, and

```
sed '1,10s/[:alpha:]//g'
```

will display the first ten lines only, with all letters deleted. By using option -n, we can simulate simple use of Grep using Sed, since the following are equivalent:

```
grep 'BRE'
sed -n '/BRE/p'
```

Worked example 10.11

Write a filter to display the last line of the input prepended by The last line is.
Solution: Use $ to match the last line of input, option -n of sed to ignore other lines in the input, and command p to print it out after substituting The last line is for the beginning of the line:

```
sed -n '$s/^/The last line is /p'
```

10.5 Splitting a file according to context

We have already met split as a method of splitting a file into smaller units, and have indicated its use when mailing large text files. Another reason for splitting a file is if you know that the file contains separate identifiable portions. For instance, suppose you had a simple text file consisting of paragraphs of English separated by blank lines, and you wanted the paragraphs to be in separate files. The blank lines would identify where to break the file, and you can specify a blank line by means of the BRE, `^$`.

ACRONYM

csplit = 'context split'

The command `csplit` splits a file into sections where the sections either contain specified numbers of lines or are delimited by text that can be described by a basic regular expression. To start with a simple example,

```
$ csplit data 10
```

will take file `data`, and create two new files called `xx00` and `xx01`. File `xx00` will contain lines 1 through 9 of file `data`, and `xx01` will contain line 10 up to the end of file `data`. File `data` remains unaltered. When each new file is created, `csplit` will print the size (in bytes) of that file, on the standard error stream (this can be suppressed with option `-s`). ('silent')

The first argument to `csplit` is the name of a file (or `-` (hyphen) if standard input) and the following one or more arguments indicate where the file is to be split. An argument that is a line number instructs a break to be made at the beginning of that line (hence in the previous example line 10 is sent to the second file). The new, smaller, files are named `xx`*nn*, where *nn* starts at `00` and counts upwards. With option `-f` followed by a string that string will be used as the **prefix** instead of `xx`. Any number of arguments can follow the filename.

Worked example 10.12

Split `/usr/dict/words` into three files called `words00`, `words01` and `words02`, the first two containing 10000 lines, the final one containing the rest of `/usr/dict/words`.
Solution: Use `csplit` to split the file with option `-f` to specify that the prefix is `words`. The next argument is `/usr/dict/words`, and this is to be split at lines 10001 and 20001.

```
$ csplit -f words /usr/dict/words 10001 20001
```

Now use `wc` to check that the files you have created are of the specified length:

```
$ wc words??
```

The three files you have created are fairly big, so don't forget to delete them.

If an argument to `csplit` is a number *n* and is then followed immediately by an argument of the form {*count*}, then it will be split at line *n* and then repeatedly every **n** lines up to a maximum of *count* times. Delete any previous **xx** files you have created, and try the following:

```
$ csplit -s /usr/dict/words 1000 {2}
$ wc -l xx??
```

You will see that /usr/dict/words has been split into four files. The first split is at the start of line 1000, so the first file is 999 lines long, then the subsequent two splits are each 1000 lines longer. The final file **xx03** contains the rest of /usr/dict/words.

If you specify that the file be split at too many places, no split files will be created and an error message will be generated. For instance, to try to split /usr/dict/words into 50 files of 10000 lines each (which we clearly cannot do):

NOTE

82985 *is the number of bytes in* xx01, *etc.*

```
$ csplit /usr/dict/words 10000 {50}
82985
82982
csplit: {50} - out of range
```

The reason for this behaviour is to encourage you to be aware of how you are splitting your files, and `csplit` errs on the side of caution. Mistakes when specifying the arguments to `csplit` would otherwise be prone to causing large volumes of unwanted split files to be generated, thus wasting valuable storage space. There are some instances, however, when this behaviour is undesirable, especially when the length of a file is not initially known. If you give `csplit` option `-k` it will warn you if you try to split the input file too many times, but it will create the **xx** files anyway. So, to split /usr/dict/words into as many files as possible each containing (roughly) 5000 lines:

```
$ csplit -k /usr/dict/words 5000 {10000}
```

Worked example 10.13

Split /usr/dict/words into three files called w0, w1 and w2, each containing a roughly equal number of lines.
Solution: Use `wc` to count the lines in /usr/dict/words, then arithmetic expansion to calculate one-third and two-thirds of that number.

```
$ LINES=$( wc -l < /usr/dict/words )
$ ONETHIRD=$(( $LINES / 3 ))
$ TWOTHIRDS=$(( $ONETHIRD + $ONETHIRD ))
```

```
$ csplit -f w -n 1 /usr/dict/words $ONETHIRD
$TWOTHIRDS
```

When performing wc we redirected the standard input from the file /usr/dict/words; by doing that, wc does not include the filename on its output. Had we used wc -l /usr/dict/words it would have been necessary to pipe the output to cut in order to isolate the first field, as the output from wc would have included the filename /usr/dict/words.

An argument to csplit can be a basic regular expression enclosed between two / (slash) symbols, in which case the file being split will be broken at the start of the next line matching that expression.

Worked example 10.14

Split /usr/dict/words into two files, the first containing all words commencing with characters up to and including m, the second containing words commencing n through z.
Solution: Use csplit with argument '/^[Nn]/' indicating that /usr/dict/words should be split at the start of the first line commencing either N or n.

```
$ csplit /usr/dict/words '/^[Nn]/'
```

Consider the problem posed at the start of the section, namely splitting a text file into paragraphs. The BRE that denotes a blank line is ^$, so if we have in file X some such text, we might have:

```
$ csplit X '/^$/'
```

This will not work; it will split the file at the first blank line only. Just as with number arguments we can follow a BRE argument to csplit by a number in braces, to indicate that the split should occur multiple times. If we don't know how big X is, we must use option -k as above:

```
$ csplit -k X '/^$/' {10000}
```

Create a small file containing a few paragraphs of text and try this command.

Worked example 10.15

The file book contains the text for a book, with each of 10 chapters commencing with a line starting Chapter ... so:

```
Title: ...
 ...
Chapter 1: Introduction
 ...
Chapter 2: Getting started
 ...
```

Split this file into several files, called `chapter00`, etc., one for each chapter.

Solution: Use `csplit` with option `-f` (to denote the names of the split files), and split at the start of each line commencing `Chapter`. The split will need to be repeated an extra 9 times:

```
$ csplit -f chapter book '/^Chapter/' {9}
```

10.6 Choosing between the three filters

It will be apparent that anything Grep or `tr` can do, Sed can also do (though possibly not as elegantly). Why do we need Grep and `tr`?

Speed may be important if the data you wish to filter is large, or your UNIX system is small and not very powerful. Since Sed does more than the other two utilities, it is almost certainly slower. Unless you really need the facilities offered by Sed, then it will be easier to remember how to use the other two utilities. Extended regular expressions are only available to Grep. Finally, some operations are not easy to perform using Sed — try coding the following using only Sed:

```
tr A-Z a-z
grep -l abc *
```

10.7 More on Vi

At this point, mention should be made of Vi commands which are almost identical to those of Sed, and which rely on BREs. First of all, / and ? are used for searching for strings. Followed by a BRE, each will locate the next (or previous) string matching that BRE. So, to move the cursor to the next blank line, and assuming you are in command-mode, type

```
/^$
```

or, if the apparently blank lines in your file may contain spaces also,

```
/^ *$
```

In colon-mode the commands available are, like Sed, of the form

address command arguments

Addresses constructed are the same as for Sed, with the addition of two extra symbols. These are ^, which means the first line of the file, and . (*dot*), denoting the current line as indicated by the cursor.

There is a command s ('substitute') which can be used to exchange occurrences of a string (denoted by a BRE) for another string. Suppose that, in the file you are editing, the cursor is on a line containing

```
Jack and Jill went up the hill
```

you could swap up for down by

```
:s/up/down/
```

The : gets you into colon-mode, s is the command to perform a substitution, and following s are three slashes. Between the first two is the BRE you wish to be changed. Between the final two is the string (just a string, not a BRE) it is to be changed to.

Normally, a substitution will occur once on the current line. That is, the address . is assumed by default. If the BRE to be substituted does not exist, then no change will happen. If you follow the command by a g ('global') the substitution will be made for all occurrences of the BRE on that line. So, to change all words on the current line commencing J to the string someone, you would type

```
:s/J[a-zA-Z]*/someone/g
```

Before a substitution command you can indicate which lines it is to be performed on by indicating an address explicitly. Preceding the command with % (percent) will cause it to be performed on every line in the file, but preceding it by a single line number will do the substitution on that line only. A pair of line numbers, separated by a comma, will apply the substitution to that range of lines. The start of the file is denoted by ^ and the end by $. Thus

```
:10,20s/Hello/Bonjour/
```

will substitute the first occurrence of Hello for Bonjour on lines 10 through 20 inclusive.

Worked example 10.16

> You are using Vi to edit a file, and wish to change all occurrences of Chris to Sam on all lines.
>
> **Solution**: Use the substitution command in colon-mode, and apply it from the start of the file to the end, and globally on every line:
>
> ```
> :^,$s/Chris/Sam/g
> ```
>
> Be careful if your file contains (say) Christine — this solution changes it to Samtine

NOTE

The symbol % can be used instead of ^,$ to mean the whole of the file

The Vi colon-mode commands which were discussed in Chapter 4 can be preceded by an address and/or followed by arguments. The command w assumes the address %, and so will normally write the whole file; if a filename follows the w as an argument to the command, it will be that file written to, and the original file will remain unchanged. The command

```
:1,10w   xyz
```

will write the first ten lines of the file to the file named xyz.

Often you will wish to perform an action on many lines, and the same action on each. The colon mode command g ('global') is used to apply a command to all lines matching a regular expression:

```
:g/BRE/action
```

For instance, to delete all completely empty lines,

```
:g/^$/d
```

or to insert an asterisk at the start of each line containing Chris

```
:g/Chris/s/^/*/
```

CHAPTER SUMMARY

Table 10.3
Commands introduced
in this chapter

csplit	split a file according to context
grep	select lines matching regular expression
sed	stream editor
tr	translate characters

EXERCISES

1 Write a filter to extract from /usr/dict/words all words containing all five vowels in alphabetical order.

2 A utility known as rot13 is a very simple encryption mechanism which replaces every letter by the letter 13 further on (or previous to it) in the alphabet. Thus

The quick brown fox jumped over the lazy dog

would be changed to

Gur dhvpx oebja sbk whzcrq bire gur ynml qbt

Write a script to encrypt standard input using the rot13 algorithm.

3 List the names of all files (excluding directories) in the current *directory which contain the string* `program` (or some other string).

4 The file `/etc/group` contains lines of the form
group-name GID list-of-members
For instance, a line defining group `ateam`, with group ID 99, and consisting of users `chris`, `jo` and `sam`, would be

```
ateam:99:chris,jo,sam
```

Write a script to list the names of all the groups of which `jo` is a member.

5 Write a filter, `numbers`, which considers its input as consisting of whole numbers (containing only digits), together with other text, and displays a list of those numbers, one per line, sorted into numerical order with duplicates removed, so:

```
$ numbers <<END
1st Blankshire Bank Ltd.,
17-19 High Street,
Anytown,
Blanks.,
AN1 4GQ.
END
1
4
17
19
```

6 How many words in `/usr/dict/words` contain at least three vowels?

7 Split the file `/usr/dict/words` into two halves, the first containing all words up to (but not including) `middle`, the second containing the rest.

Awk

This chapter

▶ introduces simple use of Awk.

The utility known as Awk, and described as a 'pattern scanning and processing language', is a complete programming language, with a syntax resembling that of C.

It can be studied as a language in its own right, or can be integrated into shell programming when other utilities are found to lack sufficient power or flexibility.

11.1 What is 'awk'?

If you are familiar with high-level programming languages, you will recognise the need for such constructs as loops, variables, conditional statements, input and output facilities, and a library of predefined procedures; in other words, a rich syntax allowing many complex tasks to be performed easily and efficiently by an experienced programmer. The shell is a high-level language, although its features are tailored to a very special task, namely managing UNIX processes, and many high-level constructs are not present in the shell.

If you need to write a program that is not clearly suited to writing in the shell, you would normally choose a language such as C or Pascal in which to write it. There is a grey area, though, where the application does seem to fit in well with the ideas and methods underlying shell programming, yet the power of a full high-level language would be advantageous. A typical situation would be where the contents of a file (or output from a pipe) contains complex (numerical or textual) data, organised into records (e.g. lines) and fields (e.g. columns), and calculations are required to be performed on the data.

To illustrate this, consider data which has as its columns a person's name, followed by numbers representing that person's marks in a number of examinations. You need to process that data to determine each person's overall mark, possibly converting it to a grade, and to calculate overall statistical data for the individual examinations. Perhaps you would like a graphical display of the mark distribution. These tasks could be performed with the shell (with some difficulty), but they can be programmed naturally using Awk.

Mention has been made before of the language C — if you can program in C then Awk will look familiar to you, and vice versa. There are features of Awk, such as pattern matching and associative arrays, which are not available with C, and vice versa. If you write a program in C, then it will probably execute faster than an equivalent program in Awk. You should therefore bear in mind that significant differences do exist, and take care not to confuse the two. There is insufficient space in this book to examine Awk in great detail, so we shall concentrate on those features of Awk which complement the other shell utilities.

11.2 Invoking 'awk'

Just as with Grep and Sed, simple use of Awk involves a **script** containing the commands that Awk uses. This script can either be a string that is an argument to `awk`, or can be contained in a file named by option `-f`.

The data which the Awk script will process is either piped from standard input, or is contained in one or more files given as arguments to the command. The data is divided into **records**, each of which is subdivided into **fields**. Unless otherwise stated, each record is a single line of the data, and fields will be separated by whitespace. For instance, to represent students with their marks, a dataset might look like:

```
Cringle Chris 14 75 33
Smith Sam 56 58 45
Jones Jo 9 63 51
```

This data contains three records (lines), each record containing five fields (columns of text). An Awk script consists of a sequence of pairs

pattern { *action* }

where either the *pattern* or the *action* can be omitted. The data is read, record by record, and each record that *matches* a pattern in the script causes the corresponding action to be performed. If the pattern is omitted the action is performed on every single line of input data. For the rest of this chapter we shall concentrate on the format of the script, and assume that data is piped from standard input. The simplest Awk script is

```
{ }
```

which will do precisely nothing for each line of data — the effect is indistinguishable from `cat >/dev/null`. It can be invoked either by creating a file (say `awkfile`) containing a single line, namely the pair of braces, and

```
awk -f awkfile
```

or by

```
awk '{ }'
```

where the script is a string following `awk`. For the rest of this chapter, the word *script* will refer to an Awk script (not a shell script), unless otherwise stated.

11.3 Naming the fields

In a shell script, `$1` , `$2`, etc., name the arguments of the script, but in an Awk script `$1`, `$2`, etc., name the fields of each record of data. The whole record is referred to as `$0`. To cause Awk to display something on standard output the command `print` can be used. Whenever the action `print` is performed, a *Newline* character is always displayed afterwards, just like the shell command `echo`. The following script copies standard input to standard output:

```
{ print $0 }
```

Worked example 11.1

> Write a shell script to run Awk to display the first field of each line of standard input.
> **Solution**: The Awk script is simple for this task, so we can enclose it within single quotes in the shell script. The Awk action is `print $1` to be performed on each line. The Awk pattern to match every line is the null pattern, so that the Awk script becomes
>
> ```
> { print $1 }
> ```
>
> To run Awk from a shell script, we require the utility `awk`, followed by this script (enclosed in quotes). Don't forget the comments!
>
> ```
> # This shell script prints the first field of each
> #   line of standard input
> awk '{ print $1 }'
> ```

If you give `print` several arguments, it will concatenate their values before displaying them. The following Awk script displays each line of input enclosed in parentheses:

```
{ print "(" $0 ")" }
```

so for input

```
hello there
Chris
```

the output would be:

```
(hello there)
(Chris)
```

11.4 Formatted output

You will recall the use of `printf` as a shell utility for displaying information on standard output in a format you specify. For instance

$ printf "Hello %s!\n" $LOGNAME

will print on your screen

```
Hello chris!
```

NOTE

printf *never displays a Newline unless explicitly instructed to do so*

The *shell* utility `printf` takes a number of arguments: the first is a string specifying the *format* of the output, the second and subsequent arguments are data (such as values of variables) to be displayed according to the specification given by the format string.

In Awk there is also a command called `printf`, which is almost identical to that used by the shell. The only major difference is that the arguments are separated by commas, not by whitespace. Try this script:

```
{ printf "The first field is %s\n", $1 }
```

Worked example 11.2

Write an Awk script which, when given input in two columns representing a person's first name followed by their family name, such as

```
Abraham Lincoln
John Kennedy
Benjamin Disraeli
```

will reverse the order of the names, and separate them with a comma:

```
Lincoln, Abraham
Kennedy, John
Disraeli, Benjamin
```

Solution: Using $1 and $2 to represent the first name and the family name of each person, display them using `printf` thus:

```
{ printf "%s, %s\n", $2, $1 }
```

Alternatively, using `print`, this would be

```
{ print $2 ", " $1 }
```

Before we can experiment much further with Awk, we need some data. Consider the problem of a grocery bill — you have purchased some vegetables that are priced per kilogram, and you buy a number of kilograms of various different vegetables. Create a file containing in column 1 the names of vegetables, in column 2 the price per kilogram, and in column 3 the number of kilograms purchased, something like:

```
potatoes 0.50 5
carrots 0.80 2.5
peas 2.20 1
beans 2.10 2
artichokes 8.50 0.5
sweetcorn 0.90 3
```

Name this file `vegetables`. We shall use this file, and Awk, to perform tasks such as totalling the cost for each vegetable, and evaluating the total bill. Recall that when using `printf` to format an integer you use the format specifier `%d`; for a **floating-point** number the specifier is `%f`. You can also require a floating-point number to be displayed to a specific accuracy — if you include between the `%` symbol and the `f` a dot followed by a number, the floating-point number will be displayed with that number of digits after the decimal place. So we could copy the file `vegetables` using

```
{ printf "%s %.2f %.1f\n", $1, $2, $3 }
```

Try this, using

```
$ awk '{ printf "%s %.2f %.1f\n", $1, $2, $3 }' \
< vegetables
```

Note what happens when you have a whole number as one of the last two columns — it is printed with the relevant number of decimal places containing zeros:

```
potatoes 0.50 5.0
carrots 0.80 2.5
peas 2.20 1.0
beans 2.10 2.0
artichokes 8.50 0.5
sweetcorn 0.90 3.0
```

Simple arithmetic can be performed by Awk, with the same operators and conventions as `bc`. These are listed in Table 11.1. To evaluate the number of seconds in a day and print it out, the following would suffice:

```
$ awk '{ print 24*60*60 }'
```

Try it — but remember that this will be done for each line of input, so if you pipe the contents of a file to this command, the output will have the

*Table 11.1 Operators
used by Awk*

+	addition
−	subtraction
*	multiplication
/	division
%	integer remainder
^	power
==	is equal to
!=	is not equal to
>	is greater than
>=	is greater than or equal to
<	is less than
<=	is less than or equal to
&&	and
||	or

same number of lines as the input, each line being the number 86400. If you just wish to do an arithmetic calculation, use bc.

Worked example 11.3

Write an Awk script to reformat the data in `vegetables` as follows:

```
I bought 5.0 kilos of potatoes at 50p per kilo
I bought 2.5 kilos of carrots at 80p per kilo
  ...
```

Solution: Use `printf` with the `%f` specifier to display the 'number of kilos' field to one decimal place accuracy, and calculating the number of pence per kilo as 100 times the price in pounds. Since the pence per kilo is an integer, use the `%d` format specifier.

```
{ printf "I bought %.1f kilos of %s at %dp per kilo\n",
        $3, $1, 100*$2 }
```

If you wish to do floating-point arithmetic in Awk, and your script contains some whole numbers, then Awk will automatically convert those integers to floating-point numbers when it is sensible to do so. Thus 1/2 will evaluate to 0.5. Similarly, if Awk is expecting a field to be a string, and receives a number as input instead, that number will be treated as a string of digits (together with decimal point or minus sign, if appropriate).

Worked example 11.4

Write an Awk script which uses the data in `vegetables` to calculate
the total amount of money spent on each vegetable, displaying it in
the following format:

```
potatoes cost 2.50
carrots cost 2.00
 ...
```

Solution: We can calculate the total cost for each vegetable by
multiplying the second and third fields together.

```
{ printf "%s cost %.2f\n", $1, $2*$3 }
```

Earlier on, we used `cut` to extract fields from lines of input. You may
find it easier to use Awk in some instances.

Worked example 11.5

Display the current year.
Solution: We could use `date` and pipe the output to `cut`, as before,
or we could use a format argument with `date`. Another method is to
pipe the output of `date` to `awk`, using `awk` to print out the sixth field.

```
$ date | awk '{ print $6 }'
```

For comparison, the other two methods would be written:

```
$ date | cut -d' ' -f6
$ date +"%Y"
```

It is up to you to decide which one you think is clearest.

11.5 Patterns

In the previous examples, we have performed a task on every line of the
standard input by using a null pattern. There are two simple patterns
that are very useful — they are called BEGIN and END. An action
associated with pattern BEGIN will be executed once, when the awk script
starts and before any lines are read from the standard input. The action
associated with END is performed after all other actions, and immediately
prior to awk terminating. The following Awk script will copy its standard
input to the standard output, but also write Start of file at the
beginning of the output, and End of file at the end:

NOTE

*Just as in shell scripts,
comments can, and
should, be inserted into
Awk scripts*

```
BEGIN { print "Start of file" } # Done at the start
{ print $0 }                     # for each line of input
END { print "End of file" }      # done at the end
```

NOTE

See Chapter 10 for a
detailed discussion of
regular expressions

Try this with the input coming from `vegetables`. More generally, many sorts of pattern are available. An ERE enclosed between slashes (/) is a pattern which will match any line of input matched by that ERE. So to print the cost per kilo of every vegetable whose name commences with a vowel, we could have

```
/^[aeiou]/ { printf "%s costs %.2f per kilo\n", $1, $2 }
```

The pattern specified by the ERE normally applies to the whole record. It can be restricted to a single field by preceding the ERE with the field number and a tilde. Since in the above example we are interested in the first field commencing with a vowel, we could restrict the pattern match to the first field thus:

```
$1 ~ /^[aeiou]/ { printf "%s costs %.2f per kilo\n", $1,$2 }
```

The behaviour of Grep can be mimicked by Awk — the following two shell commands have the same effect:

```
grep -E 'ERE'
awk '/ERE/ { print $0 }'
```

The pattern can also be an expression that evaluates to true or to false. The following displays the cost per kilo of all expensive (more than 1 pound per kilo) vegetables:

```
$2 > 1.00 { printf "%s costs %.2f per kilo\n", $1, $2 }
```

Worked example 11.6

Display the total costs for vegetables only if that cost is at least 2.50. **Solution**: For each line, evaluate the total cost (`$2*$3`), and perform `printf` if that value is greater than or equal to 2.50:

```
$2*$3 >= 2.50 { printf "%s cost %.2f\n", $1, $2*$3 }
```

More complicated patterns can be constructed using `&&` ('and') and `||` ('or'). These are *boolean* operators:

expression1 **&&** *expression2*

is true if both *expression1* and *expression2* are true, whereas

expression1 **||** *expression2*

is true if either *expression1* or *expression2* is true, or if both are true.

Worked example 11.7

Display the names of each vegetable purchased which either cost at most 1 pound per kilo, or for which less than 1 kilo was purchased.
Solution:

```
$2 <= 1 || $3 < 1 { printf "%s\n", $1 }
```

11.6 Variables

11.6.1 Accessing Values

In the shell, we use variables, which we name, and access their values by placing a dollar before their names. In Awk we also have variables, to which we can assign values in the same way as the shell, but to *use* a variable we do not need the dollar. The reason that the shell needs the dollar is a technical one, relating to ensuring that each shell statement is unambiguous. The ambiguities that might arise in the shell do not occur in Awk.

Suppose we require a total grocery bill. We could use a variable (`total`, say) to keep a 'running total' of the cost of each vegetable and print it out at the end:

```
# Initialise total to 0
BEGIN { total = 0 }

# For each line of input, that is, each vegetable, add
# the total cost to variable total
{ total = total + $2*$3 }

# At the end, print out the total
END { printf "Total cost is %.2f\n", total}
```

Some explanation is required for the action `total = total + $2*$3`: the *current* value stored in the variable `total` has the values of `$2*$3` added to it, and the resulting number is stored back in `total`. So the value of the variable `total` has been updated. Another way of stating this action is to use the symbol `+=`, so:

```
total += $2*$3
```

Thus, `total += ...` is just shorthand for `total = total + ...`
Analogous to `+=` are `-=`, `*=`, `/=`, `%=` and `^=` .

Worked example 11.8

Calculate the average price per kilo of the vegetables you have purchased.

Solution: We need to total the amount of money spent, and also the number of kilograms. The final answer is calculated by dividing one by the other.

```
# Use variable totalcost for the money spent
# Use variable totalweight for the total kilos
# Initialise totalcost and totalweight to 0
BEGIN { totalcost = 0
        totalweight = 0 }

# For each line of input update the running totals
{ totalcost = totalcost + $2*$3 }   # Cost
{ totalweight = totalweight + $3 }  # Weight

# At the end, print out the average
END { printf "Average cost is %.2f pounds per kilo\n",
        totalcost/totalweight}
```

11.6.2 Special variables

Just as the shell can use predefined variables such as HOME, so can Awk. There are many of these, all of which use capital letters only (so variable names you choose yourself should use lower-case letters). Some of them, which we discuss here, are listed in Table 11.2.

Table 11.2
Predefined Awk
variables

FILENAME	The pathname of the current input file
FS	Input field separator, usually *Space*
NF	Number of fields in current record
NR	Number of current record from start of input
FNR	Number of current record from start of current input file
OFS	Output field separator used by **print**, usually *Space*
ORS	Output record separator used by **print**, usually *Newline*

ACRONYM

NR = *'number of record'*

Each input record is counted, starting at 1. Given that the variable NR contains the number of the current record, the following script will prepend each input line with the line number (unless otherwise specified, a record is assumed to be a single line). The format is that of cat -n, where six spaces are allowed for the line numbers, which are separated from the line contents by two blanks. The format specification %6d indicates an integer right-justified within six spaces.

```
{ printf "%6d  %s\n", NR, $0 }
```

Try this Awk script, and also `cat -n`, with a file such as `vegetables`.

Worked example 11.9

> Using `awk`, select the first three lines of standard input, in the
> manner of `head -3`.
>
> **Solution**: Display only those lines whose number, as given by `NR`, is at
> most three. When `NR` is equal to three, the program should finish —
> otherwise it will continue reading input until the input terminates.
> The action `exit` causes `awk` to terminate.
>
> ```
> NR <= 3 { print $0 }
> NR == 3 { exit }
> ```

ACRONYM

FNR = *'File Number of
Record'*

The variable `NR` starts off with value 1 on the first line of input, and
continues counting however many files you have given as argument to `awk`.
There is another variable `FNR`, which is similar to `NR`, but is reset to 1
each time a new file is read as input. The variable `FILENAME` holds the
name of the current data file being read in.

Worked example 11.10

> Write an Awk script `firstlines` to read from a number of files and
> display the first line of each file preceded by the message `The first
> line of` *filename* `is:` in the following manner:
>
> ```
> $ awk -f firstlines vegetables /usr/dict/words
> The first line of vegetables is:
> potatoes 0.50 5
> The first line of /usr/dict/words is:
> AAAA
> ```
>
> **Solution**: Use variable `FNR` to form the pattern to find the first line of
> each input file, then `printf` to display that line (`$0`).
>
> ```
> FNR == 1 { printf "The first line of %s is:\n%s\n",
>                        FILENAME, $0 }
> ```

ACRONYM

NF = *'number of fields'*

Each record consists of a number of fields. The variable `NF` is the
number of fields contained in the current record. Try the following:

```
$ awk '{ print NF }'
hello there
2
A B C D E
```

5
(blank line)
0
ctrl-D

Worked example 11.11

> If some data in `vegetables` had been mistyped, there might be lines
> in the file containing either less than or more than three fields. Such
> lines cannot be processed correctly by the previous Awk scripts.
> Write an Awk script to read a file and display a list of those lines
> containing a number of fields different to three.
>
> **Solution**: Use the pattern `NF != 3` to choose those lines, and the
> value of `NR` to indicate which lines they are:
>
> ```
> NF != 3 { printf "Line %d has %d fields\n", NR, NF }
> ```
>
> Use this script to check that your file `vegetables` is indeed of the
> correct format. Try it on some other files you own and see what
> happens.

11.7 Arguments to 'awk' scripts

Suppose we wished to write a shell script called `price`, which would take
one argument, representing a vegetable name, and interrogate the file
`vegetables` as before to display the total price paid for that vegetable.
One solution would be to get Awk to evaluate the total cost for all
vegetables, and then use Grep to filter out the single line of output from
`awk`:

NOTE

In `grep $1`*, the* `$1` *refers
to the first argument of
the shell script*

```
awk '{ printf "%s %.2f\n", $1, $2*$3 }' vegetables | grep $1
```

This is a perfectly acceptable solution. Another would be to use a pattern
for `awk` so that only that single line would be processed by `awk`. But here
is a problem — we cannot use the following:

```
awk '/$1/ { printf "%s %.2f\n", $1, $2*$3 }' vegetables
```

The pattern `/$1/` is an ERE pattern. The character `$` in an ERE matches
the end of a string, and since each record Awk processes is a line, `$`
matches the end of an input line. The ERE `$1`, and thus the `awk` pattern
`/$1/`, will match all lines containing the digit 1 as the character after the
end of that line. This an impossible pattern, so it will not be matched by
any line. Try it — you should expect not to get any output. The point to
remember is that the `$1` has nothing to do with the `$1` that would
represent the first argument to a shell script.

There is, fortunately, a way around this problem. When invoking `awk`
you can preset Awk variables by specifying their initial value on the

command line. So, we could assign an Awk variable called `veg` (say), which would start off with the value that was the first argument to the script:

```
awk '{ if (veg == $1)
         printf "%s %.2f\n", $1, $2*$3 }' veg=$1 vegetables
```

By placing `veg=$1` immediately after the Awk script, it will set the value of `veg` to `$1` — the first argument to the shell script — as soon as `awk` starts up. Another method would be to use `veg` as part of a pattern:

```
awk ' veg == $1
         { printf "%s %.2f\n", $1, $2*$3 }' veg=$1 vegetables
```

Worked example 11.12

Write a shell script to take a single argument, representing a cost in pence, and print out the names of all vegetables listed in file `vegetables` that cost more than that number of pence per kilo.
Solution: Use `awk`, but pass a variable `cost` to it that is set to the first argument of the shell script.

```
# First, check the shell script has one argument
if   [ $# -ne 1 ]
then echo "One argument needed"
     exit 1
fi

# Now fire awk ...
awk '{ if ($2 * 100 >= cost)
          printf "%s\n", $1 }' cost=$1 vegetables

# Exit cleanly
exit 0
```

11.8 Arrays

Most high-level languages include **arrays**. An array (or **associative array**) is a collection of variables with a **name**, and each variable in that array has an **index**. An array index can be a string or a number. For example, we might have an array called `daysin` consisting of 12 variables, indexed by the names of the months of the year. These 12 variables would have names `daysin["January"]`, `daysin["February"]`, and so on up to `daysin["December"]`.

Worked example 11.13

Write an Awk script to read as input a sequence of lines, each containing the name of a month. Output should be the name of the month read in followed by the number of days in it. For instance, for input

```
March
November
```

we would have as output

```
March has 31 days
November has 30 days
```

Solution: Use an array indexed by the names of the months, so that each array element has as its value the number of days in the month that is its index. At the start of the script, the array must be initialised.

```
BEGIN {   # Initialise the array daysin
    daysin["January"] = 31;   daysin["February"] = 28
    daysin["March"] = 31;     daysin["April"] = 30
    daysin["May"] = 31;       daysin["June"] = 30
    daysin["July"] = 31;      daysin["August"] = 31
    daysin["September"] = 30; daysin["October"] = 31
    daysin["November"] = 30;  daysin["December"] = 31
    }
# For each input line, output month name and no. of days
    { printf "%s has %d days\n", $1, daysin[$1] }
```

Note that we can place multiple Awk commands on a single line by separating them with semicolons. Try this example. If you enter a month name that is incorrectly spelled, Awk will see that the element of the array with that index has not been assigned a value, and will assume it is therefore 0.

Returning to our shopping expedition, we may wish to store the data on each vegetable to be used later on. For example, if we purchased several bags of potatoes at different shops, we would need to enter several lines starting with `potatoes`. The scripts we have written already will not be able to total the costs for potatoes, they will just total the cost of each item on each line of input; that is, for each separate purchase. What we could do is to have an array `costs` indexed by the names of the vegetables, which we can update each time a new line of data is read in:

```
{ costs[$1] += $2*$3 }
```

The symbol `+=` indicates that the variable on the left of the symbol has its value updated by adding to it the number on the right of the symbol. At the start of the script, we would not initialise `costs`, since we do not at that point know the names of the vegetables to be mentioned in the input. When the first line of `vegetables` is read in, which is

```
potatoes 0.50 5
```

the following action is performed:

```
costs["potatoes"] += 0.50*5
```

The value of `costs["potatoes"]` starts off at 0, since it begins uninitialised, and its value is increased by 2.50.

Just as in the shell, Awk contains `for` loops. In fact, Awk allows several types of `for` loop. One of these allows you to loop through arrays and pick out those indices that have been used. The `for` statement looks like:

```
for (variable in array) statement
```

So, we could examine the values of the elements of `costs` for all indices by using

```
for (veg in costs) printf "%s costs %.2f\n",
            veg, costs[veg]
```

A complete Awk script for totalling the costs for all vegetables would then be

```
{ costs[$1] += $2*$3 }
END  { for (veg in costs)
            printf "%s costs %.2f\n", veg, costs[veg] }
```

Worked example 11.14

Calculate the average cost per kilo for each vegetable.
Solution: The *total cost* and the *total weight* for each vegetable must be calculated.

```
# Use arrays costs and weights to store the total costs
#   and total weight for each vegetable.
{ costs[$1] += $2*$3; weights[$1] += $3 }

# At the end, for each vegetable, divide its total costs
#   by the total weight, and output the value
END { for (veg in costs)
        printf "%s: %.2f pence per kilo\n",
            veg, costs[veg]/weights[veg] }
```

There is a special array `ENVIRON` which contains all the (exported) shell environment variables. To display the value of your `PATH`, the following Awk statement could be used:

```
printf "%s\n", ENVIRON["PATH"];
```

11.9 Field and record separators

The fields in a record are normally separated by whitespace. This is not always convenient. Suppose a file (**ages**, say) contains a list of people's names and their ages:

```
John 13
Sue 12
James Smith 15
James Jones 14
```

The number of fields on each line varies. This is a potential problem. Let us suppose we wish to write a simple Awk script to display

```
John is 13 years old
Sue is 12 years old
James Smith is 15 years old
James Jones is 14 years old
```

There are several possible solutions. One that you will already be able to find checks the number of fields and performs a separate action each time:

```
NF == 2 { printf "%s is %d years old\n", $1, $2 }
NF == 3 { printf "%s %s is %d years old\n", $1, $2, $3 }
```

This solution is fine if you know how many names a person is likely to have — but it is not elegant since there is a lot of duplication in the Awk script. If you were to allow persons with many forenames to appear in the list the Awk script would become unmanageable. Loops, such as `for` and `while` loops, are provided in Awk, and although we do not discuss them here, they could be used to 'count over' the first few fields. However, the solution begins to get moderately complex if that method is adopted.

The reason that the Awk scripts to perform this apparently simple task are less straightforward than you might expect is that the data has been coded unwisely. The fields are separated by characters which themselves appear in one of the fields, namely blanks. If the data had been

```
John:13
Sue:12
James Smith:15
James Jones:14
```

so that a colon (say) was used to separate the names from the numbers, then each line would have precisely two fields, and the spaces in the names would not matter. We can instruct Awk to use a different **field separator** to the usual whitespace by resetting the value of the variable FS; this should be done at the very start of the Awk script. Create a file

ACRONYM

FS = 'field separator'

called `ages` with the above names and ages in the 'colon-separated' format, and run the following Awk script:

```
BEGIN { FS=":" }
{ printf "%s is %d years old\n", $1, $2 }
```

The field separator can be any ERE, and can also be changed by giving `awk` the option `-F` followed by that ERE. For instance, to allow a sequence of one or more blanks, commas and colons to separate fields, you might have

```
awk -F "[ ,:]+"
```

On your UNIX system there should be a file called `/etc/passwd` which contains information about users on your system. This file consists of a sequence of lines which look like:

```
chris:hi64MH4uhJiq2:1623:103:Chris Cringle:/cs/ugrad/chris:
sam:a8PyPVSiPVXT6:1628:103:Sam Smith:/cs/ugrad/sam:/bin/sh
jo:9gqrX4IOig7qs:1631:103:Jo Jones:/cs/ugrad/jo:/bin/sh
geo:58esMw4xFsZ9I:1422:97:George Green:/cs/staff/geo:/bin/sh
    ...
```

Each line contains seven colon-separated fields; these represent the following:

1   A user's username (e.g. `chris`)

2   That user's *encrypted* password (e.g. `hi64MH4uhJiq2`). Passwords are usually stored in a coded form; if you know a password, it's easy to encrypt it, but virtually impossible to take an encrypted password and *de*code it. So it's safe for the encrypted passwords to be accessible by everyone. Having said this, some UNIX implementations — especially networked systems — impose a higher degree of security and do not allow the encrypted passwords to be accessed. In that case, the second field will be replaced by some other value.

3   The user's user-id (see Chapter 5).

4   The user's group-id (see Chapter 5).

5   The user's 'real' name; sometimes this field will also include other information, such as the user's office phone number or course of study.

6   The user's home directory.

7   The user's login shell (if empty, defaults to `/bin/sh`).

ACRONYM

NIS = 'Network Information Service'

Some systems which 'hide' the encrypted passwords will also have another mechanism for storing the data normally in `/etc/passwd`. If you find that this file either does not exist, or does not contain the information just described, then it is likely to be available using a special command. A common method of organising users' data over a network uses a system called **NIS**. To display the password file using NIS you should type

ACRONYM

yp = 'yellow pages'

```
ypcat passwd
```

and the data will be sent to standard output.

Worked example 11.15

Using Awk and /etc/passwd write a shell script findname to take an argument, which is a usercode, and display the name of the user who owns that usercode.
Solution: We need to look at fields 1 and 5 of the password file; if field 1 is the shell script argument we display field 5.

```
# As usual, make sure the script has one argument ...
if   [ $# -ne 1 ]
then echo "findname requires one argument"
     exit 1
fi

awk '
     # Set field separator to :
     BEGIN { FS=":" }
     {
       # Is the first field the usercode?
       if ($1 == usercode)

         # If yes, print out field 5, the user's name
         printf "%s\n", $5 }

   ' usercode=$1 </etc/passwd
   # Run awk with usercode set to the value of the
   #    first argument of the shell script, and read
   #    the data from /etc/passwd
```

Just as we can specify what should separate fields within a record, so we can specify what should separate records. Unless otherwise specified, a record is a line of input, so the **record separator** is the *Newline* character. The special variable used to change this is RS.

ACRONYM

RS = 'record separator'

Worked example 11.16

Write an Awk script to read standard input containing a list of company names and phone numbers, together with other information. All companies in the input with the keyword Anytown as part of their data should be displayed. The data for each company should be separated by a single line containing a single % symbol:

```
Toytown Telecom
Birmingham
0121 123 4567
Sells phones and answering machines
%
Sue, Grabbit and Runne
Solicitors
London
020 7999 9999
%
Chopham, Sliceham and Son
Anytown 234
family butchers
```

So with this data, the output would be:

```
Chopham, Sliceham and Son
Anytown 234
family butchers
```

Solution: Set the record separator to a %.

```
BEGIN     { RS="%" }      # Set RS
/Anytown/ { print $0 }'   # Print records matching "Anytown"
```

NOTE

WARNING!

You must be *very* careful if you reset the record separator. If the *Newline* character is no longer the record separator, any *Newline*s will be a part of the record. Unless the field separator is an ERE which allows a *Newline*, it will also be part of one of the fields. You will seldom need to reset the record separator.

Although the function `print` has been mentioned briefly, we have so far used the function `printf` as the usual means of displaying output from `awk`. This is because `printf` is very flexible. For simple output, `print` can be 'tailored' to individual requirements by use of the **output field** and **output record** separators `OFS` and `ORS`. When `print` takes several arguments, they will be printed out separated by the value of `OFS` (normally *Space*), and each record will be terminated by `ORS` (normally *Newline*).

Worked example 11.17

Write an Awk script to read in the password file and display users' names and home directories, in the following format:

```
Chris Cringle has home directory /cs/ugrad/chris.
Sam Smith has home directory /cs/ugrad/sam.
```

```
    . . .
```

Solution: Use `print` to display the fifth and sixth fields of
`/etc/passwd`. Set the input field separator to a colon, the output
field separator to

```
has home directory
```

and the output record separator to *Newline*.

```
awk ' BEGIN { FS=":"
              OFS=" has home directory "
              ORS="\n" }
  { print $5,$6 }' </etc/passwd
```

11.10 Functions

Just as `bc` and `expr` have functions defined that you can use with them
(such as `exp`), so does `awk`. Some of these are listed in Tables 11.3 and
11.4.

Table 11.3
Arithmetic functions
used by `awk`

`sin(x)`	returns the sine of x
`cos(x)`	returns the cosine of x
`atan2(x,y)`	returns the inverse tangent of x/y
`exp(x)`	returns the exponential of x, viz. e^x
`log(x)`	returns the natural logarithm of x
`sqrt(x)`	returns the square root of x
`int(x)`	truncates x to the nearest integer to 0
`rand()`	returns a random number x with $0 \leq x \leq 1$

Worked example 11.18

Write a script to 'roll a die'. Each time a line of input is entered, the
script should display a number between 1 and 6 to mimic someone
throwing a die.
Solution: Use `awk`. All the input should be discarded, but whenever a
line is entered from standard input the function `rand` is called to
generate a number between 0 and 1 (but not including 1). This is
multiplied by 6 to get a number between 0 and 6 (but not including
6). Adding 1 to this produces a number between 1 and 7, and giving
this as argument to `int` yields a whole number between 1 and 6
inclusive.

```
awk '{ printf "%d\n", int(rand()*6 + 1) }'
```

Table 11.4   Other functions used by awk

tolower(*s*)	returns string *s* with all upper-case letters in *s* lower-cased
toupper(*s*)	returns string *s* with all lower-case letters in *s* upper-cased
split(*s, a, fs*)	splits string *s* into array elements $a[1]$, $a[2]$, ..., $a[n]$, and returns *n*; separation is done with the regular expression *fs*
length(*s*)	returns the length in characters of string *s*
getline	moves on to the next input record; $0, NF, etc., are reset to their new values
match(*s, ERE*)	returns the position in string *s*, starting at 1, where *ERE* occurs; 0 is returned if *ERE does not occur* in *s*
sub(*ERE, rep*)	substitutes string *rep* for the first occurrence of *ERE* in the current record
sub(*ERE, rep, in*)	substitutes string *rep* for the first occurrence of *ERE* in the string *in*
substr(*s,m*)	returns the substring of *s* beginning at position *m*
substr(*s,m,n*)	returns the substring of *s* beginning at position *m* of length *n* (or up to the end of the string, if sooner)
system(*expression*)	evaluates *expression* as a *shell* command and returns its exit status

The trigonometric functions use radians, not degrees, and the number returned by rand might be 0, but will be strictly less than 1.

Worked example 11.19

> Write a shell script to read the password file and display each user's name in capitals.
> **Solution**: Use awk to pass the fifth field of its input to the function toupper, the result of which is then displayed.
>
> ```
> awk ' BEGIN { FS=":" }
>  { print toupper($5) }' </etc/passwd
> ```

Where a function takes a string as argument, that string is not itself altered, so that if you passed $0 to one of those functions, $0 would stay the same, but the function would return a new string based on $0.

Worked example 11.20

A certain Birmingham electrical retail company offers free delivery of its products to customers living in the Birmingham area, defined as having addresses with postcode commencing B followed by at least one digit. Delivery outside this area is charged at a flat rate per delivery. It is company practice for the driver of its delivery van to collect that fee. The company stores part of its customer data in the following format:

invoice number, customer, road, town, postcode

For example,

```
6152,J. Smith,1 High St.,Birmingham,B99 9ZZ
6183,F. Bloggs,5 Long Ave.,Dudley,DY1 1AA
```

The company requires a document to instruct the delivery driver whom to visit and whom to collect a delivery fee from.
Solution: This is an exercise that could be accomplished using Sed, although it would be quite messy. Using Awk we can use function `match` to examine the postcode. The ERE that matches a Birmingham postcode is

```
^B[0-9]
```

namely a B at the start of the postcode followed by one digit. What follows the digit — if anything — does not concern us. The Awk script might be:

```
# Set the field separator to be a comma
BEGIN { FS="," }


# For each line, $5 is the postcode
# Check if it is a Birmingham one
{ if ( match($5, "^B[0-9]") > 0)
     fee = "no fee"
 else
     fee = "standard fee"
 # Print out message for driver
 printf "%s, %s, %s, %s: %s\n", $2, $3, $4, $5, fee
 }
```

CHAPTER SUMMARY

We have described very basic use of the Awk language.

EXERCISES

1 A railway company operates trains that travel between a number of
cities. The company offers three types of *service*: *local*, *fast* and
express. Its fares are based on 10p per km travelled per passenger for
local trains, 12p for fast trains, and 15p for express. The company
keeps a log of all journeys made. For each year this data is kept in a
file (**trainlog**, say), which contains a number of fields. These are, in
order, the *departure* city, the *destination* city, the *distance* travelled
(in kilometres), the number of *passengers* carried, and the service
(**local**, **fast** or **express**). The final two fields represent the *day* and
month the journey took place. A typical part of the log file might
look like:

```
...
Edinburgh Glasgow 71 23 local 14 5
Aberdeen London 805 675 express 14 5
Manchester Birmingham 128 534 fast 15 5
Exeter Exmouth 8 112 local 15 5
...
```

The costs to the company of running trains are a fixed cost of 100
pounds per journey made plus 5 pounds per km travelled. Write Awk
scripts to take input from **trainlog** and display the following
information:

a The number of trains run.

b The number of trains run in May.

c The number of fast trains run in May.

d The total number of passengers carried in the year.

e The total fares collected in the year.

f The percentage of revenue which was generated by local trains.

g For each train, the profit or loss made on the journey; the output
should be a sequence of lines formatted so:

```
...
14/5 Edinburgh-Glasgow: loss 291.70
14/5 Aberdeen-London: profit 77381.25
15/5 Manchester-Birmingham: profit 7462.24
15/5 Exeter-Exmouth: loss 50.40
...
```

2 The Anytown and Blankshire Historical Society has decided to computerise its membership records. There are three classes of membership:

▶ *Annual*, renewable on the anniversary of joining and subject to a fee of 10.00 pounds each year.

▶ *Life*, subject to a single payment of 250.00 pounds.

▶ *Honorary*, which gives the same rights and privileges as Life membership, but is awarded by the Committee and no fee is payable.

Its membership secretary proposes to store its membership records in a file containing single-line records. Each record contains a number of colon-separated fields, the number of which depend on the class of membership.

For annual members, the fields have the following meaning:

1 Surname

2 First name(s) or initials

3 Class of membership, the string 'annual'

4 Address

5 Home phone number

6 Date of first joining (dd/mm/yy)

7 Date renewal due

For life and honorary members, field 3 is 'life' and 'honorary' respectively, and there are only six fields. For example,

```
Bloggs:Fred:annual:1 High Street:1234:03/12/90:03/12/97
Smith:John J.:annual:2 High Street::13/01/97:13/01/98
Doe:Jane:life:3 High Street:123 4567:22/02/93
Jones:Cllr. A.:honorary:New House:123 2345:22/02/93
```

Write shell scripts to read a membership file from standard input and produce the following information:

a A list of members' names, sorted by category of membership, then alphabetically by surname.

b A list of annual members whose membership has expired and is due for renewal.

c The total number of annual members due to renew in the current year.

d The total dues paid already by each member during their membership of the society.

e A list of honorary members who will have been of 10 years' standing in the current year.

f Combine (a–e) to produce a single shell script to display a comprehensive report. Take care to include messages in the output so that the report is easy to read.

3 For each of these tasks, ask how else you might solve the problem under UNIX, for instance with Grep or Sed. Is Awk the most appropriate tool?

Perl

This chapter discusses

▶ simple use of Perl; and

▶ how to use Perl effectively in combination with other UNIX tools.

12.1 Introduction

12.1.1 Why yet another utility?

A theme we have been following through this book is "keep it simple" — that is, if there is a simple utility to do what you need, then use it. However, there will *always* be situations where you need something more heavyweight than what we have already introduced.

We have discussed Awk, and seen that it can process data streams and files in a relatively complex fashion. However, Awk was never designed for sophisticated calculations, and as soon as an application deviates from straightforward processing of character streams, Awk is messy to use. Since Awk was devised in the early days of UNIX, our understanding of how to write a programming language has moved a long way, and the result is *Perl*. This is not to say that Awk is a bad language — it's not, it's just dated. However, an understanding of Awk is helpful when learning Perl, and as you will see there are tasks for which Awk is still a very appropriate solution.

Perl stands for *Practical Extraction and Report Language*. Don't let that put you off! To the serious UNIX programmer it's the best thing since sliced bread.

So what actually *is* Perl? It's a programming language, with a syntax similar to "C", and it comes complete with a full set of *libraries* — predefined functions — that access the UNIX kernel. It also has libraries

for performing almost any other function you care to name, including
database access, cryptography, graphics and internet access. The syntax
of Perl is well-designed, but is very terse — it is a language for the skilled
programmer, and a beginner would be well-advised to learn another
language first before attempting a Perl exercise. Perl is also free, and is
open source, which means that it is evolving, and new libraries for it are
being continually written. It also means that there is no concept of a
"standard" for Perl. The latest version of Perl is version 5, and it is
normally contained in all UNIX and Linux distributions. In addition, Perl
can be used on other operating systems including MacOS and Windows.

12.1.2 Beginning Perl

We will assume that the previous chapters have made sense to you. Our
goal is to identify the types of tasks for which the other tools you are now
familiar with are inappropriate, and to show how to begin to code them
in Perl. Our starting point will be processing a stream of characters, just
as we did with Awk.

However, before we start, there is a fundamental difference between
Perl and Awk. Whereas an Awk script assumes its data is naturally
separated into records which themselves are subdivided into fields, a Perl
program does not. Perl is a *general purpose* programming language, and
although it can perform the same tasks as Awk (very easily, in fact) there
are no constraints on its manner of use. Perl is *not* an "interactive shell".
While the shell can be used to "talk to" the operating system in real
time, Perl is not designed to. If the data you wish to process is not very
well structured you should consider using Perl.

12.1.3 Invoking Perl

Just as with Grep, Sed and Awk, simple use of the `perl` command
involves a **program** containing the commands Perl uses. This program can
either be a file which is an argument to `perl`, or can be contained in a
string named by option `-e`. Note that this is slightly different from the
convention used by Awk. Thus, to print out `Hello World!` we can either
invoke

```
perl -e 'print "Hello World!\n"'
```

or alternatively create a file (`perlprogram`, say) containing the print
statement `print "Hello World!"` and then invoke `perl` on the file thus:

```
perl perlprogram
```

As we shall see, although Perl embraces all the concepts we have
already encountered (such as standard input and output, pipes, processes,
and so on), the syntax it uses for them is quite different.

12.1.4 Documentation on perl

Extensive documentation is provided using the command `perldoc`. By default, this documentation is *not* available via the standard UNIX `man` command (although the manual pages can be be created if required). For an overview of how `perldoc` works, type

```
perldoc perldoc
```

12.1.5 Perl Scripts

Superficially a Perl script looks similar to a shell or an Awk script, and consists of a sequence of *statements*. Blocks of code can be enclosed in braces, and many of the basic commands, such as `printf`, are the same. There is one initial difference that often confuses, which is that *every* statement must be *terminated* by a semicolon. The end of a line has no significance to Perl.

12.2 Variables

In the shell (and Awk also), there is only one type of variable, which is a string of characters. If those characters are digits, and the variable is used in a context where a number is expected, then the variable will be understood to be a number. In Awk, arrays are also provided for.

In the shell, the value of a variable is accessed by placing a dollar symbol in front of the name of the variable, but its value is set by just using the name. In Awk, the dollar symbol is not needed at all.

In Perl, the situation is more complex. First of all we consider *scalar variables*. These are similar to variables you have already met, and can contain strings of characters, which are interpreted appropriately. The difference between Perl and shell/Awk variables is that the name of a scalar variable is *always* prepended with a dollar. For example, to set the value of `$i` to 0 and the value of `$x` to `$i+1`:

```
$i=0;
$x=$i+1;
```

Arrays are indicated by the @ symbol before the name, and square brackets are used to access individual elements of an array, which *must* be indexed by *integers* commencing with 0. Individual elements of an array, since they are scalars, are prepended with a `$`. A predefined array you will often use is `@ARGV`, which is the list of arguments to the Perl program. Its first element is `$ARGV[0]`.

In Awk, an array could be indexed by *any string*, and we referred to such an array as an *associative array*. In Perl it is called a *hash*. It is distinguished from an array in three ways. First, the @ symbol is replaced

---

by % to refer to the whole hash. Second, square brackets are replaced by braces, and finally the indices are strings, not integers.

Simple use of Perl seldom requires the @ and % symbols, since most of the time we access the individual elements of the arrays directly. As an example, suppose array @month is an array of 12 strings containing the names of the months, and %age is a hash containing the ages of some people. The following fragments of code set the first and last elements of @month and the ages for Chris and Sam.

```
$month[0]='January';
$month[11]='December';
$age{'Chris'}=22;
$age{'Sam'}=19;
```

Either single or double quotes can be used to denote strings, but like the shell, dollars and escape characters will be interpreted within double quotes but not within single quotes.

Strings can be *concatenated* — that is, joined together — by use of the operator . ("dot"). For instance, the concatenation of strings

```
"Hello " . "world!"
```

is equivalent to the single string

```
"Hello world!"
```

12.3 Input and output

A feature of the shell is that input and output, as simple data streams, are fundamental to its working. In other languages, such as Java or C, input and output can be much more complex, and programmers need to be aware of the type of data they are reading in or sending to an output device or file.

For example, if a program were to write data to many different files, then a shell program that relied on redirection of the standard output stream would become unwieldy and difficult to write.

Perl retains the simplicity of the shell whilst allowing the programmer a greater variety of methods for reading and writing data. It is equipped with five predefined variables for input and output (known as *filehandles*), shown in Table 12.1.

Table 12.1 The five predefined input and output variables

STDIN	is the *standard input stream*
STDOUT	is the *standard output stream*
STDERR	is the *standard output stream*
ARGV	is an array containing the arguments to the program
DATA	is the Perl equivalent of a here-document

12.3.1 Files and redirection

Files can be accessed directly by associating a new filehandle with the actual name of a file, using the function open. The syntax is curiously familiar. To open a file (tempfile, say) for *reading*, using the filehandle TMP, either of the following will work:

```
open(TMP, "tempfile");
open(TMP, "<tempfile");
```

To open tempfile, for *writing* using the TMP filehandle, use the following if you want the current contents of the file to be deleted (just as for the > file redirection mechanism in the shell):

```
open(TMP, ">tempfile");
```

The data written to the file can to be *appended* using the following syntax (as the >> file redirection mechanism in the shell):

```
open(TMP, ">>tempfile");
```

For the time being, use printf (syntax virtually identical to that in the shell) to send output using a filehandle (if you omit the filehandle, STDOUT is assumed). To display Hello World in file tempfile, the code fragment would be:

```
open(TMP, ">tempfile");
print TMP "Hello World!\n";
close(TMP);
```

Note the use of close — there are system limits on the number of files than can be opened at any one time, and it is good practice to "close" files when you have finished writing to (or reading from) them.

Reading a text file or stream is performed by enclosing the filehandle in angle brackets. Look at the following dialogue:

```
$v = <STDIN>;
open(TMP, "tempfile");
$w = <TMP>;
close(TMP);
```

The scalar variable v is set to the next line of standard input, and w to the *first* line of tempfile. Both v and w contain the newline character at the end of the line (unlike the shell command read or Awk) — this can be removed by use of the command chomp:

```
chomp($v);
```

A while loop can be used to go through all the lines in a file or stream. The syntax is

```
while (<filehandle>) { ... }
```

The variable $ contains the *current* line of input that has been read in.

Worked example 12.1

> Write a Perl script to take the name of a file as its first argument, and then read standard input and copy it to that file.
> **Solution**: The `ARGV` array contains the filename as its first element. Open that file for writing with a filehandle, and loop through the lines of standard input, not forgetting to close the file after use.
>
> ```
> # Set the filename variable to the first argument
> $filename=$ARGV[0];
>
> # Open the file
> open(FILE, ">$filename");
>
> # Repeatedly read in lines from standard input
> while (<STDIN>) {
>     # Print each line to the file
>     print FILE $_;
> }
>
> # Finally, close the file
> close(FILE);
> ```

12.3.2 Pipes

A similar method of working allows access to pipes. Suppose we wish to open a pipe to filter data *into* a command (`cmd`, say), which is both valid and exists on the current machine, and giving the data stream the filehandle `TMP`. To do this, use:

```
open(TMP, "| cmd");
```

Similarly, to take the output of a command as a stream, simply place the pipe symbol the other side of the command name:

```
open(TMP, "cmd |");
```

Worked example 12.2

> Write a Perl script to take a string as first argument, then read standard input and copy all lines containing that string to standard output.
> **Solution**: This is a job for `fgrep`. The `ARGV` array contains the string as its first element. Construct the command `fgrep` with the string as

its argument (note that since the string may contain spaces, you need to enclose the argument in single quotes). Open a pipe *into* the command, and loop through the lines of standard input, not forgetting to close the file after use. The output of `fgrep` by default goes to standard output, so a second pipe is unnecessary. Closing the filehandle is required even though no named file is used.

```
# Set the value of variable string to the first argument
$string=$ARGV[0];

# Create a shell command to search for that string
$command="fgrep '$string'";

# Open a pipe to that command
open(FGREP, "| $command");

# Repeatedly real lines from standard input ...
while (<STDIN>) {
  # ... and send them to the pipe
  printf FGREP $_;
  }

# Finally, close the pipe
close(FGREP);
```

12.3.3 The DATA filehandle

The DATA filehandle allows access to data in the same physical file as the Perl program itself (similar to a shell "here" document). The program and data should be separated by a line containing the string __END__, and unlike the shell this terminator *cannot* be changed to a different one.

Worked example 12.3

Write a Perl script to read into an array @days the names of the seven days of the week and then display them on standard output. **Solution**: Use the DATA filehandle and place the data at the end of the Perl script. One loop is needed to do both the assignment and the printing.

```
# Set variable i to count the lines of data read in
$i=0;

# Repeatedly read lines of data
```

```
while (<DATA>) {

    # Remove the trailing newline character
    chomp($_);

    # Set the array value indexed by i to the line
    $weekday[$i]=$_;

    # Print the line on standard output
    printf "$weekday[$i]\n";

    # Increment i
    $i++;
}
# The Perl program ends and the data follows
__END__
Monday
Tuesday
Wednesday
Thursday
Friday
Saturday
Sunday
```

12.4 Fields

In previous chapters we have frequently considered text files as being divided into *records* (usually lines) and *fields* (usually columns separated by whitespace or colons).

In Perl, we can take a string and decompose it into fields using the Perl operator `split`. This takes two arguments, a *pattern* enclosed in forward slashes, and the string, and returns an array whose values are the fields of the string using the pattern to describe what separates the fields. For example, suppose string `$play` is set to the string "Much Ado About Nothing"; then the following will create an array `@words` containing four elements (indexed from 0 to 3) containing strings "Much", "Ado", "About" and "Nothing" respectively:

```
@words = split / /, $play;
```

If the second argument is omitted, `$_` is assumed; if the first argument is *also* omitted, the split is performed on whitespace.

Worked example 12.4

> The file /etc/passwd contains colon-separated fields specifying the users of the machine. The first field is always the username. Write a Perl script to read the password file and display, one per line, all the usernames.
>
> **Solution**: use `split` to extract the fields into an array, using pattern : to describe the field separator, and print out the first element of the array (index 0).
>
> ```
> open(PASSWORDS, "/etc/passwd");
> while (<PASSWORDS>) {
>   @cols = split /:/;
>   print "@cols[0]\n";
> }
> close(PASSWORDS);
> ```

12.5 Control structures

The phrase *control structures* refers to the statements in the language that allow for choices and repetitions. In practice, this usually means *if* statements and loops.

The *condition* can be anything that evaluates to *true* or *false*. Similarly, a *while* statement will repeatedly execute until the *condition* ceases to be true:

```
while ( condition ) {
    code to execute while condition is true
  }
```

We have already met a `while` loop in the previous section, in the context of repeatedly reading in lines of input. In that case, the *condition* `<STDIN>` is assumed to be true if there is another line to read in, and false if the input has terminated. Let's look at a more typical use of `while` in an example.

Worked example 12.5

> Read in two numbers from standard input, and prompt the user to enter their product. Continue to do so until the correct answer is entered.
>
> **Solution**: Read the two numbers, on separate lines of input, into variables $n1 and $n2, then prompt the user to multiply them together. Read in the user's answer into $answer, check whether this

is different to $n1*$n2, and if so tell the user their answer is wrong, ask them to try again, and read in $answer again. Repeat until the user enters a correct answer.

```
# Prompt for input, and read two numbers
print "Type in the first number: ";
$n1 = <STDIN>;
print "Type in the second number: ";
$n2 = <STDIN>;

# Prompt for, and read, answer
print "Type in their product: ";
$answer = <STDIN>;

# Loop until correct answer input
while ($answer != $n1*$n2) {
  print "Wrong - try again: ";
  $answer = <STDIN>;
}
print "Correct - the answer is $answer\n";
```

Similarly, at its simplest, an *if* statement takes the following form:

```
if ( condition ) {
     code to execute if condition true
  } else {
     code to execute if condition false
  }
```

There is also a variant of the syntax for `if`. Instead of

```
if ( condition ) { statement }
```

we can write

```
condition && { statement }
```

and instead of

```
if (! condition ) { statement }
```

we can write

```
condition || { statement }
```

The symbol **&&** is pronounced *and*, and **||** is pronounced *or*. The words **and** and **or** can be used in place of **&&** and **||** respectively. This is simply a way of making code easier to read. For instance, if you wished to open file **myfile** for reading, and wanted Perl to inform you if the file could not be read, the following one line of code could be used:

```
open(INPUT, "myfile") || die "Cannot open myfile";
```

The **die** command causes the message following **die** to be displayed on the *standard error* stream and the Perl program to terminate immediately with non-zero exit status.

Worked example 12.6

> Your login shell reads in commands from the first of the following two files which may exist in your home directory: .bash_profile, .profile. Write a Perl script *either* to display the contents of that file, *or* to inform you that neither file exists.
>
> **Solution**: Try to open each of the files in turn, and if both fail **die**. If one has been opened, display its contents.
>
> ```
> # Try to open the one of the two files
> open(INPUT, ".bash_profile") ||
>   open(INPUT, ".profile") ||
>   die "Neither .bash_profile nor .profile found";
>
> # If one is open, use filehandle INPUT to read from it
> while (<INPUT>) {
>   print "$_";
> }
>
> # Finally, close the file
> close(INPUT);
> ```

12.6 Predefined Perl

12.6.1 Functions

There are *many* functions predefined in Perl, too many to list here. Some are almost identical to standard utilities available on UNIX/Linux, such as **chmod**, **mkdir**, **grep** and **sort**. We present here a brief (and simplified) description of a set of standard Perl functions that we feel are particularly useful. For a full list, and a detailed explanation of each, you should consult the Perl web site at **www.perl.com**.

Table 12.2   Some predefined Perl functions

`chdir`	changes the working directory to its (string) argument
`do`	executes as a Perl program the file that is its (string) argument
`eof`	returns true if its (filehandle) argument is at end of file
`eval`	evaluates its argument as if it were a Perl program
`exec`	executes the shell command that is its (string) argument
`exit`	ends program immediately, exit status its argument
`lc`	returns its (string) argument changed to lowercase
`length`	returns the number of characters in its (string) argument
`scalar`	returns the number of elements in its (array) argument
`uc`	returns its (string) argument changed to uppercase

12.6.2 Modules

A Perl *module* is a collection of Perl programs written to be used in other programs. You can write your own, or you can use modules written by other people. Some modules are included with each distribution of Perl, and others are made freely available on the Web.

The web site `www.cpan.org` ("Comprehensive Perl Archive Network") is the main place to go to find out what is available. The site is continually growing, and at the time of writing contained over 1600 modules, including modules in the following areas:

ACRONYM

HTML = 'HyperText Markup Language'
HTTP = 'HyperText Transfer Protocol'

▶ security, encryption and authentication;

▶ database support for most commercial databases;

▶ web support, including HTML parsers and HTTP servers;

▶ email clients and servers;

▶ mathematics;

▶ image manipulation;

▶ archiving and file conversion;

▶ interfaces to operating systems, including MacOS, OS/2 and Windows;

▶ hardware drivers; and

▶ specialised computational modules, such as Neural Networks and Artificial Intelligence.

In order to use a module, include the line

use *name-of-module*;

at the start of your program.

Worked example 12.7

> Write a Perl script to take two arguments, considered to be
> filenames, and copy the contents of the first file to the second.
> **Solution**: Use the `copy` function in the `File::Copy` module:
>
> ```
> use File::Copy;
>
> copy($ARGV[0], $ARGV[1]) or die "Cannot perform copy"
> ```
>
> Note that we have checked the successful completion of the `copy`
> function and generated an error message if it failed.

12.7 Regular expressions

Regular expressions have been used extensively in the previous chapters,
and it will come as no surprise that Perl also uses them. The difference
between Perl's approach to regular expressions, and that of other utilities,
is that they are *central* to the use of Awk, Sed and Grep. In Perl, the use
of regular expressions is just one of many possibilities available to the
programmer. Typical use of regular expressions in Perl involves the
comparison or *editing* of *strings*.

   The operator used to manipulate regular expressions is `=~`, known as
the *pattern binding operator*. Perl does not use the phrase *regular
expression*, preferring instead *pattern*, but it is synonymous.

   The simplest use of patterns is to match strings. The expression

   string `=~` */pattern/*

evaluates to true if the string is matched by the pattern, and

   string `!~` */pattern/*

evaluates to true if the string is *not* matched by the pattern.

Worked example 12.8

> Write a Perl fragment to take the variable `$word` and enclose its
> contents in single quotes *only if* it does not already contain single
> quotes as both its first and last characters.
> **Solution**: Use a pattern match — the pattern `^'.*'$` matches a
> single quote at the left (anchored by the `^`) and at the right
> (anchored by the `$`). The pattern `.*` matched zero or more
> occurrences of anything.
>
> ```
> if ($word !~ /^'.*'$/) {
>   $word = "'" . $word . "'";
> }
> ```

12.7.1 Single character translation

We start by considering character-by-character translation. You will recall the use in Chapter 10 of the shell command `tr`, and there is an almost identical facility available in Perl. The syntax is almost identical, except that

▶ the arguments are separated and enclosed by three slashes, and

▶ the options (such as `d`) appear at the *end*.

The string which appears between the first two slashes is called the *search string*, and the string between the last two slashes is the *replace string*. For example, the following command lowercases each letter in `$word`:

```
$word =~ tr/A-Z/a-z/;
```

The following command replaces each vowel in `$word` by an @ symbol:

```
$word =~ tr/AEIOUaeiou/@/;
```

NOTE

This behaviour is slightly more complex than the shell command `tr`

The option `d` to *delete* characters is supported, and causes all characters in the search string *which do not have replacements in the replacement string* to be deleted. For example, to delete all vowels in `$word` we could type:

```
$word =~ tr/AEIOUaeiou//d;
```

Worked example 12.9

Write a Perl script to copy standard input to standard output with all digits deleted and the symbol @ replaced by #.
Solution: Use a `while` loop to iterate through the lines of standard input; for each line, the variable `$_` contains the line, and we can then use `tr` with option `d` search string `@0-9` to delete the digits, and raplacement string `#` to replace the first character of the search string (the @):

```
while (<STDIN>) {
  $_ =~ tr/@0-9/#/d;
  print $_;
}
```

12.7.2 String editing

Just as the Perl command `tr` is similar to the shell command `tr`, the Perl command `s` is similar to Sed. The syntax is the same as for `tr`:

s/*search-string*/*replacement-string*/*options*

For example, to replace `Hello` or `hello` in variable `$greeting` by `Howdy`, we might have:

```
$greeting =~ s/[Hh]ello/Howdy;
```

Write a Perl script which takes one argument, assumed to be the name of a file which is itself a Perl program, and copies that file to standard output with all comments removed. Assume that # is not contained in any quoted string in the argument program.

Solution: A comment commences with # and continues to the end of the line, so a search string matching a comment is `#.*$` (note the use of $ to anchor the search string to the end of the line, and `.*` to match an arbitrary length sequence of characters). The script then becomes

```
open (FILE,$ARGV[0]);
while (<FILE>) {
  $_ =~ s/\#.*$//;
  print "$_" ;
}
```

Write a Perl script to read text from standard input, and send to standard output the text with all leading/trailing whitespace removed, and all sequences of tabs/spaces replaced with a single space character.

Solution: This is another use of the s, with a simple enclosing loop. The substitution is performed in two stages: first, remove the leading space, then the trailing space, then the excess whitespace. Note that a tab is whitespace, and is entered as a `\t`.

```
while (<STDIN>) {
  $_ =~ s/^[ \t]*//;        # remove leading spaces
  $_ =~ s/[ \t]*$//;        # remove trailing spaces
  $_ =~ s/[ \t][ \t]*/ /g;  # squash internal whitespace
  print "$_" ;
}
```

12.8 Perl and the Kernel

We have already mentioned some of the functions available in Perl, and have noted that functions often appear similar in name and in what they do to shell utilities. This is no accident.

Recall that a UNIX system contains at its core the *kernel*. The interface to this kernel is specified both in the C language (POSIX.1) and as shell commands (POSIX.2). The shell command names mimic — as far as is sensible — the names of the corresponding C procedures. For example, to create a new directory, the shell command `mkdir` is used, and the corresponding C procedure is called `mkdir`. The Perl function is also called `mkdir`.

The C language has been used to code the kernel, and much of the shell and Perl is written in C (or its more recent object-oriented derivative C++). The use of the names used by C to interface with the kernel thus gives the shell or Perl programmer a consistent window into the kernel. Anything (almost!) that can be coded in C on a UNIX system can be written in the shell or in Perl.

12.9 Quality code

There has been much debate since programming languages were invented as to what constitutes "good code". At the time of writing, *object-oriented* programming languages are commonly seen as encapsulating a natural, intuitive, and solid programming style, in which it is easy to write readily understandable programs. Like the shell, Perl was invented by capable and confident system programmers, people who perhaps did not feel the need for their code to be easily read by others.

Perl is not object-oriented. Perl does not come with interactive development environments which will help you write code. Perl is not forgiving of mistakes — it allows the programmer full licence to do what she or he wants.

It is possible to write Perl in variety of obscure ways so that your code is extremely difficult to read. This can be taken to extremes, for instance in the form of **JAPH** scripts. See `http://www.perl.com/CPAN-local/misc/japh` for examples. The onus is on you, the programmer, to write Perl so that your code is "good code". What does this mean in practice?

Use comments
Your program should be well commented, and perhaps a quarter of the code should be comments. Help the reader to understand what you're doing, since the Perl code itself might not.

Use meaningful variable names
It is tempting to use single letter names, since they are quicker to type, and make your programs smaller. This is false economy, and it's easy to forget what you were using variables for.

ACRONYM

JAPH = 'Just Another Perl Hacker'

Check for error conditions

If you know that your program only requires one argument (say), make sure that your code does something sensible when presented with 0 arguments or with more than one.

Structured your programs in a modular fashion

Use modules and functions. We have only touched on them in this chapter, but when you have gained experience programming Perl, and are used to writing longer programs, this will be helpful. In the meantime, if a program has several distinct phases, then ensure that they are distinguished. This can be done easily by separating them with blank lines and commenting them. Indenting the bodies of loops is another simple technique which clarifies the structure of the code.

Use standard libraries if appropriate

Perl comes supplied with libraries. Many of the tasks you may wish to accomplish can be written easily using modules from those libraries. Don't re-invent the wheel!

Worked example 12.12
Good style

Write a Perl script, which takes one integer argument, and displays a message to inform the user whether the number is prime. Ensure your code is of good quality.

Solution:

Suppose the argument is n. We solve this problem by successively trying to divide numbers from 2 up to $n/2$ into n. If any of these divides exactly, then n is not prime.

```
# Program to calculate whether a number is prime

# Part 1: Check the input data
if ($#ARGV != 0) {
    printf "Exactly one argument required\n";
    exit 1;
}

if ($ARGV[0] <= 0) {
    printf "The argument must be positive\n";
    exit 1;
}

# Part 2: Perform the calculation

# Variable number is the integer we are testing
$number = $ARGV[0];
```

```
$isPrime = 0;

# loop through all possible divisors
for ($divisor=2; $divisor <= $number/2; $divisor++) {
    if ($number % $divisor == 0) {
        $isPrime = 1;
        }
    }

# Part 3: output the result
if ($isPrime == 1) {
    printf "%d is not prime\n", $number;
}
else {
    printf "%d is prime\n", $number;
}
```

Worked example 12.13
Bad style

The task is identical to the previous worked example. The solution in this case ignores our advice on good coding. We hope that the point is made!

Solution:

```
$n=$ARGV[0];$i=0;
for ($j=2;$j<=$n/2;$j++){if($n%$j==0){$i=1;}}
if($i==1){printf "%d is not prime\n", $n;}
else {printf "%d is prime\n", $n;}
```

12.10 When do I use Perl?

Use Perl whenever you want. Anything you can program in the shell can be done in Perl. It is up to you to decide when the extra complication of using Perl actually saves you time. If you want to view the first line of a file, use head. It's easy, and a Perl program would be overkill. However, if you cannot identify simple UNIX utilities to perform the task you need done, then think about Perl. Complicated shell programming gets messy, and Perl is more suitable for non-trivial tasks.

There is one other reason to use Perl — *security*. Suppose you write a command to be used and owned by root, and to be accessible by a general user. An example might be a program for sending email, which requires write access to system files (including log files). It is *dangerous* to write such a program as a shell script, since under certain circumstances a user can use their knowledge of the shell environment to gain a subshell with root privileges. This can be prevented if the program is written in Perl.

CHAPTER SUMMARY

We have described very basic use of the Perl language.

EXERCISES

1 Write a Perl script which takes one argument, assumed to be the URL of a web site (such as `www.any.site.com`), and displays on standard output the email address of `postmaster` at that site (`postmaster@any.site.com`). Ensure your script outputs suitable error messages if the script is run without exactly one argument.

2 Write a Perl script to mimic a simple version of `fmt`. It should read text on standard input, and write the words (a word is a string of characters terminated by a space or the end of a line) one by one to standard output. As many words as possible, separated by single characters, are to be on each output line. Each output line has a maximum width of 72 characters.

3 You are provided with a file of coordinate data generated by a GPS ('Global Positioning System') device which has logged a journey. This takes the form of a text file in which each line consists of two decimal numbers, representing a map coordinate in kilometres, the first line being the start of the journey and the last line the end. Write a Perl script, taking one argument which is a filename, and outputs a message which is the calculated total length of the journey.

Maintaining your Linux OS

13

This chapter

▶ documents key features of Linux system maintenance;

▶ presents a number of alternative tools for Linux file management;

▶ provides an introduction to Linux networking;

▶ introduces guidelines on Linux security; and

▶ shows you how to uninstall Linux.

UNIX is a very stable operating system and all of the well-known distributions of Linux also provide very reliable day-to-day computing environments. This said, you will have to maintain your system both routinely — monitoring disk usage, changing user passwords, etc. — and also on a more occasional basis — configuring network usage, installing new software, and so on. The Web is a very good source of information on Linux administration and maintenance; this chapter is intended only to provide you with a basic toolkit, the key components of which will be sufficient for the day-to-day management of your Linux system. It may well be the case that you want to do more with Linux; this chapter also provides a basis from which you can begin to explore the exciting world of Linux networking. With the introduction of networking comes the responsibility of security; if so this is also covered towards the end of the chapter. Finally, if you are not happy with your Linux installation then you will want to uninstall the operating system, and details of how to do so are provided at the end of the chapter.

NOTE

`linuxconf` *is a sophisticated administration system for Linux*

13.1 Basic management

Maintenance and administration can take place at various levels in your system. Most Linux installations have with them a copy of the `linuxconf` tool. This is a versatile tool with which a number of administrative tasks can be performed, including setting the system time, changing the network settings, performing user administration and setting up file systems etc.

Maintenance can also be coordinated through tools supplied by the Linux desktop environment. These tools differ according to the Linux distribution you are running. KDE, for example, comes with a built-in Control Center (which can be reached through the K menu). The KDE Control Center is similar to the Settings menu that is found in the Windows operating system. It therefore provides a convenient interface with which to manage processor and memory configuration, device information, the windows environment, the configuration of the file manager, and so on.

A number of maintenance tasks can also be performed using the YaST set-up tool which was introduced in Section 3.6.1.

It is worth noting that some of these tools will look different (that is, they will provide you with different options and capabilities) under different user logins. You can expect to be provided with the full capabilities of the tools if, and only if, you are logged in as the root user.

The following subsections provide a useful summary of basic management tasks, which should probably form part of your administrative routine. Beyond this, the following web sites are recommended sources of information for more detailed Linux management and administration issues:

▶ `www.linuxdoc.org`
  This is the home of the Linux documentation project, including online guides, HOWTO pages, frequently asked questions and manuals for a number of Linux activities;

▶ `www.linuxnewbie.org`
  Contains news and articles including help for new and more advanced users;

▶ `www.freshmeat.net`
  Reportedly contains the largest index of UNIX software and applications on the Web. This is a good source of free Linux software and will probably contain all the applications that you, or the users of your system, will require.

NOTE

For more information on the `passwd` command, see Section 4.3.1

13.1.1 Passwords

If the security of your system is of concern, then you will need to update your passwords regularly. This is best done through the `passwd` command which can be issued from a terminal window. It allows the current user (that is, the user who is currently logged in) to change their password. If you want to change the password of other users on the system, it can be done using the command

```
passwd user
```

Note, however, that in order to change the password of other users, you must be logged in as the root user.

NOTE

`df` was discussed in Section 5.2

13.1.2 Checking storage space

The `df` command provides a report of the available disk space on your system. It is worth checking the disk usage from time to time as, if you exceed the space allocated to your Linux partition, then you are likely to run into difficulties. If your disk usage appears to be very high, particularly in the `/var` directory, then you should explore the contents of the `/var/spool/mail` directory. It is in this directory that mail is stored before it is processed by your chosen mail tool. Sometimes the mail tools are not configured to remove the data from the `mailbox` file in `/var/spool/mail` and, as a result, this file can grow very large. It is also worth keeping an eye on the hidden directories that are maintained and updated by your web browser. For example, if you are using Netscape, then you might find that the `.netscape/cache` directory can also become very large, particularly if you download large quantities of multimedia files from the Internet.

NOTE

`ps` was discussed in Section 6.1.1

NOTE

This output is the result of running the command `ps -af`. For more on the runtime flags of `ps` type `man ps`

13.1.3 Checking processes

Using the command `ps` it is possible to view the processes which are currently running on your system. By including a combination of run-time flags it is possible to output the user (`UID`), process identifier (`PID`), parent process identifier (`PPID`), start time (`STIME`), cumulative execution time (`TIME`) and command name (`CMD`) of each process on the system. The output will look something like this:

```
UID    PID    PPID    C   STIME      TTY      TIME    CMD
Croe   29527  16663   0   15:55:44   pts/37   38:24   netscape
Jara   29793  29792   0   16:25:55   pts/17   0:01    gs
sue    27128  1       0   12:02:30   pts/35   0:01    ttsession
```

It is worth checking the processes on your system from time to time, as occasionally when you close down an application, or something crashes, the associated processes remain. If processes are defunct, usually written DEFUNCT in the CMD column of the ps output, or are simply unwanted, then they can be removed using the command kill. It is a rule that processes can only be killed by their owners or by the root user; this is useful as it saves you (or anyone else) inadvertently killing the active processes of other users.

13.1.4 Managing users

Managing users, as with most administrative tasks, can be done through interaction with a graphical user interface such as the Kuser tool supplied with KDE or, if you prefer, through a terminal window.

Kuser will do most of the tasks described below. It is designed to allow you to act as an administrator to the users or groups of users that have access to your Linux system; this includes the tasks of creating, disabling and removing users from the system.

The command line tools that provide the same functionality through a terminal window can be found in the /bin directory in the Linux installation. The command for creating a new user is adduser and can be run by typing the command /bin/adduser in a terminal window. This command should be disabled to all users but root.

Users can be disabled by editing the /etc/passwd file. This file contains a list of user names and their associated passwords (stored in an encrypted form for security reasons). To disable a user, replace their encrypted password with the * (asterisk) character; this change will make it impossible for the user to sign on. Again, you will only be able to do this as the root user.

If you want to completely remove a user from the system then you should use the command userdel. This command can only be run by root users and comes with a variety of command line options (type man userdel for details). If the -r flag is added to this command then this will not only remove the user's name from the password file, but will also remove their home directory.

13.1.5 Shutting down and restarting your computer

You can shut down your computer from a terminal window using the shutdown command:

```
/bin/shutdown -r now
```

This has the same effect as pressing *ctrl-alt-delete* on the keyboard, and will close down all the processes on the machine, shutdown the machine, and then reboot. You can halt your machine (a shutdown without a subsequent reboot) by substituting the -r flag in the above command with the **-h** flag. Linux will tell you that your computer has halted, at which point you can safely turn the power off. This is useful if you are preparing your computer for transit.

13.1.6 Automating tasks

In Chapter 6 we discussed a facility called **crontab** for the automatic scheduling of repetitive tasks. This allows you to program an activity to be performed as often as every minute, or as infrequently as every year.

When managing your system, **crontab** is an invaluable tool for performing tasks, such as backups, which are important for the system to run reliably, but which can be forgotten if left to you to perform yourself.

Worked example 13.1

> How can Sam arrange for his mailbox to be backed up to
> **.mailbackup** in his home directory each morning at 6 am?
> **Solution**: Sam should use **crontab -e** to edit his personal crontab
> file so that it includes:
>
> ```
> # At 6.00am each day
> # copy /var/mail/sam to ~sam/.mailbackup
> 0 6 * * * /bin/cp /var/mail/sam ~sam/.mailbackup
> ```
>
> This will perform the file copy, and if any error message is generated,
> it will be mailed to Sam. Note the use of ~**sam** to denote Sam's home
> directory.

Many Linux distributions, including Red Hat and SuSE, include directories **/etc/cron.hourly**, **/etc/cron.daily** and **/etc/cron.weekly**. The executable scripts placed in these directories are run on an hourly, daily or weekly basis.

13.2 Linux file management

13.2.1 File compression and archiving tools

Files and file hierarchies which are no longer in use, but are nonetheless still required, can be compressed or archived. This can reduce the amount of disk space they occupy by as much as 60–70%. Compression and archiving are not only convenient ways of optimising disk usage, but also of storing and creating back-ups of important data and system files.

There are a number of tools for compressing and archiving files. These can be broadly categorised as those which can be run from a console window and those which can be run through a graphical user interface.

> **NOTE**
>
> *Details of the* compress *and* tar *commands can also be found in Section 5.7*

Console-based tools suitable for Linux file management include the following:

- ▶ `compress` — a utility that attempts to reduce a file using a *lossless* data compression algorithm. The compressed file (identified by the `.Z` extension) replaces the original, while the ownership modes and the change and modification times remain the same. The amount of compression depends on the type and size of the input file; for a typical text file it is of the order of 50–60%.

- ▶ `gzip` — is a compression utility designed to replace the `compress` command. The main advantages of `gzip` over `compress` are the better compression ratio and the freedom from patented algorithms. `gzip` produces compressed output files which can be identified by the `.gz` extension. To uncompress the `.gz` file, the command `gunzip` is used. `gzip` may not have been included in your Linux installation and if this is the case, then the utility can be downloaded free of charge from `www.gzip.org`.

- ▶ `tar` — archives and extracts files to and from a single file called a tarfile. Common operations include

  ```
  tar -cvf resultsfile *
  ```

  which archives all the files in the current and any nested subdirectories, and

  ```
  tar -xvf resultsfile
  ```

  which retrieves these files while maintaining the original directory structure.

There are a large number of file compression and archiving desktop tools. The (current) pick of the pack include:

- ▶ Karchiver — a KDE-based utility which allows you to create `.Z`, `.gz`, and `.tar` files via a graphical user interface.

- ▶ StuffIt — a tool that provides support for nearly all possible archive formats including those created by the Windows and Macintosh operating systems. StuffIt claims to produce the smallest files of any compression program; if you would like to test this claim then the toolkit can be found at `www.stuffit.com`.

- ▶ RAR — is a Linux (and Windows) archiving utility that contains a powerful compression algorithm. The tool is particularly good for the compression of multimedia data, but it can also be used to create self-extracting archives and recover damaged archives. It can be downloaded from `www.rarsoft.com`.

13.2.2 File managers

The version of Linux you have installed will no doubt have a built in file manager. KDE2, for example, has a very respectable file manager known as Kcommander, which features the mounting and unmounting of CDROMs and floppy drives, the ability to compress files and to create its own archives, built-in (Samba) networking support and a configurable menu system.

It is now possible to use file managers that provide web-based interfaces rather than the Windows style look and feel of files and folders. PHPFileExchange is a free web-based file interchange system which features authenticated user login, user groups, read and write access control at the user and group level, user privilege levels and a MySQL backend. For more information see `www.seattleserver.com`.

Nautilus is a file management system and a graphical shell found as an integral part of the GNOME desktop environment. Its features include 'advanced file management' and a look and feel that is unsurpassed. Most Linux installations have GNOME as an option. If your version does not support GNOME then you can download it for free from `www.gnome.org`.

NOTE

For more information on the `split` *command see Section 9.6.2*

13.2.3 File splitters

As well as the UNIX `split` command there are a number of graphical packages that allow the splitting and joining of large files. GfileSplit comes with the GNOME desktop environment and allows a file of any size to be split into smaller fixed size pieces; for more information see `www.gfilesplit.sourceforget.net`. ProSplitter is a fast Windows and Linux compatible tool for splitting and joining files. It has a simple graphical user interface and a number of advanced features such as DES encryption and robustness and reliability data checks. ProSplitter can be downloaded for free from `www.prosplitter.co.uk`.

13.3 Linux networking

13.3.1 Getting started

There is a lot to Linux networking and it is not the intention of this section (or indeed this book) to provide a comprehensive Linux networking tutorial. However, this section should serve as an introduction to the material that you will find in many of the good Linux networking tutorials and books. It will familiarise you with the terminology that you will need to understand and proceed with these more detailed manuals. This said, later subsections provide some detail on 'how to add your Linux machine to an existing network' and 'how to build your own private Linux network'.

For further Linux networking information see the following sources:

▶ `www.linux.org` — follow the links to 'Linux Networking HOWTO'. Incidentally, there are lots of other HOWTOs at this web site that contain useful information, from how to configure a CD-ROM under Linux to how you should go about installing Chinese.

▶ `comp.os.linux.networking` — this is a useful newsgroup dedicated to networking and related matters. If you have any networking problems, be they large or small, you will probably find someone on this newsgroup who has experienced the problem before.

There are a variety of ways of networking collections of UNIX-based computers. Probably the most common is through the use of Ethernet.

13.3.2 MAC and IP addresses

If you are planning on adding your computer to an existing UNIX network, or if you are planning on building your own local network, then you will probably already have ensured that your computer has an Ethernet card. Each Ethernet card has a unique Media Access Control (or **MAC**) address. Despite this being unique, these addresses are not commonly used as network identifiers and instead the MAC address is mapped to a higher level IP (Internet Protocol) address.

IP addresses are 32-bit numbers, usually represented in dotted decimal notation (i.e. xxx.xxx.xxx.xxx), which uniquely identify each interface of a host or network router. Using this notation, each decimal number can represent eight bits of binary data and therefore the numbers between 0 and 255. The first of these decimal numbers is important, as it determines the *class* of network to which this IP address belongs — see Table 13.1.

ACRONYM

MAC = 'Media Access Control'

Table 13.1 Network classes and their IP addresses and Netmasks

Class	Range	Netmask
A	0.0.0.0 to 127.255.255.255	255.0.0.0
B	128.0.0.0 to 191.255.255.255	255.255.0.0
C	192.0.0.0 to 223.255.255.255	255.255.255.0

Network classes are used to break networks down according to their size. Class A networks can have up to 16,777,214 hosts, class B networks 16,384 hosts and class C networks 254 hosts. This might look restrictive (and there are proposals to update this 32-bit IP version 4 to a 128-bit version 6), but sharing IP addresses across many hosts makes this less of a problem than it might first seem.

There are certain IP addresses that are reserved for special purposes. The number 0, for example, is used to refer to the current network or host, the number 127 (known as a *loopback*) is used for diagnostic purposes and the number 255 is used for broadcasting packets of data to the entire network.

Each machine IP address in a local network will share a common 'network portion' and contain a unique 'host portion'. One of the machines that I use the most has the IP address 137.205.227.85; my neighbour in the office next door has a computer with the IP address 137.205.227.84. The host portion of this address is represented by the last (the far right) numbers — the 227.84 or 227.85; the network portion of the address is the 137.205 part of the address; the 227 part is in fact a sub-part of the main university network (a subnet). As it is conventional for the number of hosts to be contiguous, there are at least 85 hosts in subnet 227.

To retrieve the network portion of an IP address a *subnet mask* (or Netmask) is used. When this is 'bitwise ANDed' with the IP address, the address of the network to which the address belongs is revealed (see Table 13.1). This mask also allows the network to be further subdivided. Table 13.2 shows how an IP address can be decomposed into its associated masks, portions and addresses.

Table 13.2
Decomposing IP
addresses

Host address	137.205.227.85
Network mask	255.255.255.0
Network portion	137.205.227.
Host portion	.85
Network address	137.205.227.0
Broadcast address	137.205.227.255

13.3.3 Domain names

IP addresses are not easy to remember and therefore computers are usually referred to using their domain name. You will be familiar with the use of domain names when accessing sites on the Internet. These domain names are mapped to IP addresses through a Domain Name Service (a **DNS**).

The domain name for the IP address 137.205.227.85 is `cement.dcs.warwick.ac.uk`. The host machine `cement` maps to the host portion 85 in the IP address; the 227 part of the network portion of the IP address corresponds to the `dcs` (Department of Computer Science) network; the 137.205 part of the IP address maps to `warwick.ac.uk`. The University of Warwick may not own all the class B 137.205 network addresses; the slice of addresses they own is coordinated by UKERNA — the organisation that administers all of the `.ac` and `.gov` domain names in the UK.

13.3.4 Adding a Linux host to an existing network

If you are planning on adding your Linux machine to an existing network then you will need to know how the IP addresses on the network are already arranged. You will need to know the following information:

▶ The host IP address that can be allocated to your machine. Your network administrator will have a list of those IP addresses that are allocated and those that are free.

▶ The IP network address.

▶ The IP broadcast address (as it might not necessarily be your network address followed by 255).

▶ The IP netmask.

▶ The router address.

▶ The Domain Name Server address (DNS address) which you have assigned to your machine.

Once you have this information, networking the machine is in fact quite easy. The best way to do this is to configure the network entries of your machine through the 'network configuration' menu of the YaST tool. This simply means copying the IP and DNS information into the appropriate fields of the network configuration menu. It is also possible to set this network information using `linuxconf`.

13.3.5 Building a private network

If you are building your own private network then you can choose whatever IP addresses you like. You will still need to:

▶ choose an IP address for each machine in your network;

▶ choose an appropriate netmask; and

▶ assign each machine a DNS address.

If you are configuring your network through YaST or `linuxconf` then it it recommended that you log in as root before working through the administration procedure.

13.3.6 Configuring the network interface

When Linux was installed on your machine it is likely that the networking device (such as the Ethernet card) on your machine was detected by the Ethernet device driver and assigned a unique interface identifier (for example, 'eth0'). The final stage of networking requires you to link this device to your chosen IP address. Again, the best way to do this is to use the YaST tool, and then to test that your modem still works using the program `wvdial`. There are more manual ways of doing this setup (for example using the command `ifconfig`), but these are less easy to master than the network administration parts of YaST.

13.4 Security

Whatever anyone tells you about security, unfortunately the only way to be completely sure that your computer is safe from a security breach is to disconnect it from the Internet and never to load any program or document that supports macros. This is clearly not going to be practical, so the answer is to find a number of ways of making security breaches to your networked computer more difficult. A number of possibilities are listed below.

▶ It is possible to set up your system so that logins to your machine can only be done from other computers on your own local network and not from machines on the Internet. To do this you need to look at the files `/etc/hosts.allow` and `/etc/hosts.deny`.

▶ You should make sure that your root password is secure. It is no use using short dictionary words, as these can easily be broken using simple password generator programs. Do not be tempted to set up users with blank passwords; it might seem like a good idea at the time, but this is very insecure. Finally, if you have more than one server, then you should make sure that the passwords are different for each. This ensures that if one machine is breached you do not compromise the whole system.

> **NOTE**
>
> `ssh` *can be downloaded for free from* `www.ssh.com`

▶ Denying host access will not completely secure your system as it is possible to intercept messages from your machine, strip out the important data, such as the identifiers of other machines on your network, and then by a mechanism known as 'spoofing' pretend to be another machine. The best way of getting around this problem is to use the `ssh` tool when connecting to other machines in your network. This ensures that the data packets sent between machines are encrypted. If you use ssh-level security for all your network traffic, then you make spoofing much harder.

▶ Another way of maintaining security is to monitor the system log files. In the directory `/var/log` you will find a number of files in which information regarding all the system and network information on your machine is stored. While this information takes a bit of interpretation, you will find that you can use it to study most of the activity on your system and on your network.

▶ Firewalls provide a means of protection between private devices such as computers or local networks and the wider Internet. The simplest form of firewall protection is to set up a Linux machine with a single Internet connection (through an Ethernet card or modem) which acts as a buffer between the Internet and any local network. This machine then blocks direct communication between the local network and the Internet (in either direction). The advantage of this approach is that anything inside the firewall is protected; the disadvantage is that it is a little complicated to set up — you need to configure the machine for two Ethernet cards and then connect the two cards through an **IP-chain** to filter the data between them.

13.5 Uninstalling Linux

There are a number of ways of removing a Linux installation and the method which you choose will depend on the type of installation that you carried out in the first place. Essentially, you need to delete the partitions on which Linux is installed and then remove the `lilo` from the master boot record.

▶ Method 1 — Run `fdisk` from a Linux rescue disk and delete the Linux partitions. This will remove the partition table entries and effectively 'wipe' the Linux partition. You can then reformat these areas of disk from the MS-DOS boot floppy by typing `fdisk /mbr`.

▶ Method 2 — Run `fdisk` and delete the Linux partitions, as above. Then instead of using `fdisk /mbr`, use the command `lilo -U`, which should restore the boot file your system previously used before Linux was installed. This will only work if a backup copy was stored at install time.

▶ Method 3 — If you are not worried about retaining any of the existing partitions on your machine and want a clean way of reformatting the hard drive for a completely new operating system, then you can use the MaxBlast tool. This can be downloaded from `www.maxtor.com` and reports are that it is both very easy to use and effective.

There is plenty of advice on the Internet if you are unsure about this procedure.

CHAPTER SUMMARY

`passwd`	change login password (see 4.3.1)
`df`	reports available disk space (see 5.2)
`ps`	reports process status (see 6.1.1)
`kill`	terminates processes (see 6.1.4 and 9.1)
`adduser`	creates new user
`useradd`	creates new user
`userdel`	removes a user
`shutdown`	close down processes and shut down machine
`compress`	reduces file to compressed form (see 5.7)
`gzip`	reduces file to compressed form
`gunzip`	uncompresses gzip file
`tar`	file and directory archive tool (see 5.7)
`split`	splits and joins large files (see 9.6.2)
`ypmatch`	prints values from Network Information System
`ssh`	secure shell for remote login
`fdisk`	modifies disk partition table (see 3.3)

Other Issues

CHAPTER OVERVIEW

This chapter

▶ introduces some issues not covered elsewhere in the book;

▶ provides a brief description of relevant software packages; and

▶ identifies other resources for software, documentation and information relating to UNIX and Linux.

If you have made it this far, it should be clear that UNIX and Linux are very powerful tools that give a large amount of control to the user, and offer a very high degree of flexibility. The previous chapters have covered very many different aspects of UNIX and Linux, ranging from core issues of installing and maintaining the system, through aspects of files, processes and shells, to the more applied side of tools that can be used with UNIX. However, much more can be added to the basic system to increase its power and usefulness dramatically.

This chapter will review some of the things that are important to mention in the context of a general introduction to UNIX and Linux, but which may have had no obvious place in earlier chapters. Inevitably, the contents will be somewhat random, but provide pointers to places to look for further resources.

We give web sites for some of the resources we mention, but you should not forget that your system may have some of them already installed. To find out, see if a `man` page exists, or check the online documentation provided on the system.

14.1 Programming languages

Perhaps the most powerful thing you can do with computers is to develop your own programs. While we have looked at some ways of writing programs through shells, Awk and Perl, for example, high-level programming languages offer many more facilities.

Java, for example, is a very powerful language that is increasingly being used across a range of platforms and for a variety of applications. It is particularly interesting because of its use in web applications, and being run through web browsers, which is increasingly common. Under UNIX and Linux, Java can be installed by downloading the appropriate software from `java.sun.com`. There are different versions available for Solaris (a version of UNIX) and Linux, with full instructions.

Many other languages are also available for download. Table 14.1 below offers a quick summary of a selection of these, but is not at all exhaustive, because there are far too many. However, a quick web search will usually reveal the necessary information.

Table 14.1
Programming
languages

Language	Further information
Java	`java.sun.com` Based on the idea that the same software should run on many different kinds of computers, consumer electronics and embedded devices.
Tcl/Tk	`www.scriptics.com` Tcl is a scripting language with a simple syntax, and comes with Tk, a graphical user interface toolkit. They are highly portable.
GCC	`gcc.gnu.org` The GNU Compiler Collection includes compilers for C, C++, Fortran and several other languages.
GNU Prolog	`gnu-prolog.inria.fr` A free Prolog compiler.
GCL	`www.gnu.org/software/gcl/` GNU Common Lisp is a portable and efficient compiler and interpreter for Lisp.
Perl	`www.perl.com` Extensive resources about Perl.
	`www.perl.org` Support for Perl users.
PHP	`www.php.org` A general-purpose scripting language that is especially suited for Web development and can be embedded into HTML.

14.2 Document Preparation

One of the interesting points of contention about using UNIX relates to the choice of popular word-processing packages. Some common application software is not available under UNIX, but there are very good alternatives. For example, this book was typeset using the LaTeX text formatting package, which offers one of the most effective ways of writing documents. Unlike word processors, text formatters do not have the best user-interface, but can provide far better layout of mathematical and other sophisticated output. Table 14.2 lists various different kinds of software available for UNIX and Linux, with their sources.

Table 14.2
Document
preparation software

Package	Further information
TeX	www.tug.org High-quality typesetting software designed for the production of scientific documents.
LaTeX	www.latex-project.org The most common set of macros for TeX.
Acrobat Reader	www.adobe.com Allows PDF files to be viewed and printed.
Framemaker	www.adobe.com A desk-top publishing package which is suitable for large content-rich documents.
Ghostscript	www.cs.wisc.edu/~ghost/ Allows you to view and print PostScript and PDF files, and to convert files between formats.
Ghostview	www.cs.wisc.edu/~ghost/ A user-friendly interface to Ghostscript.
GSView	www.cs.wisc.edu/~ghost/ Another user-friendly interface to Ghostscript, similar to Ghostview.
Emacs	www.gnu.org/software/emacs/ A very sophisticated text editor with an extensive range of features.
KOffice	www.koffice.org KDE Office application suite.
StarOffice	www.sun.com/software/star/staroffice/ A suite of programs similar to Microsoft's Office, including word processor, spreadsheet, etc.
OpenOffice	www.openoffice.org An Open Source implementation of StarOffice.

14.3 Other Software

UNIX comes with a large number of utilities, and in Table 14.3 we list some we have found particularly useful (some of which may not be installed on your system).

Table 14.3   General Software for Linux

Package	Further information
VMware	`www.vmware.com` Allows you to run more than one operating system simultaneously.
WINE	`www.winehq.com` Allows most Windows applications to be run natively under Intel versions of UNIX.
StuffIt	`www.stuffit.com` A tool to support a large range of archiving formats and purposes.
gzip	`www.gzip.org` A compression utility designed to replace `compress`, with better compression ratios.
RAR	`www.rarsoft.com` Another powerful archiving utility.
prosplitter	`www.prosplitter.co.uk` A fast tool for splitting and joining files.
XV	`http://www.trilon.com/xv/xv.html` An image display utility, good for previewing pictures, which also has simple editing facilities.
GIMP	`www.gimp.org` The GIMP is the GNU Image Manipulation Program, a powerful image drawing and editing tool.
XMMS	`www.xmms.org` The X MultiMedia System is a cross-platform multimedia player, suitable for playing audio files in most formats.
CVS	`www.cvshome.org` Concurrent Versions System, an open-source network-transparent version control system.
VNC	`www.uk.research.att.com/vnc/` A remote display system which allows you to view your 'desktop' from anywhere on the Internet.

14.4 Useful Resources

There is a wealth of information available about different UNIX versions, UNIX systems administration, and the various kinds of software that can be run under UNIX and Linux. Table 14.4 lists some of the more popular web sites.

Table 14.4 Other resources

Resource	Further information
Linux	www.linux.org An Web site which aims to be a central source of information about Linux.
	www.linux.com An independent site that provides news and information about Linux and Open Source, as well as links to software and learning resources.
	www.linuxnewbie.org Contains news and articles for new and experienced users.
	www.linuxdoc.org The Linux Documentation Project, as the name suggests, offers lots of documentation and guides on various aspects of Linux.
	www.freshmeat.net The largest index of Open Source software on the Web.
	www.OSDN.com Information about Open Source software, with many links to relevant sites.
	sourceforge.net A repository of Open Source software.
GNU	www.gnu.org Intimately entwined with Linux, the GNU project (GNU's Not Unix) started in 1984 with the aim of developing a free Unix-like operating system. GNU offers a large range of useful software for Linux.
News	www.slashdot.org News about Linux (and other techie topics).
	www.theregister.co.uk Independent IT news, with a Linux flavour.

14.4.1 Web Tools

It is almost essential now to be able to browse the web, and several web browsers and servers are easily available, as listed in Table 14.5. All of the web broswers listed, with the exception of Lynx, are "fully functional", though the look-and-feel varies considerably.

Table 14.5   Web resources

Resource	Further information
Mozilla	`www.mozilla.org` An open-source web browser which includes a powerful email client.
Netscape	`www.netscape.com` The most common web browser for UNIX and Linux, which uses much of Mozilla's code.
Opera	`www.opera.com` A newer entrant to the web browser market — a free version is available for Linux.
Konqueror	`www.konqueror.org` An Open Source web browser distributed with KDE.
Galeon	`galeon.sourceforge.net` An Open Source web browser distributed with GNOME, and which shares some of its code with Mozilla.
Lynx	`lynx.browser.org` A text-only web browser, useful if you have a slow Internet connection.
Apache	`www.apache.org` An Open Source web server, which will allow you to host and serve web pages from your own system.

14.4.2 Network Tools

It is likely that your system is connected to a network, and you may have access to more than one other system. Table 14.6 lists tools which are available for you to move data between those systems, and to remotely connect to and find information about them.

Table 14.6   Network resources

Resource	Further information
FTP	A common protocol for transferring data between systems, using commands such as `ftp` and `ncftp`.
Telnet	A protocol for connecting to remote systems via the command `telnet`.
`rlogin`	A command for connecting to remote systems, similar to `telnet`.
`rcp`	A command for copying files to a remote system.
SSH	`www.openssh.org` OpenSSH is an open source version of the SSH protocol suite of secure (encrypted) network tools. OpenSSH replaces (for example) `rlogin`, `rcp` and `ftp` by `slogin`, `scp` and `sftp`.
`putty`	`www.chiark.greenend.org.uk/~sgtatham/putty/` A free implementation of Telnet and SSH for Windows platforms, along with an `xterm` terminal emulator. Strictly not a UNIX or Linux utility, but if you have access to a UNIX server and need to connect from a Windows PC it will allow a secure connection.

CHAPTER SUMMARY

▶ A large amount of software can be downloaded and installed under UNIX and Linux.

▶ The World Wide Web provides a quick and easy way of finding and installing freely available software.

▶ The resources available to support UNIX and Linux users are almost boundless.

Answers to selected problems

Chapter 4

1   Whenever you need to find out information about a command, you should use `man`. With option `-k` followed by a keyword, `man` will display commands related to that keyword. In this case, a suitable keyword would be `login`, and the dialogue would look like:

```
$ man -k login
...
logname (1) - print user's login name
...
```

The correct answer is therefore `logname`. Try it:

```
$ logname
chris
```

3   As in problem 4.1, you should use `man` to find out more information on `date`. In this case, however, you need specific information on `date`, so the command you use is

```
$ man date
```

The manual page for `date` is likely to be big, but this is not a problem. Remember that the manual page is divided into sections. First of all, notice that under section `SYNOPSIS` the possible format for arguments to `date` is given:

```
SYNOPSIS
        date [-u] [+format]
```

NOTE

The POSIX standard specifies only two arguments to `date` – some systems may in addition allow others

This indicates that date may have up to two arguments, both of which are optional (to show this, they are enclosed in square brackets). The second one is preceded by a + symbol, and if you read further down, in the `DESCRIPTION` section it describes what **format** can contain. This is a string (so enclose it in quotes) which

includes **field descriptors** to specify exactly what the output of
`date` should look like. The field descriptors which are relevant are:
`%r` (12-hour clock time), `%A` (weekday name), `%d` (day of week), `%B`
(month name) and `%Y` (year). The argument you would give to
`date` would therefore be:

```
+"%r on %A %d %B %Y"
```

so that the command you would type would be

```
date +"%r on %A %d %B %Y"
```

5　The first decision to be made is which command to use to display
the machine's users. Use `man` with a suitable keyword:

```
$ man -k logged
...
who (1) - show who is logged on
...
```

The script should therefore `echo` the one-line message and then run
`who`:

```
echo "The following are logged in:"
who
```

Chapter 5

By this stage, you should be getting used to using `man` to decide which
commands to use, and to decide which options to give to commands.

1　Use `ls` with options `-a` (to include listing 'dot' files), `-1` (to list
filename on each line of output) and `-t` (to list in order of
modification time). Pipe this output to `head`, with option `-n 3` (to
select the first three lines in the list):

```
ls -1at | head -n 3
```

3　Use `ls` with option `-i` (to list inodes as well as filenames), and pipe
the output to `sort` with option `-n` (to indicate numerical rather
than lexical order):

```
$ ls -i | sort -n
```

5　Running `ls` with options `-l` and `-d` followed by a dot (the current
directory) will display details about the current directory. The
owner of the file begins in character column 16 and may continue
until column 23, so use `cut` with option `-c` to select columns 16 to
23:

```
ls -ld . | cut -c 16-23
```

7 Use `ls` with option `-l`, and pipe the output to `sort`. Since the fifth field is the field which is to be used for sorting comparisons, argument `+4` should be given to `sort` (the fields are counted starting from 0). The sort should be according to numerical order rather than lexical, so `sort` requires option `-n` also:

```
ls -l | sort -n +4
```

Chapter 6

1 Use `crontab -e` to edit the `crontab` file, adding the following line to that file:

```
0 8 * * 1 echo "Good Morning"
```

This instructs `crontab` to run

```
echo "Good Morning"
```

(whose output will be mailed to you) at 0 minutes past 8 o'clock every first day (i.e. Monday) of every week regardless of the month or the date.

3 Use `at` to schedule the alarm call by giving it argument `now + 1 hour`. Remember that `at` will **mail** you the standard output from the commands you give it, so you must send the message directly to the device which is your terminal. You can find out the device name using `tty`:

```
$ tty
/dev/ttypf
$ at now + 1 hour
at> echo "Your alarm" >/dev/ttypf
at> ctrl-D
```

5 This is an exercise in knowing the names of the environment variables which store the relevant information. These were presented in Table 6.1.

```
echo "Your username is $LOGNAME"
echo "Home directory is $HOME"
echo "You are using a terminal which is a $TERM"
echo "The default lineprinter is $PRINTER"
```

7 Set `MY_NAME` to be the string containing your first and family names, and enclose that string in quotes so that the blank space between the two names is part of that string:

```
$ MY_NAME="Chris Cringle"
```

Chapter 7

1   Use `find` followed by a tilde (the current directory) to select files from the current directory, and argument `-print` to list them. Other arguments are needed to perform the selection, and as there are many possible arguments you should read the manual page. Argument `-type f` selects regular files. To check on the file size, argument `-size` followed by an integer n selects all files whose size is between $(n-1)$ and n blocks of 512 bytes. The command becomes:

```
$ find ~ -type f -size 1 -print
```

3   The script must initially check that all the arguments are readable; then it can simply pass them all to `cat`:

```
for i in "$@"            # For each argument
do
    if [ ! -r "$i" ]     # if it is not (!) readable (-r)
    then exit 1          # then bomb out
    fi
done

cat "$@"                 # cat the files
```

5   Use `printf` to format and `who` to find the users. With option `-q` two lines will be displayed by `who`, the first contains the users, the second the number of them. Use `head` to select the first line of the output of `who -q`, then a `for` loop to print out each of them in turn. A count must also be made so as to know when to finish a line of output.

```
COUNT=""                           # Use to count to 4
ALLUSERS=$(who -q | head -1)       # Get the list of users
for i in $ALLUSERS                 # Loop through in turn
do
    printf "%10s" $i               # Print each in width 10
    COUNT=$COUNT"x"                # Add an "x" to COUNT
    if   [ "$COUNT" = "xxxx" ]     # If 4 "x"s in COUNT
    then printf "\n"               #    terminate the line
        COUNT=""                   #    and reset COUNT
    fi
done

# At the end, if the final line contains less than
# four columns, that line must be terminated
if   [ "$COUNT" != "" ]
then printf "\n"
fi
```

7   You need to keep a count of the number of the line, which can be
incremented with the aid of `bc`. Use `read` to read in the standard
input line-by-line, and `printf` to ensure that the format is the
same as `cat -n` (i.e. six character columns for the line number,
followed by two blank spaces, followed by the line).

```
LINENUMBER=1              # To store the line number
while read LINE          # 'read' returns false at end
do                       #              of input
    # Print the line number and the line
    printf "%6d  %s\n" $LINENUMBER $LINE
    # Add one to the line number
    LINENUMBER=$( echo "$LINENUMBER + 1" | bc )
done
```

Chapter 8

1   This is an exercise in arithmetic expansion only.

```
printf "Enter cm: "          # Prompt
read CM                      # Read number of cm
FEET=$(( $CM / 30 ))         # FEET is easy to calculate
CM=$(( $CM % 30 ))           # Replace CM by residual cm
                             #    above the previous feet
INCHES=$(( $CM * 12 / 30 ))  # Convert residual cm
                             #    to inches

printf "%d cm is %d foot %d inches\n" $CM $FEET $INCHES
```

3   This exercise requires the use of the `test` command at the start to
perform the checks on the filename given as argument to the script,
followed by a miscellany of UNIX utilities.

```
# Check number of arguments
if      [ $# -ne 1 ]
then    echo "Requires one argument"
        exit 1
# If a single argument, check it's readable
elif [ ! -r $1 ]
then    echo "File is unreadable"
        exit 1
fi

LINES=0            # To count number of lines
COL=0              # To count number of characters
while read LINE    # read returns false at end of input
do
```

```
    # Characters on line (including Newline)
    COLONLINE=$( echo "$LINE" | wc -c )
    # Add to COL and subtract 1 for the Newline
    COL=$(( $COL + $COLONLINE - 1 )
    # Increment line count
    LINES=$(( $LINES + 1 )
done <$1              # Input from the file

# Since 2 decimal places needed, must use bc to
#   calculate the average, not arithmetic expansion
AVERAGE=$( echo "scale=2; $COL / $LINES" | bc )

# Finally, display the average
printf "Average is %s\n" $AVERAGE
```

5   Use date to display the hour, then pattern match on the output:

```
# Format %H gives the hour as 2 digits, 00-23
case $( date "+%H" ) in

    # Any hour 00 to 09, also 10 or 11
    0?|1[01]) echo Good Morning ;;

    # Any hour 12 to 17
    1[2-7])   echo Good afternoon ;;

    # Any other time is evening
    *)        echo Good evening ;;
esac
```

7   This solution involves a moderately complex while loop.

```
# Check number of arguments
if   [ $# -ne 1 ]
then echo "Requires 1 argument"
     exit 1
fi

# Check the argument is between 1 and 15
case $1 in
    [1-9]|1[0-5]) ;;
    *)              echo "Require number 1-15"
                    exit 1
esac

LINE=1      # Use to count through the lines
while [ $LINE -le $1 ]
```

```
do
        # For the top and bottom lines of the square
        if [ $LINE -eq 1 ] || [ $LINE -eq $1 ]
        then    printf "+"       # First column
                COL=2            # Column to print in next
                while [ $COL -lt $1 ]
                do      printf "-"
                        COL=$(( $COL + 1 )
                done
                printf "+\n"   # Last column, and end line
        # The middle lines
        else    printf "|"       # First column
                COL=2            # Column to print in next
                while [ $COL -lt $1 ]
                do      printf " "
                        COL=$(( $COL + 1 )
                done
                printf "|\n"   # Last column, and end line
        fi
        LINE=$(( $LINE + 1 )
done
```

9 This could be solved using pattern matching on the arguments, but
   since there are many possibilities for running **eurhello** with
   options, the clean way to solve the problem is with **getopts**.

```
# Set the string GREETING to the usual greeting
GREETING="Hello"

# Use getopts to go through the possible options
# These can be f or g, or G followed by an argument
# An option is stored in OPTIONNAME when encountered
while getopts fgG: OPTIONNAME
do
   # Check the three possibilities
   case "$OPTIONNAME" in
           # French
       f) GREETING="Bonjour";;
           # German
       g) GREETING="Guten Tag";;
           # Argument to -G held in OPTARGS
       G) GREETING="$OPTARG";;
   esac
done

# If the script is called with invalid options,
```

```
# getopts will discard them and display an error
# message

# Now get rid of the options which have been processed
shift $(( $OPTIND - 1 )

# Check a name string is an argument to the script
if [ $# -eq 0 ]
then echo "usage: $0 [-f] [-g] [-G greeting] name"
    exit 1
fi


# Finally, produce the output
echo "$GREETING $*"
```

Chapter 9

1   This is a straightforward function, just requiring two commands between the braces.

```
thisyear() {
    printf "This year is "
    date "+%Y"
    }
```

Alternatively, this could be done using echo:

```
thisyear() {
    echo "This year is $( date +%Y )"
    }
```

Note that the argument to **date** does not **need** to be enclosed in quotes, as in this case it contains no characters with special meaning to the shell. In the first solution they are included for clarity, in the second one they were omitted to avoid clashing with the quotes enclosing the argument to **echo**.

3   The body of this function is the same as a script, if you had written it as a script instead. It must be written as a function in order that the value of PATH in the current shell can be altered — you cannot **export** from a child process to its parent.

```
addtopath() {
    printf "Enter directory name: "      # Prompt
    read NEW                             # Read name
    if [ -d "$NEW" ] &&                  # Check directory
        [ -r "$NEW" ]                    # Check readable
    then PATH="$PATH":"$NEW"             # Update PATH
```

```
                                fi
                                }
```

5   The only complication with this example is that you must
remember to enclose the `sh -x` in quotes, since there is a blank
which is part of the alias:

```
$ alias debugsh='sh -x'
```

7   This is simple use of `eval`.

```
printf "Type in a variable name: "
read VARIABLE


# Construct the name of the variable
#   and echo its value
eval echo \$$VARIABLE
```

Chapter 10

1   We require a Grep pattern which matches the five vowels, either
upper- or lower-case, separated by zero or more other characters.
The pattern `[Aa]` matches an upper- or lower-case 'a', and the
pattern `.*` (dot followed by an asterisk) any sequence of other
characters:

```
$ grep '[Aa].*[Ee].*[Ii].*[Oo].*[Uu]'
/usr/dict/words
```

3   Use `grep` with option `-l`:

```
$ grep -l program *
```

5   Begin by replacing all characters which are not digits by blanks,
then translate each blank to a newline, remove all empty lines, and
finally sort the result to be in numerical (rather than lexical) order,
removing duplicates:

```
sed 's/[^0-9]/ /g' |    # Pattern [^0-9] matches
                        #       any non-digit
    tr " " "\n"  |      # Replace blanks by newlines
    grep -v '^$' |      # Select all lines NOT
                        #       matching ^$
    sort -u -n          # Sort, remove duplicated lines
                        #       into numerical order
```

7   Use `csplit` to split the file at the position denoted by the BRE
`^middle$` – we have to 'anchor' the `m` and the `e` to be at the start
and end of a line so that it does not split the file earlier if there is
another word **containing** middle.

```
$ csplit /usr/dict/words '/^middle$/'
```

Chapter 11

For these problems, the solutions are in no way unique. See if you can devise different answers.

1a   The number of trains run is simply the number of lines in the file, which is the value of NR at the end of processing the data.

```
END { print NR }
```

1b   Use a variable count (say) to count the lines where the seventh field is 5:

```
$7 == 5 { count++ }
END { print count }
```

1c   Similar to the previous problem, but the count is incremented when field 7 is 5 and field 5 is fast:

```
$7 == 5 && $5 == "fast" { count++ }
END { print count }
```

1d   Rather than incrementing count by one each time a line of input relates to May (field 7 is 5), sum all the values of field 4:

```
{ passengers += $4 }
END { print passengers }
```

1e   As the previous example, but the incremented fare total depends on the value of field 5. The solution presented here does the calculation in pence, and converts to pounds only at the end.

```
$5 == "local" { fares += 10*$3*$4 }
$5 == "fast" { fares += 12*$3*$4 }
$5 == "express" { fares += 15*$3*$4 }
END { printf "%.2f\n", fares / 100 }
```

1f   In this case we have three variables for the different fare categories.

```
$5 == "local" { localfares += 10*$3*$4 }
$5 == "fast" { fastfares += 12*$3*$4 }
$5 == "express" { expressfares += 15*$3*$4 }
END { printf "%.2f\n", localfares*100/ \
              (localfares+fastfares+expressfares) }
```

1g   In this solution, floating-point arithmetic is used throughout, all the calculations being performed in pounds.

```
BEGIN { rate["local"] = 0.10
        rate["fast"] = 0.12
        rate["express"] = 0.15 }
```

```
{ cost = 100 + 5*$3
  revenue = $3*$4*rate[$5]
  profit = revenue - cost
  printf "%d/%d %s-%s: ", $6, $7, $1, $2
  if (profit > 0)
      printf "profit %.2f\n", profit
  else
      printf "loss %.2f\n", -profit
}
```

Chapter 12

As for the Awk solution, there are many other possible solutions to the Perl problems

```
2   $available_chars=72;
    $output_line="";
    while (<STDIN>) {

      # remove newline
      chomp;

      # remove leading spaces
      $_ =~ s/^[ ]*//;

      # remove trailing spaces
      $_ =~ s/[ ]*$//;

      # create an array of the words on the input line
      @words=split;

      # loop through the words in turn ...
      for ($i=0; $i <= $#words; $i++) {
        $word = $words[$i];

        # ... and if it will not fit on an output line ...
        if (length($word) >= $available_chars) {

          # ... print the current output line ...
          print $output_line . "\n";

          # ... and reset the variables
          $available_chars=72 - length($word);
          $output_line=$word;
        }
```

```
          # add the word to the output line (not forgetting a
          # blank space) and reset the variable storing the
          # available space
          $available_chars = $available_chars - length($word) - 1;
          $output_line = $output_line . " " . $word;
       };
    }
    print $output_line . "\n";
```

3

```
# Process the first argument
open(DATA, $ARGV[0]) || die "Cannot open data file";


# Initialise running total
$length=0.0;


# Data file must have at least one line
# @oldcoordinate holds the previous line, and
#  @coordinate the current line

if (<DATA>) {
  # Extract the fields in the first line into
  # the array @oldcoordinate
  @oldcoordinate = split;
} else {
  # Terminate if the data file is empty
  die "No data";
}


# Loop through the lines of the file
while (<DATA>) {
  # The current leg is calculated by
  # subtracting the new coordinated from
  # the old
  @coordinate = split;
  $x = $coordinate[0] - $oldcoordinate[0];
  $y = $coordinate[1] - $oldcoordinate[1];

  # Use Pythagoras' Theorem!
  $d = sqrt ( $x*$x + $y*$y);

  # Update the running total
  $length += $d;

  # The new line now becomes the previous
```

```
              # coordinate
              @oldcoordinate = @coordinate;
          }

          # Tidy up the open file handle
          close (DATA);

          # Finally, output the answer
          printf "The journey length is %0.2f km.\n", $length;
```

Appendix – summary of utilities

Table 14.7   Utilities a–c

Utility	Description	Chapter
adduser	creates new user	13
alias	define or display aliases	9
ar	maintain a library archive	9
at	execute commands at a specified time	6
awk	pattern scanning and processing language	11
basename	display non-directory part of filename	5
batch	execute commands when system load permits	6
bc	calculator	7
bg	run a job to the background	6
break	exit from for, while or until loop	7
cat	concatenate and print files to standard output	4
cd	change working directory	5
chgrp	change file group ownership	5
chmod	change file access privileges	5
chown	change file ownership	5
cksum	file checksum utility	9
cmp	compare two files	5
comm	select/reject lines common to two files	9
command	execute a simple command	9
compress	reduces file to compressed form	5
continue	continue for, while or until loop	7
cp	copy files	5
crontab	schedule periodic background work	6
csplit	split a file according to context	10
ctags	create a 'tags' file	9
cut	select columns or fields from each line of a file	5

Table 14.7 (cont.)
Utilities d–j

Utility	Description	Chapter
date	display current time and date	4
dd	convert file format	9
df	display free disk space	5
diff	show differences between two files	5
dirname	display directory part of a pathname	5
du	display file space usage	5
echo	write arguments to standard output	4
ed	basic text editor	4
env	set environment for a command	6
eval	construct command by concatenating arguments	9
exec	execute command by replacing shell process	9
exit	cause the shell to exit	8
expand	replace tabs by spaces	9
export	set export attribute for a variable	6
expr	evaluate an arithmetic expression	8
ex	text editor (see vi)	4
false	returns 'false' value, exit status 1	7
fc	process command history list	6
fdisk	modifies disk partition table	3
fg	run a job to the foreground	6
file	describe file contents	5
find	find files	7
fold	fold lines	5
getconf	get configuration variables	9
getopts	parse options for a utility	8
grep	select lines matching regular expression	10
gunzip	uncompresses gzip file	13
gzip	reduces file to compressed form	13
head	show the first few lines of a file	5
id	display information about a user's identity	5
jobs	list the jobs in the current session	6
join	relational database operator	9

Table 14.7   (cont.)
Utilities k–p

Utility	Description	Chapter
kill	send a signal to a process	6
ln	link files	5
locale	display information about the 'locale'	9
localedef	define the 'locale'	9
logger	log message for the system administrator	9
logname	display your login user name	4
lp	send files to a printer	5
ls	list files (directory contents)	4
mailx	process electronic mail messages	4
make	maintain and update groups of programs	9
man	display manual pages	4
mesg	allow or deny messages on your terminal	4
mkdir	create new directories	5
mkfifo	create a FIFO file	9
more	'pager'	4
mv	move files	5
newgrp	change your current group-id	5
nice	run a command with changed priority	6
nm	display name list of an object file	9
nohup	run a command immune to hangups	6
od	dump files in various formats	5
passwd	change login password	4
paste	merge corresponding lines of text files	5
patch	apply changes to files	5
pathchk	check pathname is valid	9
pax	file archiver and format translator	5
perl	'Practical Extraction and Report Language'	12
pr	a very basic formatter for text files	5
printf	write formatted output	7
ps	display information about processes	6
pwd	display working directory	5

Table 14.7 (cont.)
Utilities r–t

Utility	Description	Chapter
read	read a line from standard input	6
readonly	set read-only attribute for variables	6
renice	change the priority of a running process	6
return	return from a function	9
rm	remove a file	4
rmdir	remove empty directories	3
sed	stream editor	10
set	set options and positional parameters	8
sh	the shell	4
shift	shift positional parameters	7
shutdown	close down processes and shut down machine	13
sleep	suspend execution for a time interval	6
sort	sort or merge text files	5
split	split a file into pieces	9
ssh	secure shell for remote login	13
strings	display printable strings in a file	5
strip	remove unnecessary data from executable files	9
stty	set terminal options	9
tabs	reset the tab positions	8
tail	show the last few lines of a file	5
talk	talk to another user	4
tar	file and directory archive tool	5
tee	duplicate standard input	4
test	evaluate expression	7
time	display execution time for a command	6
touch	change last modification time of a file	5
tput	change terminal characteristics	8
tr	translate characters	10
trap	intercept a signal	9
true	returns 'true' value, exit status 0	7
tty	display the terminal name	4

Table 14.7 (cont.)
Utilities u–x

Utility	Description	Chapter
umask	change access privileges when files are created	5
unalias	remove alias definition	9
uname	display the system name	4
unexpand	replace spaces by tabs	9
uniq	filter out repeated lines	5
unset	unset options and positional parameters	8
useradd	creates new user	13
userdel	removes a user	13
uudecode	decode a file which was coded with uuencode	9
uuencode	encode a binary file	9
vi	full-screen text editor	4
wait	suspend process until completion of another process	6
wc	word, line and byte count	5
who	list who is using the system	4
write	write a message on another user's terminal	4
ypmatch	prints values from Network Information System	13
xargs	construct argument list and execute command	7

Index

D

dw (Vi) 42

200, 225

M

N

R

RAM 18

rand (Awk random number) 233

range 195

RAR 274

rcp 277

RE 199

read 96

readonly 111

read permission (file) 69

real time 108

recommended (installation) 22

record 215

record separator 231

Red Hat 22

redirection 45

regular expression 199

regular file 129

relative filename 61

release 34

renice 107

repetitive strain injury 32

Return (key) 5

Return (**more**) 54

return 177

rlogin 277

rm 48

rmdir 64

root 60

root (account) 24

RS 231

RSI 32

running process 89

running program 34

S

s (bc sine function) 127

scale (bc) 126, 127

scandisk 23

scheduling 92

scp 277

screen 3

screensaver 32

script 50, 159

script (Awk) 215

script (Grep) 201

script (Sed) 203

Sed 203

SEE ALSO (manual page) 56

sequential list 120

server 22

set 161

sftp 277

sh 12

sh 50

shell 5, 11, 12

SHELL 93

shell options 161

shift 144

shutdown 261

SIGALRM 175

SIGEXIT 175

SIGHUP 107, 175

SIGINT 174, 175

SIGKILL 92, 175

signals 92

SIGQUIT 174, 175

SIGTERM 175

SIGTTIN 103

simple command 120, 121

sin (Awk sine function) 233

single boot 19

single quote 94, 110

slash 61

sleep 91

slogin 277

soft link 165

software 2, 4

solidus 61

sort 79

Space (**more**) 54

SPARC 2

split (Awk) 234

split (Perl) 246

split 182, 206, 264

spool (directory) 168

sqrt (bc) 127

sqrt (Awk square root) 233

ssh 268

SSH 277

standard error 44

standard input 44

standard output 44

StarOffice 273